I ~~know~~ ~~a side path along a bank~~

I know a path running along a bank,
a parapet that ~~runs~~ says the level road
from the precipitous wood below. The path
serves children for looking down the long smooth steep
Between the legs of yew & beech to where
A fallen one checks the ~~sigh~~ sight: while men & women
Content ~~themselves~~ with the rd. & what is seen
Over the bank, & what the children tell.
The path trickles ~~winds~~ winding like silver on,
Bordered & even invaded by thinnest moss
That tries to cover roots & crumbling chalk
With gold, olive & emerald, but in vain.
The children ~~will not bring~~ ~~for the~~
            wear it ~~they~~ have flattened the bank

On top: & silvered it between the moss
With the current of their feet, yr after yr.
But the rd is houseless. It leads not to school.
To see a child is rare there, & the eye
Has lost the rd. the wood that it overhangs
And undergauns it, & the path that looks
As if it led on to some ~~fabled~~ legendary,
~~Or fancied~~ place where men have wished to go
And stay: till sudden, it ends where the wood
                              ends.
Remove ~~along a~~ bank, a parapet
That ~~saves~~ ~~the level only~~ the precipitous wood below
The level rd, I know a path. It serves
Children who

THE
SOUTH COUNTRY

Edward Thomas

Wood engravings by
Eric Fitch Daglish

LITTLE TOLLER BOOKS
an imprint of THE DOVECOTE PRESS

This paperback edition published in 2009 by
Little Toller Books
Stanbridge, Wimborne Minster, Dorset BH21 4JD
First published in 1909

ISBN 978-0-9562545-1-1

The photograph of Edward Thomas on the cover and the page from
Edward Thomas's notebook on page 1 are reproduced courtesy of Cardiff University
Library Archive / The Edward Thomas Literary Estate
Introduction © Robert Macfarlane 2009
Illustrations © The Estate of Eric Fitch Daglish 2009
Preface © The Estate of Helen Thomas 2009

Typeset in Monotype Sabon
Printed in Spain by GraphyCems, Navarra

All papers used by Little Toller Books and the Dovecote Press
are natural, recyclable products made from
wood grown in sustainable, well-managed forests

A CIP catalogue record for this book is available
from the British Library

3 5 7 9 8 6 4 2

CONTENTS

INTRODUCTION

Robert Macfarlane

EDWARD THOMAS was a compulsive walker. 'His greatest pleasure, and certainly his greatest need, was to walk and be alone', remembered his widow, Helen. Sometimes he carried a map with him, wanting to tramp for a day 'without touching a road but to cross it'. More often, he preferred to go mapless, and to follow the leads of the landscape – to 'trace a stream up to its source in the wood', or to be 'guided by the hills or the sun'. He made a series of one-day walks in the design of 'a rough circle', 'trusting, by taking a series of turnings to the left or a series to the right, to take much beauty by surprise and to return at last to my starting-point'. Decades before Guy Debord and his Situationists devised the idea of the *dérive* or 'randomly motivated walk' (1956); decades before Richard Long inscribed 'A Line Made By Walking' in a Wiltshire meadow, and aligned walking with sculpture (1967); decades before Paul Auster's enigmatic character Peter Stillman trod the letters of the alphabet onto the Manhattan street-plan (1984), Thomas was out there, making tracks, pursuing the living and the dead, and pioneering the walk as art-act, as artefact.

Walking was, for Thomas, re-creation rather than recreation. Depression dogged him throughout his short life, and like many melancholics he developed his own rituals of relief – the most powerful of which was walking. His tours on foot – through the Welsh marches, along ancient trackways, and over the English downlands – were attempts to out-march the causes of his sadness. He found, he wrote, 'deepest ease and joy out of doors', and of all landscapes, it was 'the South Country' that most deeply eased Thomas. He took the phrase from Hilaire Belloc's chalky poem of the same name, and used it to designate the countryside 'south of the Thames and Severn and east of Exmoor', including 'the counties of Kent, Sussex, Surrey, Hampshire, Berkshire, Wiltshire, Dorset, and part of Somerset.' To Thomas this area was not a political or social entity, but a bio-region: constituted of chalk downs, clear-watered streams, beech hangars, and wild-flower meadows. East and west across 'the south country', he wrote, 'go ranges of chalk hills, their sides smoothly hollowed by Nature . . . or sharply scored by old roads . . . their ridges mak[ing] flowing but infinitely variable clear lines against the sky'.

He lived in this area for fifteen years, and he walked it for more than twenty, wandering 'far afield alone, retreading forgotten footpaths and hidden lanes'. It was his landscape of closest acquaintance, and it consoled him in the ways that religion or music consoled others. 'Solitary on the bare downs', recalled Helen Thomas, 'or in the sheltered valleys, on the ancient tracks above which the kestrel has always circled . . . there he could throw off his brooding and be content.' Shades, here, of Albert Camus's half-contemptuous, half-envious remark that 'some of my contemporaries are cured of their sadness merely by contemplation of a landscape'.

The South Country was written rapidly in the summer of 1908 and published in 1909, as part of a pastoral series that included Belloc's *The Historic Thames*, and *The Heart of England*, also by Thomas. It bears, here and there, evidence of the speed of its production: purple patches, hack-marks, daubs of sentimentalism. Thomas himself disowned *The South Country* within a year of completing it, finding it 'full of nasty jingling rhythms', of 'endless description', and with 'an insufficient thread running through and no connecting links'. It had been done, he admitted with a grin and a grimace in a letter to a friend, by 'dipping into fifteen closely written note-books for solid details to support my soarings and fluttering'.

But Thomas is too hard on himself. At its best, *The South Country* is a sustained prose-poem, strange and visionary in its disconnections, and brilliant in its noticings. Those 'brisk acid wrens' that he hears in a Sussex hedgerow, for instance, or the 'liquid confiding monotone' of the nearby sparrows. The downs that rise 'like old thatched houses'. 'The confused moonlit chequer' of a wood's floor at night. His animistic vision of how rain brings the downlands to life: 'the voices of the green growing in the rain are innumerable. The very ground has now one voice of its own, the gurgle of its soaking hollow places' (he loved thick weather of all kinds, loved the abolition of co-ordinates, edges and familiarity that rain, fog and snow bring about).

Thomas regretted the lack of 'connecting links' to the book. But it's this lack of connection – the absence of a continuous journey, or an ever-present walker-narrator – that distinguishes *The South Country* from other Edwardian nature-travelogues. The book jumps about: geographically, seasonally, meteorologically. One moment you're in Suffolk, then you're in Hampshire. One chapter it's summer, the next it's autumn. One sentence it's raining, the next it's blazing. There's something hypermodern about the book's collage-like feel, its shifts and bucks. In topographical terms, the experience of reading *The South Country* resembles a Google-Earth fly-over of the chalk counties: zooming in here, settling there, lifting off, scrolling on . . . In tonal terms, the book slides without warning from the intensely observed to the extravagantly imagined. The effect on the reader is an intriguing cognitive dissonance, brought about by this irregular movement between the empirical and the mystical.

Thomas is too hard on himself, as well, because there *is* a 'thread running through' his book, and that thread is the idea of the old road. The 1984 Everyman reissue of *The South Country* carried on its cover Paul Nash's extraordinary oil painting 'Wood on the Downs' (1929). In the foreground is a hangar of beeches, the trees high-trunked and elephant-grey, with their leaves styled into ellipses. In the background, white chalk paths ribbon away over the downs, their forks and curves rhyming with the beech branches. The painting fuses European avant-garde technique with English pastoral content: Nash's signature combination. The image of the path fascinated Nash, and 'Wood on the Downs' recalls his earlier war-work, including 'The Mule Track' (1918), in which a duck-boarded path draws the viewer's eye dangerously onwards into a trench-scape of shell-blasts and sucking mud. Echoes, too, of the desolate 'Ruined Country, Vimy' (also 1918) in which a white path runs hopefully through war-ravaged country, while high above it swoops a combat biplane.

Nash was the great twentieth-century artist of the path; Thomas its great twentieth-century writer. Again and again, Thomas's prose travels by the old ways: along 'a disused path amid almost overlapping dog's mercury', by 'a frail path chiefly through oak and hazel'. 'The long white roads and virgin beeches are a temptation. What quests they propose!', cries Thomas midway through the book. 'They take us away to the thin air of the future or to the underworld of the past.' He had absorbed the English nineteenth-century romance of the open road – there in Robert Louis Stevenson's *Songs of Travel*, so beautifully set by Vaughan-Williams, and in George Borrow's Romany fantasias – and added to it his near-morbid fascination with the marks of the long dead. The old ways were, for Thomas, sites of communion with what Stevenson once called 'the long-vanished races'. To step out along them was to fall spiritually into alignment with the ghosts of previous pedestrians. Footfall as séance. Road as rift in time. 'For centuries these roads seemed to hundreds so necessary', he wrote:

> and men set out upon them at dawn with hope and followed after joy and were fain of their whiteness at evening: tread softly because your way is over men's dreams; but not too long; and now descend to the west as fast as feet can carry you, and follow your own dream, and that also shall in course of time lie under men's feet; for there is no going so sweet as upon the old dreams of men.

Perhaps the best way to think of *The South Country*, in fact, is as a dream-map – by which I mean an act of imaginative cartography, a chart of longing and loss projected onto actual terrain. Thomas knew, I think, that this was what he had written. 'In a sense this country is all carved out of the carver's brain, and has not a name', he observes early in the book. 'This is not the South Country which measures about two hundred miles from east to west and fifty from north to south. In some ways it is incomparably larger than any country that was ever mapped, since upon nothing less than the infinite can the spirit disport itself.'

A year after the declaration of the First World War, Thomas joined

The Artists' Rifles – a large volunteer battalion for the London and Middlesex areas – and was posted first to Hare Hall Training Camp in Essex, where he worked as a map-reading instructor, using the skills of land-knowledge he had learnt as a walker. In January 1917, he was assigned to the Western Front. He wrote to Helen on 29 January, a day before leaving England, to say that once he was 'over there', he would 'say no more goodbyes'. The move to France, remembered Helen, was a move:

> farther south, but not to his south; the compass is not the index of the heart; and, when standing at the entrance of his dugout, he looked north and saw, or dreamed he saw, Sussex, with her gentle downs scattered with sheep-like grey boulders, and thorn trees bent and wracked by the wind, and the sheltering folds where the wind never came; and Kent, the Weald of Kent, whose clay oaks and hops and apples love, whose copses the nightingale seeks; Hampshire, with her hangars of beech and yew, merry tree, and white beam, and the cottage at the foot of the hill . . . these dear places he was never to visit again; never again was he to cross the sea; never again, mounting the smooth-sided down, to take in deep breaths of thyme-scented air, nor to seek the far horizon which bounded his south country, and know the peace which only that could bring him.

In the trenches, Thomas was able to pore over the dream-map – the memory-map – of the South Country that he carried in his skull. It's clear from his journals and poems that the recollection of his years of freedom on the downs were a consolation to him during the ten weeks or so that he survived the Western Front.

On 8 April 1917, Thomas made a number of jottings in his war-diary. Some were circumstantial: a shell landing two yards from him as he stood by the forward-command post; a piece of shrapnel dust scratching his neck from another shell-burst. Others were metaphysical, proto-poetry: 'The light of the new moon and every star / And no more singing for the bird . . . / I never understood quite what was meant by God'. Then comes a cryptic and troubling prose note: 'The morning chill and clear hurts my skin while it delights my mind. Neuville in early morning with its flat straight crest with trees and houses – the beauty of this silent empty scene of no inhabitants and hid troops, but don't know why I could have cried and didn't'.

Loose inside the diary was a slip of paper with a series of scrawled addresses, and a handful of images. The last of these reads: 'Roads shining like river uphill after rain'. What was Thomas recording here, one wonders. The old ways of the south country, with their glossy chalk? Or the support roads that wound down to the Front, with their gleaming mud? Both, probably, folded together.

Those roads again – drawing Thomas's mind out and up and away. And that rain again – bestowing its blessing and its glisten even on the shattered landscape of Arras. 'The end should come in heavy and lasting rain,' Thomas wrote in *The South Country*. In fact, it came in heavy and unseasonal snow, which fell through the night of 8 April, and on into dawn of 9 April – the first day of The Battle of Arras. Through the falling snowflakes fell tens of thousands of German shells, one of which killed Thomas while he was standing at his observation post, just a few minutes after dawn.

Robert Macfarlane
Cambridge, 2009

PREFACE

Helen Thomas

The South Country is one of the happiest of the prose works of Edward Thomas. It was written at a period of comparative ease and tranquillity, and was, as not many of his books could be, written for his own pleasure, and it is therefore very characteristic of the author at his best.

He had been living in the south country for eleven years, and there were still to be nearly six more years of life spent in the part of England he knew and loved best. For five years he lived in Kent, and for twelve years Hampshire was his home county. He left Hampshire to enter the army, and never knew a home again.

During those years I have in mind long evenings of talk with friends, and pipes and beer round a great fire in a low cottage room; or, with a child on each knee, reading aloud Chaucer, or singing some of his native Welsh songs till bedtime came; or digging in an old well-matured garden, bounded by thick hedges, with a yew tree over the gate in which a gold-crested wren lived, and a flycatcher snapped his beak near as we dug in the kindly soil. But almost his greatest pleasure, and certainly his greatest need, was to walk and be alone in the country he has called "The South Country." Though these days in and out of doors of which I speak were days of rare calm and contentment for others besides himself, for him the most satisfying days were when he wandered far afield alone, retreading forgotten footpaths and hidden lanes, stopping at remote and primitive inns where strangers were rare. This of all his pleasures was the deepest and the most comprehensive. For to Edward Thomas walking was not merely exercise, though he swung along with a long slow stride – a tall, slim, powerful figure: striking, too, with his fine head and uncovered hair bleached by the wind and rain and sun. Nor was he as he walked only the nature lover intent on observing birds and flowers and clouds and all the life of the hedges and copses, though his keen eye missed little of what his minute knowledge of these things knew to be there. Nor was he only the aesthete satisfying his eye with the beauty of the contours of the hills, the symmetry of the trees, and the grouping of villages. Nor was he only the wayfarer meeting fellow travellers on the roads and in the inns, talking to them, and listening to their slow shrewd talk. Nor was he only the artist transmuting all this into words. He was all these and much more. By the English country his soul was revived when it was faint with despair, and comforted as some are by religion or music. Solitary on the bare downs, or in the sheltered valleys, on the ancient tracks above which the kestrel has always circled and hovered, and where the sheep have nibbled for such ages that the very grass and flowers have adapted their growth to evade the ceaseless menace of their teeth; or leaning over a gate to talk to the ploughman who, with such skilful ease, swings his plough at the end of the furrow; or wandering among the epitaphed tombstones of the village churchyard; or sitting in a meadow by a stream reading Traherne or Chaucer, or in the evening at the inn, or anywhere where the rural life of England continued in the traditional ways – there he could throw off his melancholy brooding and be content. And *The South Country* is the expression of that content.

Edward Thomas's nature was meditative, austere, and reserved. He hated ostentation, snobbery, hypocrisy, affectation, and sentimentality. The things and people who were honest and direct appealed to him. In this book he wanders over the south country, and records all that drifted into his thoughts or memory or observation as he went. It is easy to see how he loved the poets to whom their country was dear: Chaucer, Traherne, and Vaughan seem a right trio on the Pilgrims' Way. And there were many others whom he loved to quote or be reminded of as he strides out – poets and prose writers. He read Gilbert White, Isaac Walton, and Richard Jefferies when the country was to him no more than what could be reached by a small boy on foot, from a suburb not five miles from Charing Cross. But later he got to Wiltshire, the birthplace of his first master, Jefferies, and there his own observations and his own records rivalled these authors in their interest for him. Catching his first pike, finding the earliest thrush's egg, noting the coming of the chiff-chaff, these were for the boy, Edward Thomas, the important things. In those days, when the desire was dawning not only to see and experience, but to express, if he had been conscious of a wish it *would* have been to have leisure, freedom, and knowledge, and creative skill to write just such a book as *The South Country.* He did not know then that the love of the open air and of the tradition and history and life of the English country would grow to be so strong in him that before comfort and ease and security he would choose the freedom to live away from towns, where, with a map in his pocket, he could walk all day without touching a road but to cross it; where the Pilgrims' Way would become as familiar as his native suburban street; where notebook after notebook could be filled with records of beauty and wonder and events of interest; where he could begin a day by seeing a vixen playing with her young in a dew-drenched meadow, and continue it by tracing a stream up to its source in the wood, and end it by watching ghost moths weave their mysterious dance, or an owl feeding her young huddled on the roof-ridge, or hear a mole singing his mating song. But these things, lovely and exciting as they were to him all his life, were only a part of what the country gave to Edward Thomas. With his keen sight and almost uncanny powers of observation, and his sensitiveness to the activity of the life of the countryside, he missed nothing as he walked. But beyond these things there came to him from wide horizons, clouds, rain, and solitude, and from the harsh earth, and from contact with the earthy lives of labouring men, an indefinable quality which his spirit, with its melancholy and bitter discontent, needed for its comfort and fulfilment, and without which life, as he understood it, would have been impossible. Here in Kent, Surrey, Sussex, Hampshire, and Wiltshire he lived the life he had chosen, often suffering despair and humiliation, but always in that country finding the comfort he so passionately sought, to lose it again and find it ever again.

He had to leave it to go to France, farther south, but not to *his* south; the compass is not the index of the heart; and, when standing at the entrance of his dugout, he looked north and saw, or dreamed he saw, Sussex, with her gentle downs scattered with sheeplike grey boulders, and thorn trees bent and wracked by the wind, and the sheltering folds where the wind never came; and Kent, the Weald of Kent, whose clay oaks and hops and apples love, whose copses the nightingale seeks; Hampshire, with her hangars of beach and yew, merry tree, and white beam, and the cottage at the foot of the hill; and Wiltshire with the Avon and its rich valleys, her stone-built villages, and historic manors. These dear places he was never to visit again; never again was he to cross the sea; never again, mounting the smooth-sided down, to take in deep breaths of thyme-scented air, nor to seek the far horizon which bounded his "South Country," and know the peace which only that could give him.

I cannot bring this preface to a close without speaking of Mr. Daglish's engravings. It is a joy and wonder to me that an artist so perfectly fitted for the task has been impelled to illustrate this book. For Mr. Fitch Daglish, with his austere and strong yet loving lines, his exactness to details of fact, his freedom from sentimentality, his poetic sensitiveness to, and obvious love of, the English country and tradition in art, is one with the spirit of this book to a remarkable degree, and I think many lovers of the work of both writer and artist will give a warm welcome to this new and beautiful edition of *The South Country*.

Helen Thomas, 1932

To Edward Garnett

ONE

The South Country

THE NAME OF 'South Country' is taken from a poem by Mr. Hilaire Belloc, beginning:

> When I am living in the Midlands,
> They are sodden and unkind,
> I light my lamp in the evening,
> My work is left behind;
> And the great hills of the South Country
> Come back into my mind.

The name is given to the south of England as distinguished from the Midlands, 'North England' and 'West England' by the Severn. The poet is thinking particularly of Sussex and of the South Downs. In using the term I am thinking of all that country which is dominated by the Downs or by the English Channel, or by both; Cornwall and East Anglia have been admitted only for the sake of contrast. Roughly speaking, it is the country south of the Thames and Severn and east of Exmoor, and it includes, therefore, the counties of Kent, Sussex, Surrey, Hampshire, Berkshire, Wiltshire, Dorset, and part of Somerset. East and west across it go ranges of chalk hills, their sides smoothly hollowed by Nature and the marl-burner, or sharply scored by old roads. On their lower slopes they carry the chief woods of the south country, their coombes are often fully fledged with trees, and sometimes their high places are crowned with beech or fir; but they are most admirably themselves when they are bare of all but grass and a few bushes of gorse and juniper and some yew, and their ridges make flowing but infinitely variable clear lines against the sky. Sometimes they support a plateau of flint and clay, which slopes gradually to the level of the streams. Sometimes they fall away to the vales in well-defined ledges – first a long curving slope, then a plain of cornfield, and below that a steep but lesser slope covered with wood, and then again grassland or sandy heaths and rivers. Except on the plateau, the summits have few houses and very small hamlets; the first terrace has larger villages and even a town or two; but most of the towns are beneath on the banks of the rivers, and chiefly where they are broadest near the sea, or on the coast itself. The rivers flow mainly north and south, and can have but a short course before they enter the sea on the south or the Thames on the north. Those I remember best are the Stours, the two Rothers, but especially the one which joins the Arun, the Medway, the Len, the Eden, the Holling, the Teise, the Ouse, the Itchen, the Meon, the Wey, the Mole, the Kennet, the Ray, the Winterbournes, the Wiltshire Avon, the Wylye, the Ebble, and many little waters running gold over New Forest gravel or crystal over the chalk of Hampshire, and not least of all that unlucky rivulet, the Wandle, once a nymph that walked among her sisters:

> So amiable, fair, so pure, so delicate,
> So plump, so full, so fresh, her eyes so wonderous clear:
> And first unto her lord, at WANDSWORTH doth appear,
> That in the goodly court, of their great sovereign TAMES,
> There might no other speech be had amongst the streams,
> But only of this Nymph, sweet Wandel, what she wore;
> Of her complexion, grace, and how herself she bore.

Nor can I omit the Wiltshire and Berkshire canal, as it was fifteen years ago, between Swindon and Dauntsey, an unfrequented by-way through a quiet dairy country, and full of pike and tench among the weeds and under the tall water docks and willow herbs which even then threatened to subdue it as they now have done.

The chief roads make south, south-east, south-west and west from London; almost the only road going east and west and not touching London is the old road known between Winchester and Canterbury as the Pilgrims' Way.

Most of the towns are small market towns, manufacturing chiefly beer; or they are swollen, especially in the neighbourhood of London, as residential quarters on lines of railway or as health and pleasure resorts on the sea. But any man used to maps will be wiser on these matters in an hour than I am. For what I have sought is quiet and as complete a remoteness as possible from towns, whether of manufactures, of markets or of cathedrals. I have used a good many maps in my time, largely to avoid the towns; but I confess that I prefer to do without them and to go, if I have some days before me, guided by the hills or the sun or a stream – or, if I have one day only, in a rough circle, trusting, by taking a series of turnings to the left or a series to the right, to take much beauty by surprise and to return at last to my starting-point. On a dull day or cloudy night I have often no knowledge of the points of the compass. I never go out to see anything. The signboards thus often astonish me. I wish, by the way, that I had noted down more of the names on the signboards at the cross-roads. There is a wealth of poetry in them, as in that which points – by a ford, too – first, to Poulner and Ringwood; second, to Gorley and Fordingbridge; third, to Linwood and Broomy: and another pointing to Fordingbridge, to Ringwood, and to Cuckoo Hill and Furze Hill: and another in the parish of Pentlow, pointing to Foxearth and Sudbury, to Cavendish and Clare, and to Belchamps and Yeldham. Castles, churches, old houses, of extraordinary beauty or interest, have never worn out any of my shoe leather except by accident. I like to come upon them – usually without knowing their names and legends – but do not lament when chance takes me a hundred times out of their way. Nor have I ever been to Marlow to think about Shelley, or to Winterslow for Hazlitt's sake; and I enter Buriton many times without remembering Gibbon. They would move me no more than the statue of a man and a fat horse (with beribboned tail) which a grateful countryside erected to William III in the market square at Petersfield. I prefer any country church or chapel to Winchester or Chichester or Canterbury Cathedral, just as I prefer "All round my hat," or "Somer is icumen in," to Beethoven. Not that I dislike the cathedrals, or that I do not find many pleasures amongst them. But they are incomprehensible and not restful. I feel when I am within them that I know why a dog bays at the moon. They are much more difficult or, rather I am more conscious in them of my lack of comprehension, than the hills or the sea; and I do not like the showmen, the smell and look of the museum, the feeling that it is admiration or nothing, and all the well-dressed and fly-blown people round about. I sometimes think that religious architecture is a dead language, majestic but dead, that it never was a popular language. Have some of these buildings lived too long, been too well preserved, so as to oppress our little days with too permanent an expression of the passing things? The truth is that, though the past allures me, and to discover a cathedral for myself would be an immense pleasure, I have no historic sense and no curiosity. I mention these trivial things because they may be important to those who read what I am paid for writing. I have read a great deal of history – in fact, a university gave me a degree out of respect for my apparent knowledge of history – but I have forgotten it all, or it has got into my blood and is present in me in a form which defies evocation or analysis. But as far as I can tell I am pure of history. Consequently I prefer the old brick houses round the cathedral, and that avenue of archaic bossy limes to the cathedral itself with all its turbulent quiet and vague antiquity. The old school also close at hand! I was there after the end of the term once, and two boys were kicking a football in a half-walled court; it was a bright, cold, windy April afternoon; and the ancient brick was penetrated with their voices and the sound of the ball, and I thought there could be nothing lovelier than that court, the pleasant walls, and the broad playing fields in sight of a smooth noble hill and a temple of dark firs on top. I was not thinking of Winchester or of any one older than the fondest son of that "mother, more than mother," and little of him; but was merely caught up by and with the harmony of man and his work, of two children playing, and of the green downs and windy sky.

And so I travel, armed only with myself, an avaricious and often libertine and fickle eye and ear, in pursuit, not of knowledge, not of wisdom, but one of whom to pursue is never to capture. Politics, the drama, science, racing, reforms and preservations, divorces, book clubs – nearly everything which the average (oh! mysterious average man, always to be met but never met) and the superior and the intelligent man is thinking of, I cannot grasp; my mind refuses to deal with them; and when they are discussed I am given to making answers like, "In

Kilve there is no weathercock." I expect there are others as unfortunate, superfluous men such as the sanitation, improved housing, police, charities, medicine of our wonderful civilization saves from the fate of the cuckoo's foster-brothers. They will perhaps follow my meanders and understand. The critics also will help. They will misunderstand – it is their trade. How well they know what I ought, or at least ought not, to do. I must, they have said, avoid "the manner of the worst oleographs;" must not be "affected," though the recipe is not to be had; must beware of "over-excitation of the colour sense." In slow course of years we acquire a way of expression, hopelessly inadequate, as we plainly see when looking at the methods of great poets, of beautiful women, of athletes, of politicians, but still gradually as fitted to the mind as an old walking-stick to the hand that has worn and been worn by it, full of our weakness as of our strength, of our blindness of as our vision – the man himself, the poor man it may be. And I live by writing, since it is impossible to live by not writing in an age not of gold but of brass.

Unlearned, incurious, but finding deepest ease and joy out of doors, I have gone about the South Country these twenty years and more on foot, especially in Kent between Maidstone and Ashford and round Penshurst, in Surrey between London, Guildford and Horley, in Hampshire round Petersfield, in Wiltshire between Wootton Bassett, Swindon and Savernake. The people are almost foreign to me, the more so because country people have not yet been thrown into quite the same confusion as towns-people, and therefore look awkwardly upon those who are not in trade – writing is an unskilled labour and not a trade – not on the land, and not idle. But I have known something of two or three men and women, and have met a few dozen more. Yet is this country, though I am mainly Welsh, a kind of home, as I think it is more than any other to those modern people who belong nowhere. Here they prefer to retire, here they take their holidays in multitudes. For it is a good foster-mother, ample-bosomed, mild and homely. The lands of wild coast, of mountains, of myriad chimneys, offer no such welcome. They have their race, their speech and ways, and are jealous. You must be a man of the sea or of the hills to dwell there at ease. But the South is tender and will harbour any one; her quiet people resent intrusion quietly, so that many do not notice the resentment. These are the "home" counties. A man can hide away in them. The people are not hospitable, but the land is.

Yet there are days and places which send us in search of another kind of felicity than that which dwells under the Downs, when, for example, the dark wild of Ashdown or of Woolmer, some parcel of heathery land, with tufted pines and pale wandering roads, rises all dark and stormy out of the gentle vale, or on such an evening as when the sky is solemn blue save at the horizon where it is faint gold, and between the blue and the gold, across the north-west, lies an ashen waste of level cloud. This sky and its new moon and evening star below, is barred by the boles of beeches; through them the undulations of deserted ploughland are all but white with dewy grass and weed. Underfoot winds a disused path amid almost overlapping dog's mercury. The earth is like an exhausted cinder, cold, silent, dead, compared with the great act in the sky. Suddenly a dog-fox barks – with melancholy and malice in the repeated hoarse yells – a sound that awakens the wildest past out of the wood and the old path. He passes by me at a trot, pausing a little to bark. He vanishes, but not his voice, into the wood, and he returns, still barking, and passes me again, filling the wood and the coombe below with a sound that has nothing to match it except that ashen waste in the beech-barred, cold blue and golden sky, against which the fox is carved in moving ebony. Or again, when a rude dark headland rises out of the mist of the plain into the evening sky. The woods seem but just freed from the horror of primeval sea, if that is not primeval sea washing their bases. Capella hangs low, pale, large, moist and trembling almost engulfed between two horns of the wood upon the headland, the frailest beacon of hope, still fluttering from the storm out of which the land is emerging. Then, or at home looking at a map of Britain, the West calls, out of Wiltshire and out of Cornwall and Devon beyond, out of Monmouth and Glamorgan and Gower and Caermarthen, with a voice of dead Townsends, Eastaways, Thomases, Phillipses, Treharnes, Marendaz, sea men and mountain men.

Westward, for men of this island, lies the sea; westward are the great hills. In a mere map the west of Britain is fascinating. The great features of that map, which make it something more than a picture to be imperfectly copied by laborious childish pens, are the great promontories of Caernarvon, of Pembroke, of Gower and of Cornwall, jutting out into the western sea, like the features of a grim large face, such a face as is carved on a ship's prow. These protruding features, even on a small-scale map, thrill the mind with a sense of purpose and spirit. They yearn, they peer out ever to the sea, as if using eyes and nostrils to savour the utmost scent of it, as if themselves calling back to the call of the waves. To the eyes of a child they stand for adventure. They are lean and worn and scarred with the strife and watching. Then gradually into the mind of the child comes the story that justifies and, still more, inspires and seems to explain those westward-pointing promontories. For, out towards them continually have the conquered races of the world retreated, and their settlements give those corners a strangeness and a charm to our fantastic sympathies. Out from them conquerors in their turn have gone to found a legend like the Welsh Madoc, an empire like the men of Devon. The blood of conquered and conqueror is in our veins, and it flushes the cheek at the sight or thought of the west. Each man of us is as ancient and complicated, as lofty-spired and as deep-vaulted as cathedrals and castles old, and in those lands our crypts and dark foundations are dimly remembered. We look out towards them from the high camps at Battlesbury and Barbury: the lines of the Downs go trooping along to them at night. Even in the bosom of the South Country, when the tranquil bells are calling over the corn at twilight, the westward-going hills, where the sun has fallen, draw the heart away and fill us with a desire to go on and on for ever, that same way. When, in the clear windy dawn, thin clouds like traveller's joy are upon the high air, it seems that up there also, in those placid spaces, they travel and know the joy of the road, and the sun – feeding on the blue, as a child said yesterday, as Lucretius said before – goes the desired way.

London also calls, making the needle whirl in the compass. For in London also a man may live as up " a great river wide as any sea;" and over some of the fairest of the South Country hangs the all-night glimmer of the city, warning, threatening, beckoning anon. Some of this country has already perished, or is so ramparted about that there is no stranger country in the world unless it be those perpendicular valleys cloven among the Blue Mountains, their floors level and of the purest grass, but accessible only at the end nearest the plain, where the cleft is sometimes so narrow that not even a dog can enter.

This, then, is my South Country. It covers the North Downs and the South Downs, the Icknield Way and the Pilgrims' Way, and the cross-roads between them and the Thames and the sea, a land of hops, fruit, corn, high pasture, meadow, woodland, heath and shore. But there is no man of whose powers I stand more in awe than the topographical writer, from Mr. A.G. Bradley or Mr. E.V. Lucas downwards. I shall not attempt to compete with them. I should only be showing my ignorance and carelessness were I to label every piece of country which I chance to mention or describe. Any one can point out my omissions, my blindness, my exaggeration. Nor can I bring myself to mention the names of the places where I walked or sat down. In a sense this country is all "carved out of the carver's brain" and has not a name. This is not the South Country which measures about two hundred miles from east to west and fifty from north to south. In some ways it is incomparably larger than any country that was ever mapped, since upon nothing less than the infinite can the spirit disport itself. In other ways it is far smaller – as when a mountain with tracts of sky and cloud and the full moon glass themselves in a pond, a little pond.

It would need a more intellectual eye than mine to distinguish county from county by its physical character, its architecture, its people, its unique combination of common elements, and I shall not attempt it. As often as not I have no doubt mingled parts of Kent with my Wiltshire, and so on. And positively I cannot say to which belongs one picture that occurs to me as characteristic of the South Country.

A crossing of roads encloses a waste place of no man's land, of dwarf oaks, hawthorn, bramble and fern, and the flowers of knapweed and harebell, and golden tormentil embroidering the heather and the minute seedling oaks. Follow one of these roads past straight avenues of elms leading up to a farm (built square of stone, under a roof of thatch or stone slate, and lying well back from the road across a level meadow with some willows in the midst, elms round about, willow herb waving rosy by the stream at the border), or merely to a cluster of ricks; and presently the hedges open wide apart and the level white road cools itself under the many trees of a green, wych elms, sycamores, limes and horse-chestnuts, by a pool, and, on the other side, the sign of the "White Hart," its horns held back upon its haunches. A stone-built farm and its barns and sheds lie close to the green on either side, and another of more stateliness where the hedges once more run close together alongside the road. This farmhouse has three dormers, two rows of five shadowy windows below, and an ivied porch not quite in the centre; a modest lawn divided by a straight path; dense, well-watered borders of grey lavender, rosemary, ladslove, halberds of crimson hollyhock, infinite blending stars of Michaelmas daisy; old apple trees seeming to be pulled down almost to the grass by glossy-rinded fruit: and, behind, the bended line of hills a league away, wedding the lowly meadows, the house and the trees to the large heavens and their white procession of clouds out of the south and the sea. The utmost kindliness of earth is expressed in these three houses, the trees on the flat green, the slightly curving road across it, the uneven posts and rails leaning this way and that at the edge of the pond. The trees are so arranged about the road that they weave a harmony of welcome, of blessing, a viaticum for whosoever passes by and only for a moment tastes their shade, acknowledges unconsciously their attitudes, hears their dry summer murmuring, sees the house behind them. The wayfarer knows nothing of those who built them and those who live therein, of those who planted the trees just so and not otherwise, of the causes that shaped the green, any more than of those who reaped and threshed the barley, and picked and dried and packed the hops that made the ale at the "White Hart." He only knows that centuries of peace and hard work and planning for the undreaded future have made it possible. The spirit of the place, all this council of time and Nature and men, enriches the air with a bloom deeper than summer's blue of distance; it drowses while it delights the responding mind with a magic such as once upon a time men thought to express by gods of the hearth, by Faunus and the flying nymphs, by fairies, angels, saints, a magic which none of these things is too strange and "supernatural" to represent. For after the longest inventory of what is here visible and open to analysis, much remains over, imponderable but mighty. Often when the lark is high he seems to be singing in some keyless chamber of the brain; so here the house is built in shadowy replica. If only we could make a graven image of this spirit instead of a muddy untruthful reflection of words! I have sometimes thought that a statue, the statue of a human or heroic or divine figure, might more fitly than in many another stand in such a place. A figure, it should be, like that benign proud Demeter in marble now banished to a recess in a cold gallery, before which a man of any religion, or class, or race, or time might bow and lay down something of his burden and take away what makes him other than he was. She would be at home and blithe again, enshrined in the rain or in this flowery sunlight of an English green, near the wych elm and sycamore and the walls of stone, the mortar mixed, as in all true buildings, with human blood.

TWO
The End of Winter

SUFFOLK

THERE ARE three sounds in the wood this morning – the sound of the waves that has not died away since the sea carried off church and cottage and cliff and the other half of what was once an inland wood; the sound of trees, a multitudinous frenzied sound, of rustling dead oak-leaves still on the bough, of others tripping along the path like mice, or winding up in sudden spirals and falling again, of dead boughs grating and grinding, of pliant young branches lashing, of finest twigs and fir needles sighing, of leaf and branch and trunk booming like one; and through these sounds, the song of a thrush. Rain falls and, for a moment only, the dyked marshland below and beyond the wood is pale and luminous with its flooded pools, the sails of windmills climb and plunge, the pale sea is barred with swathes of foam, and on the whistling sands the tall white waves vaunt, lean forward, topple and lie quivering. But the rain increases: the sound and the mist of it make a wall about the world, except the world in the brain and except the thrush's song which, so bright and clear, has a kind of humanity in it by contrast with the huge bulk of the noises of sea and wood.

Rain and wind cease together, and here on the short grass at the cliff's edge is a strange birth – a gently convex fungus about two inches broad, the central boss of it faintly indented, the surface not perfectly regular but dimpled so as to break the light, and the edge wavering away from the pure circular form; in hue a pale chestnut paling to a transparent edge of honey colour; and the whole surface so smooth and polished by rain as to seem coated in ice. What a thought for the great earth on such a day! Out of the wood on to this grass the thrushes steal, running with heads down and stopping with heads prouder than stags'; out also into the short corn; and so glad are they that they quarrel and sing on the ground without troubling to find a perch.

It is perfectly still; the sun splutters out of the thick grey and white sky, the white sails shine on a sea of steel, and it is warm. And now in the luxury of the first humid warmth and quiet of the year the blackbird sings. The rain sets in at nightfall, but the wind does not blow, and still the blackbird sings and the thrushes will hardly leave the corn. That one song alone sweetens the wide vague country of evening, the cloudy oak woods, the brown mixen under the elms and the little white farm behind the unpruned limes, with its oblong windows irregularly placed and of unequal size, its white door almost at a corner, and the lawn coming right to the walls.

Day breaks and sun and wind dance together in the clouds and trees, but without rain. Larks sing over the dark heavy cornland in which the watery furrows shine. The dead drab grasses wave at the feet of the hedgerows. Little pools at meadow corners bring down the sky to the dark earth. Horses nod before the plough. A slight haze exhales from the innumerable rich spongy clods, between the hedges of oak and ash. Now and then shapeless rags of white or snow-grey clouds wander up from the west and for a little while obscure the white mountains of cloud, the blue sky, the silver sun; or the sweet smoke from the fires of hedgers and ditchers rises up against the edge of a copse. The white linen flaps and glows in cottage gardens; the dung carts go by crunching the flints into the mud; and the hoofs and bells of pony traps make a music forgotten since last February.

It is only the twenty-second day of February, yet these delights of the soul through the eyes and ears are of spring. The children have begun to look for violets, and the youngest, being nearest to them in stature and in nature, has found one. There she stands, four years old, with straight brown legs, her face clear and soft but brown as a new hazel nut, her hair almost of the same colour and paler where the sun has bleached it round her temples and falling over her cheeks and neck; and through it shine eyes of a deeper brown, the hue of the most exquisite flints. The eyes shine, the teeth shine through the ever parted long red lips, the chin

'The rain sets in at nightfall . . . and still the blackbird sings.'

shines, the brow shines most of all with a lustre that seems to come from the joyous brain behind.

She is beautiful and straight as the July corn, as the ash tree standing alone by the stream. She is fearless as fire, bold and restless as wind, clear-hearted, simple, bright and gay as a mountain water; in all her actions a daughter of the sun, the wind and the earth. She has loving looks for all. From her fair broad naked foot to her gleaming hair she is, to many, the dearest thing that lives.

Beside her plays a dog, with lifted ears, head on one side, rosy tongue bright against his yellow fur, waiting upon her fancies. His rest and his motion, like hers, are careless and beautiful, gifts of the sun, the wind and the earth. As I look at them I think of such a child and such a playmate that lived two thousand years ago in the sun, and once as they played each set a foot upon the soft clay of a tile that the tile maker had not yet burned hard and red. The tile fell in the ruin of a Roman city in Britain, was buried hundreds of years in ashes and flowering mould, and yesterday I saw the footprints in the dark red tile, two thousand years old.

A day follows of rain and wind, and it is the robin that is most heard among the dripping thorns, the robin and his autumnal voice. But the sky clears for sunset and the blackbird's hour, and, as twilight ends, only the rear of the disappearing procession of day cloud is visible on the western horizon, while the procession of night has but sent up two or three dark forerunners. The sky is of palest blue, and Jupiter and Sirius are bright over the sea, Venus over the land and Mercury just over the far oaks. The sea is very dark except at the horizon which is pale with the dissolving remnant of sunset gold in it; but two ranks of breakers throw up a waving vapour of fairy foam against the dark waves behind.

Again there are roaring wet mornings and sunlit mornings, but in them all the pewits wheel over the marsh and their wild cries mingle with the sweet whimper of dunlins, the songs of larks, the glitter of the dykes, the wall of rain. All day the sky over heathery moorland is like a reduplication of the moorland, except that at the horizon the sky clears at intervals and fleets of pure white cloud sail over the dark ploughland and green pines; and the gentle sea is white only where the waves break on the sand like a line of children in white frocks advancing with wavers in the game of "Here we come gathering nuts and may." Or the west is angry, thick and grey, the snow is horizontal and fierce, and yet the south has a bay of blue sky and in it a vast sunlit precipice of white cloud, and the missel thrushes roll out their songs again and again at the edges of many woods. Or a sun appears that brings out the songs of thrush and chaffinch and lark, and leaves a chequer of snow on pine and ploughland and on the mole hills of the meadows. Again the sun disappears and the swift heavy hail rebounds on the grass with a dancing as of sand-hoppers, and there is no other sound except a sudden hedge-sparrow's song to break in upon the beating of the pellets on hard ivy and holly and tender grass. In the frosty evening the first moth comes to the lamp.

Now the rain falls rejoicing in its power, and then the sky is sunny and the white clouds are bubble-shaped in the blue, the wet roads are azure with reflected sky, the trees are all of crystal, and the songs of thrushes can be heard even through the snorting and rumbling of a train.

HAMPSHIRE

The beeches on the beech-covered hills roar and strain as if they would fly off with the hill, and anon they are as meek as a great horse leaning his head over a gate. If there is a misty day there is one willow in a coombe lifting up a thousand silver catkins like a thousand lamps, when there is no light elsewhere. Another day, a wide and windy day, is the jackdaw's, and he goes straight and swift and high like a joyous rider crying aloud on an endless savannah, and, underneath, the rippled pond is as bright as a peacock, and millions of beech leaves drive across the open glades of the woods, rushing to their Acheron. The bush harrow stripes the moist and shining grass; the plough changes the pale stubble into a ridgy chocolate; they are peeling the young ash sticks for hop poles and dipping them in tar. At the dying of that windy day the wind is still; there is a bright pale half-moon tangled in the pink whirl of after-sunset cloud, a sound of blackbirds from pollard oaks against the silver sky, a sound of bells from hamlets hidden among beeches.

Towards the end of March there are six nights of frost giving birth to still mornings of weak sunlight, of an opaque yet not definitely misty air. The sky is of a milky, uncertain pale blue without one cloud. Eastward the hooded sun is warming the slope fields and melting the sparkling frost. In many trees the woodpeckers laugh so often that their cry is a song. A grassy ancient orchard has taken possession of the visible sunbeams, and the green and gold of the mistletoe glows on the silvered and mossy branches of apple trees. The pale stubble is yellow and tenderly lit, and gives the low hills a hollow light appearance as if they might presently dissolve. In a hundred tiers on the steep hill, the uncounted perpendicular straight stems of beech, and yet not all quite perpendicular or quite straight, are silver-grey in the midst of a haze, here brown, there rosy, of branches and swelling buds. Though but a quarter of a mile away in this faintly clouded air they are very small, aerial in substance, infinitely remote from the road on which I stand, and more like reflections in calm water than real things.

At the lower margin of the wood the overhanging branches form blue caves, and out of these emerge the songs of many hidden birds. I know that there are bland melodious blackbirds of easy musing voices, robins whose earnest song, though full of passion, is but a fragment that has burst through a more passionate silence, hedge-sparrows of liquid confiding monotone, brisk acid wrens, chaffinches and yellowhammers saying always the same thing (a dear but courtly praise of the coming season), larks building spires above spires into the sky, thrushes of infinite variety that talk and talk of a thousand things, never thinking, always talking of the moment, exclaiming, scolding, cheering, flattering, coaxing, challenging, with merry-hearted, bold voices that must have been the same in the morning of the world when the forest trees lay, or leaned, or hung, where they fell. Yet I can distinguish neither blackbird, nor robin, nor hedge-sparrow, nor any one voice. All are blent into one seething stream of song. It is one song, not many. It is one spirit that sings. Mixed with them is the myriad stir of unborn things, of leaf and blade and flower, many silences at heart and root of tree, voices of hope and growth, of love that will be satisfied though it leap upon the swords of life. Yet not during all the day does the earth truly awaken. Even in town and city the dream prevails, and only dimly lighted their chalky towers and spires rise out of the sweet mist and sing together beside the waters.

The earth lies blinking, turning over languidly and talking like a half-wakened child that now and then lies still and sleeps though with eyes wide open. The air is still full of the dreams of a night which this mild sun cannot dispel. The dreams are prophetic as well as reminiscent, and are visiting the woods, and that is why they will not cast aside the veil. Who would rise if he could continue to dream?

It is not spring yet. Spring is being dreamed, and the dream is more wonderful and more blessed than ever was spring. What the hour of waking will bring forth is not known. Catch at the dreams as they hover in the warm thick air. Up against the grey tiers of beech stems and the mist of the buds and fallen leaves rise two columns of blue smoke from two white cottages among trees; they rise perfectly straight and then expand into a balanced cloud, and thus make and unmake continually two trees of smoke. No sound comes from the cottages. The dreams are over them, over the brows of the children and the babes, of the men and the women, bringing great gifts, suggestions, shadowy satisfactions, consolations, hopes. With inward voices of persuasion those dreams hover and say that all is to be made new, that all is yet before us, and the lots are not yet drawn out of the urn.

We shall presently set out and sail into the undiscovered seas and find new islands of the free, the beautiful, the young. As is the dimly glimmering changeless brook twittering over the pebbles, so is life. It is but just leaving the fount. All things are possible in the windings between fount and sea.

Never again shall we demand the cuckoo's song from the August silence. Never will July nip the spring and lengthen the lambs' faces and take away their piquancy, or June shut a gate between us and the nightingale, or May deny the promise of April. Hark! before the end of afternoon the owls hoot in their sleep in the ivied beeches. A dream has flitted past them, more silent of wing than themselves. Now it is between the wings of the first white butterfly, and it plants a smile in the face of the infant that cannot speak: and again it is with the brimstone butterfly, and the child who is gathering celandine and cuckoo flower and violet starts back almost in fear at the dream.

The grandmother sitting in her daughter's house, left all alone in silence, her hands clasped upon her knees, forgets the courage without hope that has carried her through eighty years, opens her eyes, unclasps her hands from the knot as of stiff rope, distends them and feels the air, and the dream is between her fingers and she too smiles, she knows not why. A girl of sixteen, ill-dressed, not pretty, has seen it also. She has tied up her black hair in a new crimson ribbon. She laughs aloud with a companion at something they know in common and in secret, and as she does so lifts her neck and is glad from the sole of her foot to the crown of her head. She is lost in her laughter and oblivious of its cause. She walks away, and her step is as firm as that of a ewe defending her lamb. She was a poor and misused child, and I can see her as a woman of fifty, sitting on a London bench grey-complexioned, in old black hat, black clothes, crouching over a paper bag of fragments, in the beautiful August rain after heat. But this is her hour. That future is not among the dreams in the air to-day. She is at one with the world, and a deep music grows between her and the stars. Her smile is one of those magical things, great and small and all divine, that have the power to wield universal harmonies. At sight or sound of them the infinite variety of appearances in the world is made fairer than before, because it is shown to be a many-coloured raiment of the one.

The raiment trembles, and under leaf and cloud and air a window is thrown open upon the unfathomable deep, and at the window we are sitting, watching the flight of our souls away, away to where they must be gathered into the music that is being built. Often upon the vast and silent twilight, as now, is the soul poured out as a rivulet into the sea and lost, not able even to stain the boundless crystal of the air; and the body stands empty, waiting for its return, and, poor thing, knows not what it receives back into itself when the night is dark and it moves away. For we stand ever at the edge of Eternity and fall in many times before we die. Yet even such thoughts live not long this day. All shall be healed, says the dream. All shall be made new. The day is a fairy birth, a foundling not fathered nor mothered by any grey yesterdays. It has inherited nothing. It makes of winter and of the old springs that wrought nothing fair a stale creed, a senseless tale: they are naught: I do not wonder any longer if the lark's song has grown old with the ears that hear it or if it still be unchanged.

What dreams are there for that aged child who goes tottering and reeling up the lane at mid-day? He carries a basket of watercress on his back. He has sold two-pennyworth, and he is tipsy, grinning through the bruises of a tipsy fall, and shifting his cold pipe from one side of his mouth to the other. Though hardly sixty he is very old, worn and thin and wrinkled, and bent sideways and forward at the waist and the shoulders. Yet he is very young. He is just what he was forty years ago when the thatcher found him lying on his back in the sun instead of combing out the straw and sprinkling it with water for his use. He laid no plans as a youth; he had only a few transparent tricks and easy lies. Never has he thought of the day after to-morrow.

For a few years in his prime he worked almost regularly for one or two masters, leaving them only now and then upon long errands of his own and known only to himself. It was then perhaps that he earned or received as a gift, along with a broken nose, his one name, which is Jackalone. For years he was the irresponsible jester to a smug town-let which was privately amused and publicly scandalized, and rewarded him in a gaol, where, unlike Tasso, he never complained. Since then he has lived by the sale of a chance rabbit or two, of watercress, of greens gathered when the frost is on them and nobody looking, by gifts of broken victuals, by driving a few bullocks to a fair, by casual shelter in barns, in roofless cottages, or under hedges.

He has never had father or mother or brother or sister or wife or child. No dead leaf in autumn wind or branch in flooded brook seems more helpless. He can deceive nobody. He is in prison two or three times a year for little things: it seems a charity to put a roof over his head and clip his hair. He has no wisdom; by nothing has he soiled what gifts were given to him at his birth. The dreams will not pass him by. They come to give him that confidence by which he lives in spite of men's and children's contumely.

How little do we know of the business of the earth, not to speak of the universe; of time, not to speak of eternity. It was not by taking thought that man survived the mastodon. The acts and thoughts that will serve the race, that will profit this commonwealth of things that live in the sun, the air, the earth, the sea, now and through all time, are not known and never will be known. The rumour of much toil and scheming and triumph may never reach the stars, and what we value not at all, are not conscious of, may break the surface of eternity with endless ripples of good. We know not by what we survive. There is much philosophy in that Irish tale of the poor blind woman who recovered her sight at St. Brigit's well. "Did I say more prayers than the rest? Not a prayer. I was young in those days. I suppose she took a liking to me, maybe because of my name being Brigit the same as her own."(*A Book of Saints and Wonders,* by Lady Gregory). Others went unrelieved away that day. We are as ignorant still. Hence the batlike fears about immortality.

We wish to prolong what we can see and touch and talk of, and knowing that clothes and flesh and other perishing things may not pass over the borders of death with us, we give up all, as if forsooth the undertaker and the gravedigger had archangelic functions. Along with the undertaker and the gravedigger ranks the historian and others who seem to bestow immortality. Each is like a child planting flowers severed from their stalks and roots, expecting them to grow. I never heard that the butterfly loved the chrysalis; but I am sure that the caterpillar looks forward to an endless day of eating green leaves and of continually swelling until it would despise a consummation of the size of a railway train. We can do the work of the universe though we shed friends and country and house and clothes and flesh, and become invisible to mortal eyes and microscopes. We do it now invisibly, and it is not these things which are us at all. That maid walking so proudly is about the business of eternity.

And yet it would be vain to pretend not to care about the visible many-coloured raiment of which our houses, our ships, our gardens, our books are part, since they also have their immortal selves and their everlasting place, else should we not love them with more than sight and hearing and touch. For flesh loves flesh and soul loves soul. Yet on this March day the supreme felicity is born of the two loves, so closely interwoven that it is permitted to forget the boundaries of the two, and for soul to love flesh and flesh to love soul. And this ancient child is rid of his dishonours and flits through the land floating on a thin reed of the immortal laughter. This is "not altogether fool." He is perchance playing some large necessary part in the pattern woven by earth that draws the gods to lean forward out of the heavens to watch the play and say of him, as of other men, of birds, of flowers: "They also are of our company." . . .

In the warm rain of the next day the chiffchaff sings among the rosy blossoms of the leafless larches, a small voice that yet reaches from the valley to the high hill. It is a double, many times repeated note that foretells the cuckoo's. In the evening the songs are bold and full, but the stems of the beeches are faint as soft columns of smoke and the columns of smoke from the cottages are like them in the still air. Yet another frost follows, and in the dim golden light just after sunrise the shadows of all the beeches lie on the slopes, dark and more tangible than the trees, as if they were the real and those standing upright were the returned spirits above the dead.

Now rain falls and relents and falls again all day, and the earth is hidden under it, and as from a land submerged the songs mount through the veil. The mists waver out of the beeches like puffs of smoke or hang upon them or in them like fleeces caught in thorns: in the just penetrating sunlight the long boles of the beeches shine, and the chaffinch, the yellowhammer and the cirl bunting sing songs of blissful drowsiness. The Downs, not yet green, rise far off and look, through the rain, like old thatched houses.

When a hot sun has dried the woods the wind beats a cloud of pollen like grey smoke from the yews on the beechen coombes which are characteristic of Hampshire. They are steep-sided bays, running and narrowing far into and up the sides of the chalk hills, and especially of those hills with which the high flinty plateau breaks down to the greensand and the plain. These steep sides are clothed with beeches, thousands of beeches interrupted by the black yews that resemble caverns among the paler trees, or, in the spring, by the green haze of a few larches and the white flames of the beam tree buds. Sometimes a stream rises at the head of the coombe, and before its crystal is a yard wide and ankle deep over the crumbling chalk it is full of trout; the sunny ripples are meshed like honeycomb. If there is not a stream there is a hop garden, or there is a grassy floor approached by neither road nor path and crossed only by huntsman and hounds. All the year round the coombes, dripping, green and still, are cauldrons for the making and unmaking of mists, mists that lie like solid level snow or float diaphanous and horizontal of airiest silk across the moon or the morning sun. The coombes breed whole families, long genealogical trees, of echoes which the child delights to call up from their light sleep; so, too, do fox and owl at night, and the cow on a calm evening; and as to the horn and the cry of hounds, the hangers entangle and repeat them as if they would imprison them for ever, so that the phantom exceeds the true. This is the home of the orchises and of the daintiest snails. In spring, yellow and white and yellowish green flowers are before all the rest under the beeches – the flowers of the golden green saxifrage and delicate moschatel, the spurge and the spurge laurel, the hellebore, the white violet and wood-sorrel, and the saffron-hearted primrose which becomes greenish in the light of its own leaves; to these must be added the yellow green of young foliage and of moss. Fairest of all the white flowers is the frost flower that grows about some rotten fallen branch day after day in curls that are beyond silk, or a child's hair, or wool when it is first exposed to the sun by the shearer's hand. Most conspicuous of the early green is that of the pale swords of sedge that bear purple-brown feathers of flower at the end of March. The crystal wavering water, the pale green stems and ever so slightly curving blades, and the dark bloom, make the sense smart with joy. Never was ivy more luxuriant under the beeches, nor moss so powerful

'The home of the orchises and of the daintiest snails.'

as where it arrays them from crown to pedestal. The lichens, fine grey-green bushy lichens on the thorns, are as dense as if a tide full of them had swept through the coombe. From the topmost branches hangs the cordage of ivy and honeysuckle and clematis. The missel thrush rolls out his clear song. The woodpecker laughs his loud shaking laughter as he bounds in his flight. Among the golden green mistletoe in the old shaggy apple tree at the entrance of the coombe the blackbird sings, composing phrases all the sweeter for being strangely like some in the songs that countrymen used to sing. Earth has no dearer voice than his when it is among the chilly rain at the end of the light. All day there have been blue skies and parading white clouds, and no wind, with sudden invasions of violent wind and hail or rain, followed by perfected calm and warmer sun – sun which lures the earliest tortoise-shell butterfly to alight on the footworn flints in the path up the coombe. At last the sky seems securely blue above the hangers and a clear small star or two pricks through it. But, emerging from the coombe, whose sides shut out half the heavens, you see that the west has wonderfully ordered and dressed itself with pale sky and precipitous, dark, modelled clouds and vague woods, and above them the new moon. The blackbirds sing, the dim Downs proceed, and the last shower's drops glitter on the black boughs and pallid primroses. Why should this ever change? At the time it seems that it can never change. A wide harmony of the brain and the earth and the sky has begun, when suddenly darker clouds are felt to have ascended out of the north-west and to have covered the world. The beeches roar with rain. Moon and Down are lost. The road bubbles and glows underfoot. A distant blackbird still sings hidden in the bosom of the rain like an enchanter hidden by his spells . . .

It is April now, and when it is still dark in the woods and hedges the birds all sing together and the maze of song is dominated by the owl's hoot – like a full moon of sound above myriad rippling noises. Every day a new invader takes possession of the land. The wryneck is loud and persistent, never in harmony with other birds, a complete foreigner, and yet the ear is glad of his coming. He is heard first, not in the early morning, along a grove of oaks; and the whole day is his.

Then on every hand the gentle willow wrens flit and sing in the purple ash blossoms. The martins, the swallows, have each a day. One day, too, is the magpie's: for he sits low near his mate in a thicket and chatters not aloud but low and tenderly, almost like the sedgewarbler, adding a faint plaintive note like the bullfinch's, and fragments as of the linnet's song, and chirrupings; disturbed, he flies away with chatter as hoarse as ever.

The rooks reign several days. They have a colony in a compact small oval beech wood that stands in a hollow amidst dry grey ploughland; and from the foxy-red summits of the trees, in the most genial hot day, their cawings are loud and mellow and warm as if they were the earth's own voice; and all the while the dew is sliding along the branches, dropping into other drops or to the ground as the birds flutter at their nests, and from time to time one triple drop catches the sun and throbs where it hangs like Hesperus among the small stars.

And every tender eve is the blackbird's. He sings out at the end of the long bare ash bough. Beneath him the gloomy crystal water stirs the bronze cresses, and on the banks the white anemones float above the dark misty earth and under the hazel leaves yet drooping in their infancy. The dark hollies catch the last light and shine like water. Behind all, the Downs are clear and so near that I feel as well as see the carving on their smooth and already green flanks. The blackbird gathers up all the low-lit beauty into one carol.

The flowers also have days to themselves, as the minute green moschatel when it is first found among the hedgerow roots, or the violets when, white and pale purple, they are smelt and then seen bowed with dew in the weedy sainfoin field which the chain harrow passed over but a few days before. Another notable day is when the junipers are perfectly coloured by their sloe-blue, or palest green, but chiefly grey, small berries. Another, a very great day, belongs to the willows, when their crowded fragrant catkins are yellow against the burning blue and all murmurous with bees. And the briers have their day when their green is a vivid flame in a gloomy air, against a dark immense wood and sepia sky. There is, too, a solitary maimed sycamore in one of the coombes that has a glorious hour when it stands yellow-green in separate masses of half-opened leaf, motionless and languid in the first joy of commerce with the blue air, yet glowing.

One morning, very early, when the moon has not set and all the fields are cold and dewy and the woods are still massed and harbouring the night, though a few thorns stand out from their edge in affrighted virgin green, and dim starry thickets sigh a moment and are still, suddenly the silence of the chalky lane is riven and changed into a song. First, it is a fierce impetuous downfall of one clear note repeated rapidly and ending wilfully in mid-burst. Then it is a full-brimmed expectant silence passing into a long ascendant wail, and almost without intervals another and another, which has hardly ceased when it is dashed out of the memory by the downpour of those rapidly repeated notes, their abrupt end and the succeeding silence. The swift notes are each as rounded and as full of liquid sweetness as a grape, and they are clustered like the grape. But they are wild and pure as mountain water in the dawn. They are also like steel for coldness and penetration. And their onset is like nothing else: it is the nightingale's. The long wail is like a shooting star: even as that grows out of the darkness and draws a silver line and is no more, so this glides out of the silence and curves and is no more. And yet it does not die, nor does that liquid onset. They and their ghosts people each hanging leaf in the hazel thicket so that the silence is closely stored. Other notes are shut in the pink anemone, in the white stitchwort under and about the hazels, and in the drops of dew that begin to glitter in the dawn.

Beautiful as the notes are for their quality and order, it is their inhumanity that gives them their utmost fascination, the mysterious sense which they bear to us that earth is something more than a human estate, that there are things not human yet of great honour and power in the world. The very first rush and the following wail empty the brain of what is merely human and leave only what is related to the height and depth of the whole world. Here for this hour we are remote from the parochialism of humanity. The bird has admitted a larger air. We breathe deeply of it and are made free citizens of eternity. We hear voices that were not dreamed of before, the voices of those spirits that live in minute forms of life, the spirits that weave the frost flower on the fallen branch, the gnomes of underground, those who care for the fungus on the beech root, the lichen on the trunk, the algae on the gravestone. This hazel lane is a palace of strange pomp in an empire of which we suddenly find ourselves guests, not wholly alien nor ill at ease, though the language is new. Drink but a little draught of this air and no need is there to fear the ways of men, their mockery, their cruelty, their foreignness.

The song rules the cloudy dawn, the waiting ranges of hills and their woods full of shadows yet crested with gold, their lawns of light, the soft distended grey clouds all over the sky through which the white sun looks on the world and is glad. But it has ceased when the perpendicular shafts of rain divide the mists over the hillside woods and the pewits tangle their flight through the air that is now alive with the moist gleaming of myriads of leaves on bramble, thorn and elder. Presently the rain is only a glittering of needles in the sun. For the sky is all one pale grey cloud, darker at the lowest edge where it trails upon the downs and veils their summits, except in the south-east. There the edge is lifted up over a narrow pane of silver across which fleet the long slender fringes of the clouds. Through this pane the sun sends a broad cascade of light, and up into this the fields and the Down beyond rise and are transfigured, the fields into a lake of emerald, the Down – here crowned by trees in a cluster – into a castle of pearl set upon the borders of the earth. Slowly this pane is broadened; the clouds are plumped into shape, are illumined, are distinguished from one another by blue vales of sky, until at length the land is all one gleam of river and pool and grass and leaf and polished bough, whether swollen into hills or folded into valleys or smoothed into plain. The sky seems to belong to this land, the sky of purest blue and clouds that are moulded like the Downs themselves but of snow and sun.

In the clear air each flower stands out with separate and perfect beauty, moist and bright, a beauty than which I know nothing more nearly capable of transferring the soul to the days and the pleasures of infancy. The crust of half a lifetime falls away, and we can feel what Blake expressed when he wrote those lines in *Milton*:

Thou perceivest the flowers put forth their precious odours,
And none can tell how from so small a centre comes such sweet,
Forgetting that within that centre Eternity expands
Its ever-during doors, that Og and Anax fiercely guard.
First, ere the morning breaks, joy opens in the flowery bosoms,
Joy even to tears, which the Sun rising dries; first the Wild Thyme
And Meadow-sweet, downy and soft, waving among the reeds,
Light springing in the air, lead the sweet Dance; they wake
The Honeysuckle sleeping in the Oak, the flaunting beauty
Revels along upon the wind; the white-thorn lovely May
Opens her many lovely eyes; listening the Rose still sleeps.
None dare to wake her. Soon she bursts her crimson-curtained bed.
And comes forth in the majesty of beauty; every Flower –
The Pink, the Jessamine, the Wallflower, the Carnation,
The Jonquil, the mild Lily opes her heavens; every Tree
And Flower and Herb soon fill the air with an innumerable Dance,
Yet all in order sweet and lovely . . .

Those words or such a morning – when the soul steps back many years; or is it many centuries? – might have moved M. Maeterlinck to his descriptions of certain great moments in the lives of plants. The terms of these descriptions are so chosen as to imply an intelligence and discriminating vital energy in plants. They prove and explain nothing, but they take one step towards the truth by disturbing the conventional scientific view and substituting that of a man who, passionately looking at many forms of life, finds them to be of one family. After this, it should be more and more difficult for men to think of flowers as if they were fragile toys from an exceptionally brilliant manufacturer.

And now there is a day of sun and high blue sky alternating with low, grey-yellow sky and driving snow that chequers the northern sides of the furrows and the beech boles. The sun melts the snow and all is clear, bright and cold, and the sky blue again with white and lofty clouds; many thrushes are singing; the broad vale is all one blue moorland that has buried its houses, and the Downs at the far side are close at hand. Towards evening the wind falls, and it is a glimpse of another world that is given as the sun is warm for a moment on a low curving slope of wet grass, with tall rookery beeches glowing on one hand and on the other bulging white clouds just emerging from behind the green edge into the blue, while very far away the Downs, both grass and wood, are deep blue under a broad pane of yellowish light.

The north wind makes walking weather, and the earth is stretched out below us and before us to be conquered. Just a little, perhaps, of the warrior's joy at seeing an enemy's fair land from the hill-top is mingled with the joy in the unfolding landscape. The ploughlands brighten over twenty miles of country, pale and dry, among dark woods and wooded hills; for the wind has crumbled the soil almost white, so that a sudden local sunlight will make one field seem actually of snow. The old road following a terrace of the hillside curves under yews away from the flinty arable and the grey, dry desolation round about the poultry-farmer's iron house, to the side of a rich valley of oak and ash and deepening pastures traversed by water in a glitter. The green fire of the larch woods is yellow at the crest. There and in oak and ash the missel thrush is an embodiment of the north wind, summing it up in the boldness of his form and singing, as a coat of arms sums up a history. Mounted on the plume of the top of the tall fir, and waving with it, he sings of adventure, and puts a spirit into those who pass under and adds a mile to their pace. The gorse is in flower. In the hedges the goose-grass has already set its ladders against the thorns, ladders that will soon have risen to the top of every hedge like scaling ladders of an infinite army. Down from tall yew and ash hang the abandoned ropes of last year's traveller's joy that have leapt that height – who has caught them in the leap? – but the new are on their way, and even the old show what can be done as they sway from the topmost branches. At sunset an immense and bountiful land lies at our feet and the wine-red sun is pouring out large cups of conquest. The undulating ploughland is warm in the red light, and it is broken up by some squares of old brown stubble and of misty young wheat, and lesser green squares full of bleating and tinkling sheep. Out of these fields the dense beech copses rise sheer. Beyond, in the west, are ridges of many woods in misty conflagration; in the south-west, the line of the Downs under the level white clouds of a spacious and luminous sky. In the south, woods upon the hills are dissolving into a deep blue

smoke, without form except at their upper edges. And in the north and
north-west the high lands of Berkshire and Wiltshire are prostrate and
violet through thirty miles of witching air. That also is a call to go on
and on and over St. Catherine's Hill and through Winchester until the
brain is drowsed with the colours of night and day.

The colour of the dawn is lead and white – white snow falling out of
a leaden sky to the white earth. The rose branches bend in sharper and
sharper curves to the ground, the loaded yew sprays sweep the snow
with white plumes. On the sedges the snow is in fleeces; the light strands
of clematis are without motion, and have gathered it in clots. One thrush
sings, but cannot long endure the sound of his unchallenged note; the
sparrows chirrup in the ricks; the blackbird is waiting for the end of that
low tingling noise of the snow falling straight in windless air.

At mid-day the snow is finer, and almost rain, and it begins to pour
down from its hives among the branches in short showers or in heavy
hovering lumps. The leaves of ivy and holly are gradually exposed in all
their gloomy polish, and out bursts the purple of the ash buds and the
yellow of new foliage. The beech stems seem in their wetness to be made
of a dark agate. Out from their tops blow rags of mist, and not far above
them clouds like old spiders' webs go rapidly by.

The snow falls again and the voices of the little summer birds are
buried in the silence of the flakes that whirl this way and that aimlessly,
rising and falling and crossing or darting horizontally, making the trees
sway wearily and their light tops toss and their numbers roar continually
in the legions of the wind that whine and moan and shriek their hearts
out in the solitary house roofs and doors and round about. The silence
of snow co-exists with this roar. One wren pierces it with a needle of
song and is gone. The earth and sky are drowning in night and snow.

'Snow ... One wren pierces the silence with a needle of song and is gone.'

THREE
Spring

NEXT DAY the wind has flown and the snow is again almost rain: there is ever a hint of pale sky above, but it is not as luminous as the earth. The trees over the road have a beauty of darkness and moistness. Beyond them the earth is a sainted corpse, with a blue light over it that is fast annihilating all matter and turning the landscape to a spirit only. Night and the snow descend upon it, and at dawn the nests are full of snow. The yews and junipers on a league of Downs are chequered white upon white slopes, and the green larches support cirrus clouds of snow. In the garden the daffodils bend criss-cross under snow that cannot quite conceal the yellow flowers. But the snow has ceased. The sky is at first pale without a cloud and tender as from a long imprisonment; it deepens in hue as the sun climbs and gathers force. The crooked paths up the Downs begin to glitter like streaks of lightning. The thrushes sing. From the straight dark beeches the snow cannot fall fast enough in great drops, in showers, in masses that release the boughs with a quiver and a gleam. The green leaves close to the ground creep out, and against them the snow is blue. A little sighing wind rustles ivy and juniper and yew. The sun mounts, and from his highest battlement of cloud blows a long blast of light over the pure land. Once more the larch is wholly green, the beech rosy brown with buds. A cart goes by all a-gleam with a load of crimson-sprouting swedes and yellow-sprouting mangolds that seem to be burning through the net of snow above them. Down each side of every white road runs a stream that sings and glitters in ripples like innumerable crystal flowers. Water drips and trickles and leaps and gushes and oozes everywhere, and extracts the fragrance of earth and green and flowers under the heat that hastens to undo the work of the snow. The air is hot and wet. The snow is impatient to be water again. It still makes a cape over the briers and brambles, and there is a constant drip and steam and song of drops from the crossing branches in the cave below. Loud sounds the voice of leaf and branch and imprisoned water in the languor and joy of their escape. On every hand there is a drip of gush and ooze of water, a crackle and rustle and moan of plants and trees unfolding and unbending and greeting air and light; a close, humid, many-perfumed host; wet gloom and a multitudinous glitter; a movement of water and of the shadows like puffs of smoke that fleet over the white fields under the clouds.

And over and through it a cuckoo is crying and crying, first overhead, then afar, and gradually near and retreating again. He is soon gone, but the ears are long afterwards able to extract the spirit of the song, the exact interval of it, from among all the lasting sounds, until we hear it as clearly as before, out of the blue sky, out of the white cloud, out of the shining grey water. It is a word of power – cuckoo! The melting of the snow is faster than ever, and at the end of the day there is none left except in some hollows of the Downs on the slopes behind the topmost of the beeches that darkly fringe the violet sky. In the misty shutting of the light there are a thousand songs laced by cuckoos' cries and the first hooting of owls, and the beeches have become merely straight lines of pearl in a mist of their own boughs. Below them, in the high woods, goes on the fall of the melting snow through the gloomy air, and the splash on the dead leaves. This gloom and monotonous sound make an exquisite cloister, visited but not disturbed by the sound of the blackbirds singing in the mist of the vale underneath. Slowly the mist has deepened from the woods to the vale and now the eye cannot see from tree to tree. Then the straight heavy rain descends upon the songs and the clatterings of blackbirds, and when they are silenced the moorhen's watery hoot announces that the world belongs to the beasts and the rainy dark until tomorrow.

Beautiful upon the waters, beautiful upon the mountains, is the cuckoo's song, and most rare over the snow. But of all places and hours I should choose the crags of Land's End in a dawn of June; and let it be the end of that month and the wind be grey and cold, so that the ships stagger in the foam and crag-like waves as they catch the early light

tenderly upon their sails. The cold beams, the high precipices yet full of
shadow and of the giddy calling of daw and gull, the black but white-
lipped water and the blacker cormorant flying straight across it just over
the foam, the sky golden yet still pallid and trembling from the dungeon
of night – through it floats that beloved voice breaking, breaking, and
the strong year at the summit of its career has begun to decline. The
song is memorable and fair also when the drenched gardens toss and
spread their petals in the grass. Many a one hears it who will not hear
it again, and many that once expected it impatiently hears it no more
because he is old and deaf or because his heart is closed. There is not a
broad and perfect day of heat and wind and sunshine that is not haunted
by that voice seeming to say the earth is hollow under our feet and the
sky hollow over our heads.

There are whole nights when the cuckoo will not sleep, and the woods
on either side of a road twenty miles long emit the cry of these conquerors
under the full moon and the white stars of love. If you pause it will appear
that it is not a silence that this song rules over; for what was a silence was
full of sounds, as many sounds as there are leaves, sounds of creeping,
gliding, pattering, rustling, slow wormlike continuous noises and sudden
sounds. And strangely at length is the glorious day reared high upon the
ruins of this night, of which the survivors slink away into the old forgotten
roads, the dense woods, the chimneys of deserted houses.

It is a jolly note only when the bird is visible close at hand and the
power of his throat is felt. Often two or three will answer one another,
or for half a day will loiter about a coombe for the sake of an echo. It is
one of the richest sounds in nature when two sing together, the second
note of one being almost blended with the first of the other; and so they
continue as if themselves entranced by the harmony, and the navvy leans
upon his pick to listen.

·   ·   ·   ·   ·

On the day after the great melting of the snow the white beam tree, at the
edges of high woods and in the midst of the beeches, has its hour, when

its thousands of large white buds point upward like a multitudinous candelabrum. For me the white beam is always associated with wayfaring. Its white buds are the traveller's joy of spring. The buds like blossoms or flames bewitch from afar off. They are always upon sloping ground and usually upon hillsides in the chalk land. In the autumn their leaves often shrivel before falling, and turn to a colour that looks like pink almond blossom by contrast with juniper and yew. When they have fallen, they are as much to be noticed. They lie commonly with their white undersides uppermost, and though rain soaks them and wind scatters them and they are trodden down, they preserve their whiteness until the winter or the following spring. It is a tree that belongs, above all others except the yew, to the Pilgrims' Way, and it is impossible to forget these leaves lying white on the untouched wayside sward, among the dewy purple and crimson and gold of other leaves, sparkling in the sun and entering into all the thoughts and fancies and recollections that come to one who goes in solitude along that old road when the scent of the dying year is pungent as smoke and sweet as flowers.

KENT, SURREY AND HAMPSHIRE

The beam tree is bright on the soft hills all through the days of rain following upon the snow and sun. There are days when earth is absorbed in her delights of growth and multiplication. The rain is a veil which she wraps about her that she may toil and sing low at her myriad divine domesticities untroubled. Delicate snails climb the young stalks of grass and flower, and their houses, pearly, chocolate, tawny, pure or ringed or chequered, slide after them. The leaves, with their indescribable charm of infinitely varied division, of wild clematis, maple, brier, hawthorn, and many more, come forth into the rain which hangs on their drooping points and on the thorns. The lichen enjoys the enduring mist of the woods; the blackthorns are crusted and bearded with lichens of fleshy green-silver and ochre which grow even on the thorns themselves and round the new leaves and flowers. The birch is now an arrested shower of green, but not enough to hide the white limbs of the nymph in the midst of it. The beech trunk is now most exquisitely coloured: it is stained and spotted and blotched with grey and rough silver and yellow-green lichen, palest green mould, all the greens of moss, and an elusive dappling and graining of greys, of neutral tints and almost blacks in the wood itself, still more diversified by the trickling rain and the changing night. The yew bark is plated and scaled and stained with greens and reds and greys, powdered with green mould, and polished in places to the colour of mahogany. Even the long-deserted thistly cornfields are dim purple with ground-ivy flowers and violets. The marsh, the pasture, the wood, the hedge, has each its abundance of bloom and of scent; so, too, has the still water and the running water. But this is the perfect hour of the green of grass, so intense that it has an earthly light of its own in the sunless mist. It is best seen in meadows bounded on two or three sides by the sheer dark edges of woods; for in that contrast the grass seems a new element, neither earth, nor water, nor sky – under our feet like the earth, gleaming and even as water, remote and celestial as the sky. And the voices of the green growing in the rain are innumerable. The very ground has now one voice of its own, the gurgle of its soaking hollow places.

HAMPSHIRE

The fields where the green is now greenest, those bounded on two or more sides by woods, are of a kind not peculiar to Hampshire. They are usually on the greensand and lie in smooth, often winding, hollows like the beds of rivers. Sometimes the banks of these beds are steep, and they are clothed in woods or in hedges of hornbeam, hazel, ash and thorn that have grown almost to woods. The meadows are green broad rivers running up between the dark trees that bathe their roots in primroses. Sometimes there is a stream of water running down the midst of such a field, but as the stream, being a boundary, is often lined with bushes, the particular charm is lost. In the perfect examples there is the smoothness of the long hollowed meadow, the green, the river-like form, the look of being a court or cloister between the trees. Another kind of field of great charm is made by the convexity of the land rising up from one side or both of such a hollow meadow. These heaving fields, some of a regular domed shape, are favourites of the sunset light, in spring when they are grassy, in August when they bear corn: at noon when there are cattle grazing on the steep slope, their shadows are an exact inversion of themselves, as in water.

· · · · ·

Out of the rain and mist Spring has now risen full-grown, tender and lusty, fragrant, many-coloured, many-voiced, fair to see, so that it is beyond a lover's power to make even an inventory of her lovely ways. She is tall, she is fresh and bold, sweet in her motion and in her tranquillity; and there is a soft down upon her lip as there is a silken edge to the young leaves of the beeches.

KENT

Even the motor road is pleasant now when the nightingales sing out of the bluebell thickets under oak and sweet chestnut and hornbeam and hazel. Presently it crosses a common, too small ever to draw a crowd, a rough up-and-down expanse of gorse and thorn, pierced by grassy paths and surrounded by turf that is rushy and mounded by old ant heaps; and here, too, there are nightingales singing alone, the sweeter for the contrast between their tangled silent bowers and the sharp, straight white road. The common is typical of the lesser commons of the south. Crouch's Croft in Sussex is another, in sight of the three dusk moorland breasts of Crowborough; gorse-grown, flat, possessing a pond, and walled by tall hollies in a hedge. Piet Down, close by, is a fellow to it – grass and gorse and irregular pine – a pond, too – rough, like a fragment of Ashdown or Woolmer, and bringing a wild sharp flavour into the mellow cultivated land. Yet another is at Stone Street, very small, a few oaks up to their knees in blackthorn, gorse and bramble, with dusty edge and the hum of the telegraph wire for a song.

After the little common and long meadows, oak and ash, an old stone house with seven hundred years of history quiet within its walls and dark tiles – its cedar and yew and pine, its daisied grass, its dark water and swans – the four oast cones opposite, all taste more exquisitely. How goodly are the names hereabout! – Dinas Dene, the coombe in which the old house stands; Balk Shaw, Cream Crox, Dicky May's Field, Ivy Hatch, Lady Lands, Lady's Wood, Upper and Lower Robsacks, Obram Wood, Ruffats, Styant's Mead, the Shode, and, of course, a Starvecrow. Almost due west goes one of the best of footpaths past hop garden, corn, currant plantations, rough copses, with glimpses of the immense Weald to the east, its trees massed like thirty miles of wood, having sky and cloud over its horizon as if over sea, and southward the wild ridge of Ashdown. Then the path enters tall woods of ash and oak, boulder-strewn among their anemone and primrose, bluebell and dog's mercury, and emerges in a steep lane at the top of which are five cowled oast houses among cherry blossom and under black firs. Beyond there is a hollow winding vale of meadow and corn, its sides clothed in oak, hazel and thorn, revealing primroses between. Woods shut it away from the road and from all houses but the farm above one end. A few cattle graze there, and the sun comes through the sloping woods and makes the grass golden or pale.

Then the North Downs come in sight, above a church tower amid stateliest pale-foliaged beeches and vast undulations of meadow. They are suffused in late sunshine, their trees misty and massed, under a happy sky. Those beeches lie below the road, lining the edge of one long meadow. The opposite sun pours almost horizontal beams down upon the perfectly new leaves so as to give each one a yellow-green glow and, to some a silver shimmer about the shadowy boles. For the moment the trees lose their anchor in the solid earth. They are floating, wavering, shimmering, more aerial and pure and wild than birds or any visible things, than aught except music and the fantasies of the brain. The mind takes flight and hovers among the leaves with whatsoever powers it has akin to dew and trembling lark's song and rippling water; it is throbbed away not only above the ponderous earth but below the firmament in the middle world of footless fancies and half thoughts that drift hither and thither and know neither a heaven nor a home. It is a loss of a name and not of a belief that forbids us to say to-day that sprites flutter and tempt there among the new leaves of the beeches in the late May light.

Almost every group of oast houses here, seen either amongst autumn fruit or spring blossom, is equal in its effect to a temple, though different far, even when ivy-mantled as they occasionally are, from the grey towered or spired churches standing near. The low round brick tower of the oast house, surmounted by a tiled cone of about equal height, and that again crested with a white cowl and vane, is a pleasant form. There are groups of three which, in their age, mellow hue, roundness, and rustic dignity, have suggested the triple mother goddesses of old religions who were depicted as matrons, carrying babes or fruit or flowers, to whom the peasant brought thank-offerings when sun and rain had been kind. Those at Kemsing, for example, stand worthily beside the perfect grey-shingled spire, among elm and damson, against the bare cloudy Down. And there are many others near the Pilgrims' Way of the same charm.

That road, in its winding course from Winchester to Canterbury, through Hampshire, Surrey and Kent, sums up all qualities of roads except those of the straight highway. It is a cart-way from farm to farm; or a footpath only, or a sheaf of half a dozen footpaths worn side by side; or, no longer needed except by the curious, it is buried under nettle and burdock and barricaded by thorns and traveller's joy and bryony bines; it has been converted into a white country road for a few miles of its length, until an ascent over the Downs or a descent into the valley has to be made, and then once more it is left to footsteps upon grass and bird's foot trefoil or to rude wheels over flints. Sometimes it is hidden among untended hazels or among chalk banks topped with beech and yew, and the kestrel plucks the chaffinch there undisturbed. Or it goes free and hedgeless like a long balcony halfway up the Downs, and unespied it beholds half the South Country between ash tree boles. Church and inn and farm and cottage and tramp's fire it passes like a wandering wraith of road. Some one of the little gods of the earth has kept it safe – one of those little and less than omnipotent gods who, neglecting all but their own realms, enjoy the earth in narrow ways, delighting to make small things fair, such as a group of trees, a single field, a pure pool of sedge and bright water, an arm of sea, a train of clouds, a road. I see their hands in many a by-way of space and moment of time. One of them assuredly harbours in a rude wet field I know of that lies neglected between two large estates: three acres at most of roughly sloping pasture, bounded above by the brambly edge of a wood and below by a wild stream. Here a company of meadow-sweet invades the grass, there willow herb tall with rosy summits of flowers, hoary lilac mint, dull golden fleabane, spiry coltstails. The snake creeps careless through these thickets of bloom. The sedge-warbler sings there: One old white horse is content with the field, summer and winter, and has made a plot of it silver with his hairs where he lies at night. The image of the god is in the grey riven willow that leans leafless over the stream like a peasant sculpture of old time. There is another of these godkins in a bare chalk hollow where the dead thistles stick out through a yard of snow and give strange thoughts of the sailless beautiful sea that once rippled over the Downs: one also in the smell of hay and mixen and cow's breath at the first farm out of London where the country is unsoiled. There is one in many a worthless waste by the roadside, such as that between two roads that go almost parallel for a while – a long steep piece, only a few feet broad, impenetrably overgrown by blackthorn and blackberry, but unenclosed: and one in each of the wayside chalk-pits with overhanging beech roots above and bramble below. One, too, perhaps many, were abroad one August night on a high hillside when the hedge crickets sang high up in the dogwood and clematis like small but deafening sewing machines, and the glowworms shone in the thyme, and the owl's crying did not rend the breathless silence under the full moon, and in the confused moonlit chequer of the wood, where tree and shadow were equals, I walked on a grating of shadows with lights between as if from under the earth; the hill was given over to a light happiness through which I passed an unwilling but unfeared intruder.

In places these gods preside over some harmony of the earth with the works of men. There is one such upon the Pilgrims' Way, where I

'The snake creeps careless through these thickets of bloom.'

join it, after passing the dark boughs and lightsome flowers of cherry
orchards, grass full of dandelions, a dark cluster of pines, elms in groups
and cavalcades, and wet willowy meadows that feed the Medway. Just
at the approach there is a two storied farm with dormers in the darkly
mellowed roof, protected by sycamores and chestnuts, and before it a
weather-boarded barn with thatched roof, and then, but not at right
angles, another with ochre tiles, and other outbuildings of old brick
and tile, a wagon lodge of flint and thatch beside a pond, at the edge of
a broad unhedged field where random oaks shadow the grass. Behind
runs the Pilgrims' Way, invisible but easily guessed under that line of
white beam and yew, with here and there an ash up which the stout
plaited stems of ivy are sculptured, for they seem of the same material as
the tree, and both of stone. Under the yew and white beam the clematis
clambers over dogwood and wayfaring trees. Corn grows up to the
road and sometimes hops; beyond, a league of orchard is a-froth round
farmhouses or islands of oak; and east and west sweeps the crescent of
the North Downs.

With the crescent goes the road, halfway up the sides of the hills but
nearly always at the foot of the steepest slopes where the chalk-pits are
carved white, like the concave of a scallop shell, out of the green turf.
Luxuriant hedges bar the view except at gateways and stiles. At one
place the upper hedge gives way to scattered thickets scrambling up the
hill, with chalky ruts and rabbit workings between. Neither sheep nor
crops cover the hill, nor yet is it common. Any one can possess it – for
an hour. It is given up to the rabbits until Londoners can be persuaded to
build houses on it. At intervals a road as old as the Way itself descends
precipitously in a deep chalk groove, overhung by yew and beech,
or hornbeam, or oak, and white clouds drifting in a river of blue sky
between the trees; and joins farther south the main road which winds,
parallel with the Pilgrims' Way and usually south of it, from Winchester,
through Guildford, Dorking, Westerham, Maidstone, Ashford, and
Canterbury to Dover Strait. Not only chalk-pits and deep roads hollow
the hills. For miles there is a succession of small smooth coombes, some
grown with white thorn, some grassy, above the road, alternating with

corresponding smooth breasts of turf. Towers and spires, but chiefly towers, lie beneath, and in the mile or so between one and the next there are red farms or, very rarely, a greater house at the end of a long wave of grass among trees. Above, the white full-bosomed clouds lean upon the green rampart of the hills and look across to the orchards, the woods beyond, the oaken Weald and its lesser ridges still farther, and then the South Downs and a dream of the south sea.

Rain falls, and in upright grey sheaves passes slowly before the fresh beech leaves like ghosts in shadowy procession; and once again the white clouds roll over the tops of the trees, and the green is virginal, and out of the drip and glimmer of the miles of blissful country rises the blackbird's song and the cuckoo's shout. The rain seems not only to have brightened what is to be seen but the eye that sees and the mind that knows, and suddenly we are aware of all the joy in the grandeur and mastery of an oak's balance, in those immobile clouds revealed on the farthest horizon shaped like the mountains which a child imagines, in the white candles of the beam tree, in the black-eyed bird sitting in her nest in the hawthorn with uplifted beak, and in the myriad luxuriant variety of shape and texture and bright colour in the divided leaves of wood sanicle and moschatel and parsley and cranesbill, in the pure outline of twayblade and violet and garlic.

Newly dressed in the crystal of the rain the landscape recalls the earlier spring; the flowers of white wood-sorrel, the pink and white anemone and cuckoo flower, the thick-clustered, long-stalked primroses and darker cowslips with their scentless sweetness pure as an infant's breath; the solitary wild cherry trees flowering among still leafless beech; the blackbirds of twilight and the flower-faced owls; the pewits wheeling after dusk; the jonquil and daffodil and arabis and leopard's bane of cottage gardens ; the white clouds plunged in blue floating over the brown woods of the hills; the delicate thrushes with speckled breasts paler than their backs, motionless on dewy turf; and all the joys of life that come through the nostrils from the dark, not understood world which is unbolted for us by the delicate and savage fragrances of leaf and flower and grass and clod, of the plumage of birds and fur of animals and breath and hair of women and children.

How can our thoughts, the movements of our bodies, our human kindnesses, ever fit themselves with this blithe world? Is it but vain remorse at what is lost, or is it not rather a token of what may yet be achieved, that makes these images blind us as does the sight of children dressed for a play, some solemn-thoughtful, some wholly gay, suddenly revealed to us in brilliant light after the night wind and rain?

But at morning twilight I see the moon low in the west like a broken and dinted shield of silver hanging long forgotten outside the tent of a great knight in a wood, and inside are the knight's bones clean and white about his rusted sword. In the east the sun rises, a red-faced drover and a million sheep going before him silent over the blue downs of the dawn: and I am ill-content and must watch for a while the fraying, changeful edges of the lesser clouds drift past and into the great white ones above, or hear rebellious music that puts for one brief hour into our hands the reins of the world that we may sit mightily behind the horses and drive to the goal of our dreams.

A footpath leads from the Pilgrims' Way past the divine undulations and beech glades of a park – a broad piece of the earth that flows hither and thither in curves, sudden or slow but flawless and continuous, and everywhere clothed in a seamless garment of grass. The path crosses the white main road into a lesser one that traverses a common of beech and oak and birch. The leaves make an unbroken roof over the common: except the roads there is not a path in it. For it is a small and narrow strip of but a few acres, without any open space, gloomy, much overgrown by thickets. Last year's leaves lie undisturbed and of the colour of red deer under the silky green new foliage and round the huge mossy pedestals of beech and in caves behind the serpentine locked roots. No child's shout is heard. No lover walks there. The motor-car hurries the undesirable through and down into the Weald. And so it is alone and for themselves that the beeches rise up in carven living stone and expand in a green heaven for the song of the woodwren, pouring out pearls like wine.

Southward, on either side of the steep road, the slope is, below the beeches, given to corn and hops; at the foot are all the oaks and pasture of the Weald, diversified by hop gardens on many of the slanting fields that break up its surface. Looking back from here the hills above are less finely modelled than the downs still farther behind us in the north. But they also have their shallow coombes, sometimes two tiers of them, and they are indented by deep, wide-mouthed bays. One of them begins in copses of oak and hazel and sallow, a little arable, a farm, three oast cones, and a little steep orchard in a hollow of their own, which give way to hops, followed by grass and then a tortuous ploughland among the oaks and firs of the great woods that cover the more precipitous sides of the upper end of the bay. Exquisitely cultivated, this bay is yet a possession of cuckoo and nightingale, singing under the yellow-green and black-branched oaks and above the floor of bluebell and dark dog's mercury.

Out of the coombe a deep lane ascends through beech, hazel and beam to another common of heather, and whinberry bathing the feet of scattered birch, and squat oak and pine, interrupted by yellow gravel pits.

Beyond is a little town and a low grey spire, neighboured by sycamores that stretch out horizontal boughs of broad leaves and new yellow-green flower tassels over long grass. Past the town – rapidly and continually resuming its sleep after the hooting of motor-cars – begins a wide and stately domain. At its edge are cottages doddering with age, but trim and flowery, and assuredly wearing the livery of the ripe, grave house of brick that stands on the grassy ascent above them, among new-leaved beech masses and isolated thorns dreaming over their shadows. That grove of limes, fair and decorous, leading up to the house is the work of Nature and the squire. His chestnut and pine plantations succeed. And now a pollard beech, bossy-rooted on a mound of moss and crumbling earth, its grotesque torso decorated as by childish hands with new leaves hanging among mighty boughs that are themselves a mansion for squirrel and jay and willow wren and many shadows, looks grimly down at the edge of a wood and asks for the wayfarer's passport – has he lived well, does he love this world, is he bold and free and kind? –

and if he have it not seals him with melancholy as he enters among the innumerable leaves of innumerable beeches beginning to respond to the straight, still, after-sunset rain, while the last cuckoo's cry and the last footsteps and wheels of the world die away behind. The foliage has a pale, almost white, light of its own among the darkly dripping boughs, and when that is gone the rain and leaf under a spongy grey sky have a myriad voices of contentedness. Below, invisible in the dark rain but not unfelt, is the deep hollow land of the Weald. The owls whimper and mew and croon and hoot and shriek their triumphs.

SURREY

In the morning a storm comes up on bellying blue clouds above the pale levels of young corn and round-topped trees black as night but gold at their crests. The solid rain does away with all the hills, and shows only the solitary thorns at the edge of an oak wood, or a row of beeches above a hazel hedgerow and, beneath that, stars of stitchwort in the drenched grass. But a little while and the sky is emptied and in its infant blue there are white clouds with silver gloom in their folds, and the light falls upon round hills, yew and beech thick upon their humps, the coombes scalloped in their sides tenanted by oaks beneath. By a grassy chalk pit and clustering black yew, white beam and rampant clematis, is the Pilgrims' Way. Once more the sky empties heavy and dark rain upon the bright trees so that they pant and quiver while they take if joyfully into their deep hearts. Before the eye has done with watching the dance and glitter of rain and the sway of branches, the blue is again clear and like a meadow sprinkled over with blossoming cherry trees.

The decent vale consists of square green fields and park-like slopes, dark pine and light beech; but beyond that the trees gather together in low ridge after ridge so that the South Country seems a dense forest from east to west. On one side of the hill road is a common of level ash and oak woods, holly and thorn at their edges, and between them and the dust a grassy tract, sometimes furzy; on the other, oaks and beeches sacred to the pheasant but exposing countless cuckoo flowers among the hazels of their underwood. Please trespass. The English game preserve is a citadel of woodland charm, and however precious, it has only one or two defenders easily eluded and, when met, most courteous to all but children and not very well dressed women. The burglar's must be a bewitching trade if we may judge by the pleasures of the trespasser's unskilled labour.

In the middle of the wood is a four-went way, and the grassy or white roads lead where you please among tall beeches of broad, crisp-leaved shining thorns and brief open spaces given over to the mounds of ant and mole, to gravel pits and heather. Is this the Pilgrim's Way, in the valley now, a frail path chiefly through oak and hazel, sometimes over whin and whinberry and heather and sand, but looking up at the yews and beeches of the chalk hills? It passes a village pierced by straight clear waters – a woodland church – woods of the willow wren – and then, upon a promontory, alone, within the greenest mead rippled up to its walls by but few graves, another church, dark, squat, small-windowed, old, and from its position above the world having the characters of church and beacon and fortress, calling for all men's reverence. Up here in the rain it utters the pathos of the old roads behind, wiped out as if writ in water, or worn deep and then deserted and surviving only as tunnels under the hazels.

I wish they could always be as accessible as churches are, and not handed over to land-owners – like Sandsbury Lane near Petersfield – because straight new roads have taken their places for the purposes of tradesmen and carriage people, or boarded up like that discarded fragment, deep-sunken and overgrown, below Colman's Hatch in Surrey. For centuries these roads seemed to hundreds so necessary, and men set out upon them at dawn with hope and followed after joy and were fain of their whiteness at evening: few turned this way or that out of them except into others as well worn (those who have turned aside for wantonness have left no trace at all), and most have been well content to see the same things as those who went before and as they themselves have seen a hundred times. And now they, as the sound of their feet and the echoes, are dead, and the roads are but pleasant folds in the grassy chalk. Stay, traveller, says the dark tower on the hill, and tread softly because your way is over men's dreams; but not too long; and now descend to the west as fast as feet can carry you, and follow your own dream, and that also shall in course of time lie under men's feet; for there is no going so sweet as upon the old dreams of men.

FOUR

An Adventurer

IN ONE OF the new cottages at the edge of the town beyond lives, or tries to live, a man who fought for many years in one of the suburbs a losing battle against London. His father had farmed land now covered by streets. He himself was persuaded to sell all but his house and garden to raise money for a business which promised his sons great wealth. He retained barely enough to live upon; the business, an honest one, failed; and in a short time misfortunes compelled him to open a shop. He converted the house – that was once a farm-house – into a shop, and not five years ago it could still be seen at the end of a row of gaudy, glittering windows, itself a village shop, having but a common house window for the display of wares, the interior gloomy and approached through a strip of garden where a lime tree put on and shed its leaves with the air of a princess of old romance. The back garden, half an orchard, was bordered along a side street by a high wall, and over that a broad cherry used to lean a gnarled branch and shower its blossoms upon the asphalt; the foot-passengers complained of the tree which had grown without foreknowledge of the fact that men would pass below in silk hats, and the branch was lopped. In the shop itself everything was for sale, everything that officious travellers could foist upon the little weak-eyed half-farmer, half-gardener who kept the shop – hoisery, leather bags, purses, cheap jewellery, fishing-tackle, cricket-bats, umbrellas, walking-sticks. A staircase led out of the shop to the bedrooms, just as it had done when the window on the narrow landing looked over hay-fields to Banstead Downs. When the cat was not lying upon the socks in the window, she had, very likely, been kept away by a litter of kittens somewhere among the seldom disturbed bundles of unfashionable ties, or she lay in the sun beneath the lime and watched her kittens pursuing the spiral flight of the yellow leaves.

The owner made no concessions except such as he was forced to, as when he bought the stock of jewellery because the traveller praised his cat; or allowed the cherry tree to be mutilated because the new Borough Council commanded. He dressed in breeches, gaiters and heavy boots, and never wore a coat or took his pipe out of his mouth (except to play with puss). Seldom did he leave the house, unless it was to go into the garden or to take a walk down the emptied busy street at night, when the only sound was the crickets' song from the bakers' shops. The little old house rippled over by creeper was beautiful then – the lime tree and the creeper trembling in the gusty moonlight, and the windows and doorway hollow and dark and romantic as if a poet had made them to sting men's hearts with beauty and with regret.

No one can ever say what the old man thought as he slammed the door after one of these walks and was alone with himself. Certainly he regretted the big decorous high-gated houses that used to stand opposite his, veiled by wistaria, passion flower and clematis; the limes that used to run the whole length of his father's land, but now all gone, save this one (how lovely its fallen leaves looked in the as yet untrodden streets in autumn mornings, lying flat and moistly golden under the fog!); the balsam growing through the railings; the dark yew tree that looked among bright lilac and laburnum like a negro among the women in the *Arabian Nights;* the pathway through the churchyard, in the days before they had to rail it in to preserve the decent turf – in vain, for it was now littered with newspapers and tram-tickets among the tombs of – Esquire, – Esquire, for they were all esquires. He regretted the houses and gardens, but less than their people, the men and women of some ease and state, of speech whose kindliness was thrice kind through its careful dignity, so he thought. And then the children, there were no such children now; and the young men and women, the men a little alarming, the women strong and lovely and gentle enough to supply him with incarnations at once of all those whom he read of in the novels of Scott. They had gone long ago, except those who survived vaguely in the novels. He remembered their houses better, for it was not until after some years that they were pulled down, their orchards grubbed up, and their rich mould carried away in sacks to the trumpery villas round about – dragged along the road and spilt in a long black trail. It was wonderful dark mould, and the thought of the apples, the plums, the nectarines, the roses which had grown out of it made him furious when it was taken to their gardens by people who would be gone in a year or less, and would grow in it nothing but nasturtiums and sunflowers.

There followed a period when, the old attitudes, the things that had been handed down from the last revolution, having been broken up, the gardens became a possession of nettles and docks, and fewer and fewer were the crown-imperials and hollyhocks to survive the fall of the houses. The scaffold-poles, the harsh blocks of stone, the rasping piles of bricks, the scores of cold earthenware and iron articles belonging to the rows of villas about to replace the old houses, looked more like ruin than preparation as they lay stark and hideous among the misty grass and still blue elms. There were days when the thrushes still sang well among the rioting undisturbed shrubberies. But soon men felled the elms and drove away their shadows for ever, and all that dwelled or could be imagined therein. No more would the trees be enchanted by the drunken early songs of blackbirds. The heavenly beauty of earthly things went away upon the timber carriages and was stamped with mud. The butts of the trees were used to decorate the gardens of the new houses. Two, indeed, were spared by someone's folly, and a main bough fell in the night and crushed through a whole fortnight's brickwork.

Those elms had come unconsciously to be part of the real religion of men in that neighbourhood, and certainly of that old man. Their cool green voices as they swayed, their masses motionless against the evening or the summer storms, created a sense of pomp and awe. They gave mystic invitations that stirred his blood if not his slowly working humble brain, and helped to build and to keep firm that sanctuary of beauty to which we must be able to retire if we are to be more than eaters and drinkers and newspaper readers. When they were gone he wondered, still humbly, what would do their work in the minds of the newcomers. Looking at the features of the younger people, held in a vice of reserve or pallidly leering, and hearing the snarl of their voices, he was not surprised. They had not been given a chance. How could they have the ease, the state, the kindliness of the old inhabitants? They had no gods, only a brand-new Gothic church. Often they supported this or that new movement, or bought a brave new book, but they continued to sneer timidly or brutally at everything else. They were satisfied with a little safe departure from the common way, some mental or spiritual equivalent to the door-knocker of imitation hammered copper. They did not care very much for trees though they planted them in every street, where the grammar-school boys and errand-boys mutilated them one by one in the dark; they cut off the heads of a score of tall poplars, lest perchance the west wind should one day do the same thing when one of the million was passing below.

The new people were a mysterious, black-liveried host, the grandchildren of peers, thieves, gutter-snipes, agricultural labourers, artisans, shopkeepers, professional men, farmers, foreign financiers, an unrelated multitude. They were an endless riddle to the old man. He used to stare at their houses as one might stare at a corpse in the hope of discovering that there was something alive there. They were as impenetrable as their houses, when at night the blinds of the lighted rooms were drawn and figures or parts of figures shot fantastically by. He read of their bankruptcies, their appointments, their crimes, their successes, unwittingly, in the newspapers. He could never take it as a matter of course to pass, to be continually surrounded by, thousands of whom he knew nothing, to whom he was nothing. Well did they keep their secrets, this blank or shamefaced crowd of discreetly dressed people who might be anywhere tomorrow.

He turned from them to his garden and cherry tree, and thinking of those who had walked there, and in the long garden on the other side of the fence, he felt at home again, with his cat and her long line of descendants. That long garden had survived the big house to which it had belonged. A merchant had lived there with his family of four daughters, dark, tall women, whose pride and tender speech the old trees in their garden often recalled. All were beautiful, and they were most beautiful together. They walked, they rode, they played and read in the garden, and the old man could see them there. They were said to be clever and their father was wealthy. They were nearly always together, and as often as possible with him. They were a tribe apart, of extraordinary perfection of strength and grace, holding their own against the world. And yet, as the old man thought to himself, looking at their garden in the rain, not one of them was ever married. They had moved right into London after selling their house and land. They had come to his shop once or twice after and made an excuse for going into the garden: they looked into their own as if they had lost something there. Thinking of them he went into his shop and opened a book. A minute black insect, disturbed from among the leaves, crawled over and over the white page as he pretended to read; it went in zigzags half an inch long, lost in the black and white desert, sometimes turning the sharp edge and going to the other side of the page; but as a rule the edge alarmed it and it retreated; it was never still. It reminded him of himself. They were both lost upon the vast surface of the earth.

But, of course, that was not why he left. Nobody knew why he left. In his seventieth year he ran away, bursting out of the crowd as one sheep no braver than the rest will do sometimes, inexplicably. He has brought his cats with him, and he has money enough to last until he is dead. Being considered by his niece as of unsound mind, he is free to do as he will and is happy when he is alone.

FIVE

Sussex

A FEW MILES south of that great presiding pollard beech is the boundary line between Surrey and Kent on the north and Sussex on the south. A few miles over the line the moorland organ roll of heather and birch and pine succeeds the grassy undulations and the well-grown beech and oak. The yellow roving lines of the paths cut through the heather into the sand add to the wildness of the waste, by their suggestion of mountain torrents and of channels worn in the soft rock or clay by the sea. The same likeness in little is often to be seen upon a high-pitched roof of thatch when the straw is earth-coloured and tunnelled by birds and seamed by rain. Here the houses are of stone, unadorned, heather-thatched. The maker of birch-heath brooms plies his trade. There are stacks of heath and gorse in the yard. All the more fair are the grooves in the moorland, below the region of pines, where the tiled white-boarded mill stands by the sheen of a ford, and the gorse is bright and white clothes are blowing over neat gardens and the first rose. On a day of rain and gloom the answer of the gorse to sudden lights and heats is delicious; all those dull grey and glaucous and brown dry spines bursting into cool and fragrant fire is as great a miracle as the turning of flames to roses round a martyr's feet.

It is only too easy for the pheasant lords to plant larch in parallelograms: to escape from them it is necessary to go in amongst them. Yet there are parts of the forest large and dark and primeval in look, with a few poor isolated houses and a thin file of telegraph posts crossing it among the high gloomy pines and down to the marshy hollows, to the strewn gold of dwarf willows, and up again to the deserted wooden windmill, the empty boarded cottage, the heather-thatched sheds at the southern edge of the moor. Looking at this tract of wild land the mind seems to shed many centuries of civilization and to taste something of the early man's alarm in the presence of the uncultured hills – an alarm which is in us tempered so as to aid an impression of the sublime. Its influence lingers in the small strips of roadside gorse beyond its proper boundary. Then, southward, there are softly dipping meadows, fields of young corn, and oaks thrown among the cowslips. The small farm-houses are neat and good – one has a long stone wall in front, and, over the road, tall Scotch firs above a green pond dappled by the water crowfoot's white blossoms and bordered by sallow and rush. Narrow copses of oak or wide hedges of hazel and sallow line the road; and they are making cask hoops under lodges of boughs at the woodsides. Bluebells and primroses and cuckoo flowers are not to be counted under the trees. The long moist meadows flow among the woods up and down from farm to farm and spire to tower. Each farm-house group is new – this one is roofed and walled with tiles; and opposite is a tangle of grass and gorse, with fowls and hen-coops amongst it, a sallowy pond, a pile of faggots, some crooked knees of oak, some fresh-peeled timber: old grey hop poles lean in a sheaf all round a great oak. The gates are of good unpainted oak, and some few are of a kind not often seen elsewhere, lower than a hurdle and composed of two stout parallel bars united by twenty uprights and by two pieces meeting to form a V across these. The gates deserve and would fill a book by themselves.

Green lucent calipers of flags shadow one another in little wayside ponds, white-railed; for this is the Weald, the land of small clay ponds. The hazels are the nightingale's. In many of the oak woods the timber carriages have carved a way through primroses and bluebells deep into the brown clay. The larger views are of cloudy oak woods, ridge behind ridge, and green corn or grass and grey ploughland between; and of the sun pouring a molten cataract out of dark machicolated clouds on to one green field that glows a moment and is insignificant again: the lesser are of little brambly precipitous sandpits by the road, of a white mill at a crossing, of carved yews before black-timbered inns, of a starling that has learned the curlew's call perched on a cottage roof, of abeles all rough silver with opening leaf shivering along the grass-bordered evening road, of two or three big oaks in a meadow corner and in their shadow unblemished parsley and grasses bowed as if rushing in the wind. At an inn door stands a young labourer, tall and straight but loosely made, his nose even and small, his eyes blue and deep set, his lips like those of Antinous, his face ruddy and rough-grained, his hair short and brown and crisp upon his fair round head; his neck bound by a voluminous scarf (with alternate lozenges of crimson and deep green divided by white lines) that is gathered beneath his chin by a brass ring and thence flows down under his blue coat; his trousers of grey cord, dirty and patched with drab to a weathered stone colour, fitting almost tightly to his large thighs and calves and reaching not too near to his small but heavily-shod feet. A prince – a slave. He is twenty, unmarried, sober, honest, a noble animal. He goes into a cottage that stands worn and old and without a right angle in its timbers or its thatch any more than in its apple trees and solitary quince which all but hide the lilac and massed honesty of the little garden. This is a house – I had almost said this is a man – that looked upon England when it could move men to such songs as, "Come, live with me and be my love," or –

> "Hey, down a down!" did Dian sing,
>   Amongst her virgins sitting;
> "Than love there is no vainer thing,
>   For maidens most unfitting."
> And so think I, with a down, down derry.

For a moment or less as he goes under the porch I seem to see that England, that swan's nest, that island which a man's heart was not too big to love utterly. But now what with Great Britain, the British Empire, Britons, Britishers, and the English-speaking world, the choice offered to whomsoever would be patriotic is embarrassing, and he is fortunate who can find an ideal England of the past, the present, and the future to worship, and embody it in his native fields and waters or his garden, as in a graven image.

The round unending Downs are close ahead, and upon the nearest hill a windmill beside a huge scoop in the chalk, a troop of elms below, and then low-hedged fields of grass and wheat. The farms are those of the down-land. One stands at the end of the elm troop that swerves and clusters about its tiled roof, grey cliff of chimney-stack, and many gables; the stables with newer tiles; the huge slope of the barn; the low mossy cart-lodge and its wheels and grounded shafts; the pale straw stacks and the dark hay ricks with leaning ladders. A hundred sheep-bells rush by with a music of the hills in the wind. The larks are singing as if they never could have done by nightfall. It is now the hour of sunset, and windy. All the sky is soft and dark-grey-clouded except where the sun, just visible and throbbing in its own light, looks through a bright window in the west with a glow. Exactly under the sun the grass and wheat is full both of the pure effulgence and of the south-west wind, rippling and glittering: there is no sun for anything else save the water. North of the sun and out of its power lies a lush meadow, beyond it a flat marshland cut by several curves of bright water, above that a dark church on a wooded mound, and then three shadowy swoops of Down ending at a spire among trees.

South-west, the jagged ridgy cluster of a hillside town, a mill and a castle, stand dark and lucid, and behind them the mere lines of still more distant downs.

SIX

A Return to Nature

I TURN INTO MY next inn with unusual hopes. For it was here some years ago that I met for the first time a remarkable man. It was nine o'clock on a late July evening, and the haymakers, only just set free, came stamping into the bar. The last wagon-load stopped at the door while the red-whiskered carter stood, one hand on the latch, and drank his pint before leading his horses into the stall. After the haymakers, in their pale corduroys and dirty white slops, came a tall, spare, shock-headed man, not recently shaved, dressed in grey – grey coat, grey breeches and stockings, and a tall, hard felt hat that was old and grey. He called for sixpenny ale, and wiping the hay dust from his neck sat down beside me.

No, he is not here to-day. Perhaps he will never get out of London again.

I asked him the way to the nearest village, and whether a bed was to be had there. He answered that it was some way off – paused, looked at me, drank from his tankard – and added in a lower voice that he would be glad if I would come and share his place. Such an unusual invitation enforced assent.

A quarter of a mile down the next by-way he opened a little oaken gate that slammed after us, and there, in a corner of a small, flat field, was his sleeping place, under an oak. Would I care to join him in fried bacon and broad beans and tea at six next morning?

He lit a wisp of hay and soon had a fire burning, and brought over some hay and sacks for the second bed. The lights of the farm-house shone on the other side of the little field behind lilac bushes. The farmhouse pump gave out a cry like a guinea fowl for a few minutes. Then the lights went out. I asked the name of the farm and he told me.

"I come here almost every summer for the haymaking," he said, and detecting my surprise that it was not his first year of haymaking, he continued:

"It is my tenth summer, to be exact."

He was a man of hardly over thirty, and I noticed that his hands, though small and fine, were rough and warty and dark. Thoughtlessly I remarked that he must find the winter hard if he travelled like this all the year round.

"Yes," he said, with a sigh, "it is, and that is why I go back in the winter; at least partly why."

"Go back – ?"

"Yes, to London."

I was still perplexed. He had the air of a town-bred man of the clerkly class, but no accent, and I could not think what he did in London that was compatible with his present life.

"Are you a Londoner, then?"

"Yes, and no. I was born at the village of —— in Caermarthenshire. My father was a clerk in a coal merchant's office of the neighbouring town. But he thought to better himself, worked hard in the evenings and came to London, when I was seven, for a better-paid post. We lived in Wandsworth in a small street newly built. I went to a middle-class school close by until I was sixteen, and then I went into a silk merchant's office. My father died soon after. He had never been strong, and from the first year's work in the city, I have heard my mother say, he was a doomed man. He made no friends. While I was young he gave up all his spare time to me and was happy, wheeling me, my mother walking alongside, out into the country on every Sunday that was not soaking wet, and nearly every Saturday afternoon, too.

"It was on one of these excursions, when they had left me to myself a little while to talk more gravely than they usually did when we were out like that, that there was suddenly opened before me – like a yawning pit, yet not only beneath me but on every side – infinity, endless time, endless space; it was thrust upon me, I could not grasp it, I only closed my eyes and shuddered and knew that not even my father could save me from it, then in a minute it was gone. To a more blessed child some fair or imposing vision might have risen up out of the deep and given him a profounder if a sadder eye for life and the world. How unlike it was to the mystic's trance, feeling out with infinite soul to earth and stars and sea and remote time and recognizing his oneness with them! To me, but later than that, this occasionally recurring experience was as an intimation of the endless pale road, before and behind, which the soul has to travel: it was a terror that enrolled me as one of the helpless, superfluous ones of the earth.

"I was their only child that lived, and my father's joy in me was very great, equalled only by his misery at the life which he had to lead and which he foresaw for me. He used to read to me, waking me up for the purpose sometimes when he reached home late, or if he did not do that rousing me an hour before breakfast. His favourite books were *The Compleat Angler* and *Lavengro,* the poems of Wordsworth, the diaries of Thoreau and the *Natural History of Selborne.* I remember crying – when I was twelve – with despair of human nature's fickleness to think that White, even though he was an old man, could have it in his heart to write that farewell to natural history at the end of his last letter to Barrington. My father read these books to me several times in a sad, hoarse voice – as it seemed to me, though when he paused he was happy enough – which I had often great trouble to endure as I got older and able and willing to read for myself.

So full was I of a sense of the real wild country which I had never seen – the Black Mountains of Caermarthen I hardly recalled – that I became fanciful, and despised the lavish creeper that hung like a costly dress over the fence between our garden and the next, because the earth it grew in was not red earth but a black pasty compound, full of cinders and mortar and decayed rags and kittens. I used to like to go to the blacksmith's to smell the singeing hoof and to the tram-stables and smell the horses, and see the men standing about in loose shirts, hanging braces, bare arms, clay pipes, with a sort of free look that I could not see elsewhere. The navvies at work in the road or on the railway line were a tremendous pleasure, and I noticed that the clerks waiting for their trains in the morning loved to watch these hulking free and easy men doing something that looked as if it mattered, not like their own ledger work and so on. I had the same sort of pleasure looking up the street that rose from east to west and seeing the sun set between the two precipices of brick wall at the top; it was as if a gate opened there and through it all the people and things that saddened me had disappeared and left me to myself; it was like the pit, too, that opened before me as a little child.

"My father died of consumption. I was then just able to earn my own living, so I was left in lodgings and my mother returned to Wales. I worked hard at figures; at least I went early and stayed late and never stopped to talk to the others; yet I made frequent mistakes, and the figures swam in a mist of American rivers and English waterfalls and gipsy camps, so that it was a wonder I could ever see my Thoreau and Wordsworth and Borrow without these figures. Fancy men adopting as a cry the 'right to work'.' Apparently they are too broken-spirited to think of a right to live, and would be content only to work. It is not wonderful that with such a cry they do very little. Men cannot fight hard for the 'right to work'! as I did. My office was at the bottom of a pit. The four sides of the pit were walls with many windows, and I could hear voices speaking in the rooms behind and the click of typewriters, but could not see into them. Only for two or three days in June could I see the sun out of the pit. But in the hot days blue-bottles buzzed on my panes and I took care of them until one by one they lay dead upon the window ledge. There were no spiders and they seemed to have a good life. Sparrows sometimes flew up and down the pit, and once for a week I had the company of a black-and-white pigeon. It sat day after day in a hole in the opposite wall until it died and fell on to the paved yard below. The clouds sailed over the top of the pit. Sea-gulls flew over, all golden-winged, in October afternoons. I liked the fog when all the lights were lit, and though we did not know one another in the pit we seemed to keep one another company. But I liked the rain best of all. It used to splash down from all sides and make a country noise, and I looked up and saw the quaint cowls sitting like cats on the chimney-pots, and had ridiculous fancies that took me far away for a second or two.

"The worst time of all was two or three years after my father's death. I spent most of my poor earnings on clothes; I took the trouble to talk and smoke and think as much as possible like the other nine young men in the railway carriage that took me into the city; I learned their horrible, cowardly scorn for those who were poor or outlandish, and for all things that were not like those in their own houses or in those of the richer people of their acquaintance or envy. We were slaves, and we gilded our collars."

"But the journalist and hack writer," said I, "is worse off. At least your master only asked for your dregs. The hack writer is asked to give everything that can be turned into words at short notice, and so the collar round his neck is never taken off as yours was between six in the afternoon and nine in the morning."

"Ah, but it is open to you to do good or bad. We could only do bad. All day we were doing things which we did not understand, which could not in any way concern us, which had nothing to do with what we had been taught at school, had read in books or had heard from our fathers and mothers. When he was angry the head of the firm used to say we had better take care or a machine would supersede us in ten years instead of twenty. We had been driven out of life into a corner in an underground passage where everything was unnecessary that did not help us to be quick at figures, or taking down letters from dictation, or neat in dress and obedient to the slaves who were set over us. When we were out of the office we could do nothing which unfitted us for it. The head of the firm used to say that we were each 'playing a part, however humble, in the sublime machine of modern civilization, that not one of us was unnecessary, and that we must no more complain or grow restive than does the earth because it is one of the least elements in this majestic universe.' We continued to be neat when we were away from the office, we were disobedient to everything and everybody else that was not armed with the power of taking away our bread – to the old, the poor, the children, the women, the ideas which we had never dreamed of, and that came among us as a white blackbird comes in the winter to a barbarous parish where keeper and gardener and farmer go out with their guns and stalk it from hedge to hedge until, starved and conspicuous and rather apart from its companions, it falls to their beastly shot and is sold to one of the gentry who puts it into a glass case.

"Sometimes on a Saturday or Sunday I broke away in a vague unrest, and walked alone to the pretty places where my father and mother had taken me as a little boy. Most of them I had not seen for five or six years. My visits were often formal. I walked out and was glad to be back to the lights of the street, the strong tea, the newspaper and the novel. But one day I went farther than usual to a wood where we used to go without interference and, after finding all the blackbirds' and thrushes' and robins' nests within reach, boil a kettle and have tea. I had never in that wood seen any man or woman except my father and mother; never heard a voice except theirs – my father perhaps reading Wordsworth aloud – and the singing birds' and the moorhens' in the pond at the edge; it used to shut out everything but what I had learned to love most, sunshine and wind and flowers and their love. When I saw it again I cried; I really could not help it. For a road had been made alongside of it, and the builder's workmen going to and fro had made a dozen gaps in the hedge and trodden the wood backward and forward and broken down the branches and made it noisome. Worse than all, the field, the golden field where I used to lie among the buttercups and be alone with the blue sky – where I first felt the largeness and dearness and nearness of the blue sky as a child of eight and put up my hand in my delight to draw it through the soft blue substance that seemed so near – the field was enclosed, a chapel built; it was a cemetery for all the unknown herd, strange to one another, strange to every one else, that filled the new houses spreading over the land.

"At first I was for running away at once. But the sight made me faint-hearted and my legs dragged, and it was all I could do to get home – I mean, to my lodgings.

"However, I was quite different after that. I was ashamed of my ways, and now spent all my spare time and money in going out into the country as far as possible, and reading the old books and the new ones that I could hear of in the same spirit. I lived for these things. It was now that I knew my slavery. Everything reminded me of it. The return half of my railway ticket to the country said plainly, 'You have got to be back at not later than 10.39 p.m.' Then I used to go a different way back or even walk the whole way to avoid having this thing in my pocket that proclaimed me a slave.

"It was now that I first accepted the invitation of a relation who lived on the east coast very near the sea. The sea had a sandy shore bounded by a perpendicular sandy cliff, to the edge of which came rough moorland. The sea washed the foot of the cliff at high tide and swept the yellow sand clean twice a day, wiping away all footprints and leaving a fresh arrangement of blue pebbles glistering in the bitter wind. It was impossible to be more alone than on this sand, and I was contented again. The sea brought back the feeling I had when I lay in the buttercup field – the cemetery – and looked into the sky. Walking over the moor the undulations of the land hid and revealed the sea in an always unexpected way, and often as I turned suddenly I seemed to see the blue sky extended so as to reach nearly to my feet and half-way up it went small brown or white clouds like birds – like ships – in fact they were ships sailing on a sea that mingled with the sky. It seemed a beautiful life, where clouds could not help being finely spun or carved, or pebbles help being delicious to eye and touch. But out of the extremity of my happiness came my worst grief. I fell in love. I fell in love with one of my cousins, a girl of seventeen. She never professed to return my love, but she was a most true friend, and for a time I was intoxicated with the delight; I now envy even the brief moment of pain and misery that I had in those days.

"She was clever and understanding so that I was always at my best with her, and yet, too, she was as sweet as a child and strange as an animal. The few moments of pain were when I saw her with the other girls. When they were together, running on the sands or talking or dancing they seemed all to be one, like the wind; and sometimes I thought that like the wind they had no heart amongst them – except mine that raced with the runners and sighed among the laughers. It was lovely to see her with animals! with cows or horses, her implicit motherhood going out to them in an animal kindness, a bluff tenderness without thought. At times I looked carefully and solemnly into her eyes until I was lost in a curious pleasure like that of walking in a shadowy, still, cold place, a cathedral or wintry grove – she had the largest of dark grey eyes; and she did not turn away or smile, but looked fearlessly forward, careless and unashamed like a deep pool in a wood unused to wayfarers. Then she seemed so much a child, and I longed for the days (which I had never really had) when I could have been as careless and bold and free as she was. No, I could never teach those eyes and lips the ways of love: that was for some boy to do. And I thought I will be content to love her and to have her friendliness. I was old for my years, and my life without the influence of women in office and lodgings, I thought, had made me unfit for her delicate ways. I turned away and the sunny ships in the sea were mournful because of my thoughts. But I could not wait. I told her my love. She was not angry or indifferent. She did not reject it. She was afraid. They sent her away to college. She overworked and overplayed, and they have told me she is now a schoolmistress. I see her sad and firm with folded hands. When I knew her she was tall and straight, with long brown hair in two heavy plaits, a shining, rounded brow, dark-lashed, grey eyes, and a smile of inexpressible sweetness in which I once or twice surprised her, pleased with the happiness and beauty of her thoughts and of Nature.

"When I had lost her, or thought I had –

> Not comforted to live
> But that there is this jewel in the world
> Which I may see again –

I resolved that I would not be a slave any more. For a few weeks I used to fancy it was only by a chance I had lost her, and every now and then as I mused over it I got heated and my thoughts raced forward as if in the hope of overtaking and averting that very evil chance which had already befallen, and had in fact caused the train of thought.

"I saved every penny that I could from my salary. In six months I had saved twenty pounds. Out of this I bought a new black suit, a pair of boots and a hat, and gave them to my landlady and asked her to take care of them until I returned, which might be at the end of October. It was then April. I gave notice to my employers and left them. The next day very early I left London, and walked all day and all night until I reached the sea. There I bathed and ate a hearty meal, and walking along the cliffs till I came to a small farm-house. I engaged a bedroom, and there I slept and thought and slept undisturbed for twenty-four hours. I was free. I was free to dream myself no longer one of the mob-led mob. With care my money would last until midsummer, even if I did no work.

"It was a warm, wet May, and by the end of the month there was a plentiful crop of weeds, and I had no difficulty in getting work at hoeing. Strawberry picking and cherry picking followed. I was very slow and earned little, but it was now warm enough to sleep out, and I earned my food. By the end of July, as I liked the work, I was as useful with my hayrake as any of the women and better than most of the odd hands. I wore my fingers raw at tying up barley and oats and, later on, at feeding the threshing machine. But before the end of October the weather drove me back to London, with ten shillings in my pocket.

"I put on my new clothes and got as good a berth as my first one, and in the hope of another spring and summer out of doors I passed the winter cheerfully. To save more money I went to bed as soon as I got back to my lodgings, and read myself to sleep.

"In May a spell of fine weather drove me to give notice again, and I walked as far as Maidstone the first day. My second summer was like my first. I was already known at half a dozen farms. When they could not give me work at once they gave me leave to fish in the three or four ponds to be found on all the farms in the Weald of Kent, and I had many a large, if not always savoury, meal of tench and eels. At the end of the summer I had three pounds in my pocket, and little less by the end of October.

"The winter I passed as before. For five years I lived in this way. Then, for the sake of going abroad on my savings, I worked for a whole year at a desk, and spent four months along the Loire and down to Bordeaux;

from there I worked my passage to Newport. Since then I have gone back to my old plan."

Here he paused and mused. I asked him if he still found it easy to get work in London.

"No, that's it," he replied; "my handwriting is worse and it is slow. The first weeks in London seem to undo all the good of my summer outing, especially as my salary is less than it used to be. They begin to ask me if I am a married man when I apply for work. The November rains remind me that I have rheumatism. It is my great fear that I may need a doctor, and so spend my savings, and be unable to leave London until field work is plentiful in June. But I have my freedom; I could, if necessary, take an under-cowman's place and live entirely on the land. They begin to look at my hands when I apply for clerical work, and I can't wear gloves."

"And ten years hence?"

"That is ten years too far ahead for me to look, though I am less cheerful than I used to be. I realize that I belong to the suburbs still. I belong to no class or race, and have no traditions. We of the suburbs are a muddy, confused, hesitating mass, of small courage though much endurance. As for myself, I am world-conscious, and hence suffer unutterable loneliness. I know what bitterness it is to be lacking in those strong tastes and impulses which, blinding men to what does not concern them, enable them to live with a high heart. For example, I have a sensitive palate and am glad of my food, yet whenever I taste lamb – which I do when I can – my pleasure is spoilt by the sight of the butcher carrying a lamb under his arm. There it is. I am sensitive on all sides. Your true man would either forget the sight or he would be moved to a crusade. I can do neither.

"I am weary of seeing things, the outsides of things, for I see nothing else. It makes me wretched to think what swallows are to many children and poets and other men, while to me they are nothing but inimitable, compact dark weights tumbling I do not know how through the translucent air – nothing more, and yet I know they are something more. I apprehend their weight, buoyancy and velocity as they really are, but

I have no vision. Then it is that I remember those words of Sir Thomas Browne's:

> I am sure there is a common spirit that plays within us, yet makes no part in us; and that it is the Spirit of God, the fire and scintillation of that noble and mighty essence, which is the life and radical heat of spirits . . . This is that gentle heat that brooded on the waters and in six days hatched the world; this is that irradiation that dispels the mists of hell, the clouds of horror, fear, sorrow, despair; and preserves the region of the mind in serenity. Whosoever feels not the warm gale and gentle ventilation of this spirit (though I feel his pulse I dare not say he lives; for truly without this, to me there is no heat under the tropic; nor any light, though I dwell in the body of the sun.

"I dare not say I live. And yet the cows, the well-fed, quiet cows, in this fine soft weather stare enviously at me through the gate, though they know nothing of death, and I know it must come, and that even though often desired, when it comes it will be unwelcome – Yet they stare enviously at me, I am sure.

"I have no courage. I can at least endure. I can use my freedom to become a slave again, and at least I know that I have lost nothing by my way of living. Yes, I can endure, and if after my death I am asked questions difficult to answer, I can ask one that is unanswerable which I have many times asked myself – often in London, but not here. Here I love my food and my work, my rest. My dreams are good. I am not unkindly spoken to; I make no enemies.

"But yet I cannot look forward – there is nothing ahead – just as I cannot look back. My people have not built; they were not settled on the earth; they did nothing; they were oil or grit in a great machine; they took their food and shelter modestly and not ungratefully from powers above that were neither kind nor cruel. I hope I do no less; I wish I could do more.

"Now again returns that old feeling of my childhood – I felt it when I had left my cousin – I have felt it suddenly not only in London, but on the top of the Downs and by the sea; the immense loneliness of the world, as if the next moment I might be outside of all visible things.

You know how it is, on a still summer evening, so warm that the ploughman and his wife have not sent their children to bed, and they are playing, and their loud voices startle the thought of the woods; my feeling is like that, space and quiet and my own littleness stupendously exaggerated. I have wished I could lay down my thoughts and desires and noises and stirrings and cease to trouble that great peace. It was, perhaps, of this loneliness that the Psalmist spoke: 'My days are consumed like smoke . . . I watch, and am as a sparrow alone on the housetop.' The world is wrong, but the night is fine; the dew light and the moist air is full of the honeysuckle scent. I will smoke another pipe of your tobacco and leave you for a while. I like to be alone before I sleep."

The next I saw of him was when he was frying bacon and boiling beans for our meal. "Forget my night thoughts," he said, "and be thankful for the white dry road and the blue sky. We are not so young but that we must be glad it is summer and fine. As for me, the dry weather is so sweet that I like the smell of elder flower and haycart horses' dung and dust that get into the throat of an evening. Good-bye."

He went away to wash at the pump, as the cattle spread out from the milking-stalls into the field and filled it with their sweet breath and the sound of their biting the thick grass.

I saw him again a few years later.

London was hot and dry, and would have been parched, cracked and shrivelled had it been alive instead of dead. The masonry was so dry that the eyes wearied of it before the feet wearied of the pavement, and both desired the rain that makes the city at one with Nature. The plane trees were like so many captives along the streets, shackled to the flagstones, pelted with dust, humiliated, all their rusticity ravished though not forgotten. The very sky, lofty, blue, white-clouded, was parched, the blue and the white being soiled by a hot, yellowish-grey scum that harmonizes with gritty pavements and stark towers and spires. The fairest thing to be seen – away from the river – was the intense young green of the grass-blades trying to grow up through the gratings which surround the trees of the streets. The grass was a prophet muttering wild, ambiguous things, and since his voice was very small and came from underground, it was hard to hear him, even without understanding. Thousands tread down the grass, so that except for a few hours at night it can never emerge from the grating.

Some vast machinery plunged and thundered behind the walls, but though they trembled and grew hot, it burst not through. Even so the multitude in the streets, of men and horses and machines and carriages of all kinds, roared and moved swiftly and continuously, encaged within walls that are invisible; and they also never burst through. Both are free to do what they are told. All of the crowd seem a little more securely imprisoned than him who watches, because he is aware of his bars; but they move on, or seem to do, on and on, round and round, as thoughtless as the belt of an engine.

There was not one face I knew; not one smiled; not one relaxed or contracted with a thought, an emotion, a fancy; but all were clear, hard, and fixed in a vice, so that though they were infinite in their variety – no two eyebrows set the same way, no two mouths in the same relation to the eyes – the variety seemed the product of a senseless ingenuity and immense leisure, as of a sublime philatelist. Hardly one spoke; only the women moved from left to right instead of straight on, and their voices were inaudible when their lips moved. The roar in which all played a part developed into a kind of silence which not any one of these millions could break; the sea does not absorb the little rivers more completely than this silence the voices of men and women, than this solitude their personalities. Now and then a face changed, an eyebrow was cocked, or a mouth fell; but it meant less to me than the flutter as of a bird when drop by drop the rain drips from the beeches and gives a plash and a trembling to one leaf and then another in the undergrowth.

There is a more than human force in the movement of the multitude, more than the sum of all the forces in the arched necks, the grinding chest muscles, and the firm feet of the horses, the grace of the bright women, the persistency of the tall men and thick men. They cannot stop. They look stupid or callous or blank or even cruel. They are going about another's business; they conceal their own, hiding it so that they forget (as a drunkard forgets where he has hidden his gold) where they have hidden it, hiding their souls under something stiffer and darker than the clothing of their bodies. It is hard to understand why they do not sometimes stop one another, to demand where the soul and the soul's business is hid, to snatch away the masks. It was intolerable that they were not known to me, that I was not known to them, that we should go on like waves of the sea, obeying whatever moon it is that sends us thundering on the unscalable shores of night and day. Such force, such determination as moved us along the burning streets might scale Olympus. Where was he who could lead the storming-party?

Between a pack of cabs and a pack of buses there was a quiet space of fifty yards in length; for a little while it seemed that the waves were refusing their task. There was not one black coat, not one horse, not one brightly loaded bus: no haste. It was a procession.

In front marched a tall son of man, with white black-bearded face, long black hair, more like plumage than hair in its abundance and form, and he wore no hat. He walked straight as a soldier, but with long, slow steps, and his head hung so that his bare breast supported it, for he had no coat and his shirt was half open. He had knee-breeches, bare dark legs, and shoes on his feet. His hands were behind his back, as if he were handcuffed. Two men walked beside him in other men's black clothes and black hats worn grey – two unnoticeable human beings, snub-nosed, with small, rough beards, dull eyes, shuffling gait. Two others followed them close, each carrying one of the poles of a small white banner inscribed with the words: "The Unemployed." These also were unnoticeable, thin, grey, bent, but young, their clothes, their faces, their hair, their hats almost the same dry colour as the road. It was impossible to say what their features were, because their heads hung down and their hats were drawn well on to their heads, and their eyes were unseen. They could not keep step, nor walk side by side, and their banner was always shaky and always awry.

Next, in no order, came three others of the same kind, shambling like the rest, of middle height, moderately ill-dressed, moderately thin, their hands in their pockets. In one of these I recognized the man who was born in Caermarthenshire. A cart came close behind, drawn by a fat grey donkey who needed no driving, for the one who rode in the cart had his back to the shafts, and, leaning forward on a tub into which money was expected to be thrown, he appeared to be talking to those who trailed at the back, for he waved an arm and wagged his yellow beard. He was fat, and dressed in a silk hat, frock-coat and striped trousers, almost too ancient to be ridiculous had they not kept company with a jaunty pair of yellow boots. He was midway between a seaside minstrel and a minister, had not one gesture destroyed the resemblance by showing that he wore no socks. Round about his coat also were the words: "The Unemployed," repeated or crudely varied. Those whom he addressed were the fifteen or twenty who completed the procession but seemed not to listen. They were all bent, young or middle-aged men, fair-haired, with unintentional beards, road-coloured skins and slightly darker clothes. Many wore overcoats, the collars turned up, and some had nothing under them except a shirt, and one not that. All with hands in pockets, one carrying a pipe, all silent and ashamed, struggled onward with bent knees. No two walked together; there was no approach to a row or a column in their arrangement, nor was there any pleasing irregularity as of plants grown from chance-scattered seed; by no means could they have been made, to express more feebleness, more unbrotherliness, more lack of principle, purpose or control. Each had the look of the meanest thief between his captors.

Two blue, benevolent, impersonal policemen, large men, occasionally lifted their arms as if to help forward the contemptible procession; sometimes, with a quick motion of the hand, they caused the straggling rear to double their pace for a few yards by running with knees yet more bent and coat-tails flapping and hands still deep in pockets – only for a few yards, for their walking pace was their best, all having the same strength, the same middle height, the same stride though no two could be seen keeping step.

The traffic thickened, and amidst the horses that nodded and trampled and the motor-cars that fumed and fretted the procession was closed up into a grey block behind the donkey-cart. On one side of the donkey was the black-bearded man, his right arm now resting on the animal's neck; on the other side the policemen; in front the standard-bearers hung down their heads and held up their poles. Often the only remnant visible was the raven crest of the leader.

The multitude on the pavement continued to press straight onward, or to flit in and out of coloured shops. None looked at the standard, the dark man and his cloudy followers, except a few of the smallest newspaper boys who had a few spare minutes and rushed over to march with them in the hope of music or a speech or a conflict. The straight flower-girl flashed her eyes as she stood on the kerb, her left arm curving with divine grace round the shawl-hidden child at her bosom, her left hand thrust out full of roses. The tender, well-dressed women leaning on the arms of their men smiled faintly, a little pitiful, but gladly conscious of their own security and pleasantness. Men with the historic sense glanced and noted the fact that there was a procession.

One man, standing on the kerb, took a sovereign from his pocket, looked at it and then at the unemployed, made a little gesture of utter bewilderment, and dropping the coin down into the drain below, continued to watch. Comfortable clerks and others of the servile realized that here were the unemployed about whom the newspapers had said this and that – ("a pressing question" – "a very complicated question not to be decided in a hurry" – "it is receiving the attention of some of the best intellects of the time" – "our special reporter is making a full investigation" – "who are the genuine and who are the impostors?" – "connected with Socialist intrigues") – and they repeated the word "Socialism" and smiled at the bare legs of the son of man and the yellow boots of the orator. Next day they would smile again with pride that they had seen the procession which ended in feeble, violent speeches against the Army and the Rich, in four arrests and an imprisonment. For they spoke in voices gentle with hunger. They were angry and uttered curses. One waved an arm against a palace, an arm that could scarcely hold out a revolver even were all the kings sitting in a row to tempt him. In the crowd and disturbance the leader fell and fainted. They propped him in their arms and cleared a space about him. "Death of Nelson," suggested an onlooker, laughing, as he observed the attitude and the knee-breeches. "If he had only a crown of thorns . . . " said another, pleased by the group. "Wants a bit of skilly and real hard work," said a third.

SEVEN

A Railway Carriage

I LEFT LONDON as quickly as possible. The railway carriage was nearly full of men reading the same newspapers under three or four different names, when a little grizzled and spectacled man of middle age entered – a printer, perhaps – with a twisted face and simple and puzzled expression that probably earned him many a laugh from street-corner boys. As he sat down he recognized a sailor, a tall, ponderous, kind-faced man made in three distinct stories, who supported his enormous red hands upon knees each fit to have been the mould of a hero's helmet.

"Well. I never did, and how are you, Harry?"

They looked at one another kindly but with a question piercing through the kindness and an effort to divine the unknowable without betraying curiosity. The kindness did, in fact, melt away the almost physical obstacle of twenty years spent apart and in ignorance of one another.

"When did you leave the old place?" said the sailor.

"Soon after you did yourself, Harry; just after the shipwreck of the *Wild Swan*; twenty-one, twenty-two – yes, twenty-two years ago."

"Is it so long? I could have sworn you had that beard when I saw you last," and the sailor looked at him in a way that showed he had already bridged the twenty-two years and knew the man.

"Yes, twenty-two years."

"And do you ever go back to the old place? How's Charlie Nash, and young Woolford, and the shepherd?"

"Let me see – "

"But how is Maggie Looker?" broke in the sailor upon a genial answer in the bud.

"Oh, didn't you know? She took ill very soon after you went away, and then they thought she was all right again; but they could not quite get rid of the cough, and it got bad in the winter, and all through the spring it was worse."

"And so she died in the summer."

"So she did."

"Oh, Christ! but what times we had."

And then, in reminiscences fast growing gay – the mere triumph of memory, the being able to add each to the other's store, was a satisfaction – they told the story of a pretty country girl whom they had quarrelled over until she grew too proud for both; how heavy was her hair; how she could run, and nobody was like her for finding a wasps' nest. Her boldness and carelessness filled them with envy still.

"I reckon we old ones would call her a tomboy now," said the sailor.

"I should say we would."

"Now, I wonder what sort of a wife she would have made?"

"Hum, I don't know . . ."

"Do you remember that day her and you and me got lost in the forest?"

"Yes, and we were there all night, and I got a hiding for it."

"Not Maggie."

"Not poor Maggie."

"And when we couldn't see our way any more we lifted her up into that old beech where the green woodpecker's nest was."

"Yes, and you took off your coat and breeches to cover her up."

"And so did you, though I reckon one would have been enough now I come to think of it."

"I don't know about that. But how we did have to keep on the move all night to keep warm."

"And dared not go very far for fear of losing the tree."

"And in the morning I wondered what we should do about getting back our clothes."

"You wanted me to go because my shirt hadn't any holes in it."

"But we both went together."

"And, before we had made up our minds which should go first and call, up she starts. Lord, how she did laugh!"

"Ay, she did."

"And says, 'Now, that's all my eye and Betty Martin, boys'; and so did we laugh, and I never felt a bit silly either. She was a good sort of girl, she was. Man and woman, I never met the likes of her, never heard tell of the equal of her," said the-sailor musingly.

"Married, Harry?"

"No, nor likely to be, I don't think. And yourself?"

"Well, I was . . . I married Maggie . . . It was after the first baby . . ."

A small boy in a corner could not get on with his novelette: he stared open-mouthed and open-eyed, now and then unconsciously imitating their faces; or he would correct this mere wonderment and become shy and uncomfortable at the frank ways of these men talking aloud in a crowded carriage, and utterly regardless of others, about private matters.

A trim shop assistant pretended to read about the cricket, but listened, and could not conceal his cold contempt for men so sunken as to give themselves like this.

A dark, thin, genial, pale-faced puritan clerk looked pitifully – with some wrinkles of superiority that asked for recognition from his fellow-passengers – at these *children,* for as such he regarded them, and would not wholly condemn.

Others occasionally jerked out a glance or rolled a leaderless eye or rustled a newspaper without losing the dense veil over their individuality that made them tombs, monuments, not men.

One sat gentle, kindly, stupidly envying these two their spirited free talk, their gestures, the hearty draughts of life which they seemed to have taken.

All were botanists who had heard and spoken words but had no sense of the beauty and life of the flower because fate had refused, or education destroyed, the gift of liberty and of joy.

SURREY

Then I saw a huge silence of meadows, of woods, and beyond these, of hills that raised two breasts of empurpled turf into the sky; and, above the hills, one mountain of cloud that beamed as it reposed in the blue as in a sea. The white cloud buried London with a *requiescat in pace.*

I like to think how easily Nature will absorb London as she absorbed the mastodon, setting her spiders to spin the winding-sheet and her worms to fill in the graves, and her grass to cover it pitifully up, adding flowers – as an unknown hand added them to the grave of Nero. I like to see the preliminaries of this toil where Nature tries her hand at mossing the factory roof, rusting the deserted railway metals, sowing grass over the deserted platforms and flowers of rose-bay on ruinous hearths and walls. It is a real satisfaction to see the long narrowing wedge of irises that runs alongside and between the rails of the South-Eastern and Chatham Railway almost into the heart of London. And there are many kinds of weather when the air is full of voices prophesying desolation. The outer suburbs have almost a moorland fascination when fog lies thick and orange-coloured over their huge flat wastes of grass, expectant of the builder, but does not quite conceal the stark outlines of a traction engine, some procumbent timber, a bonfire and frantic figures darting about it, and aerial scaffolding far away. Other fields, yet unravished but menaced, the fog restores to a primeval state. And what a wild noise the wind makes in the telegraph wires as in wintry heather and gorse! When the waste open spaces give way to dense streets there is a common here and a lawn there, where the poplar leaves, if it be November, lie taintless on the grass, and the starlings talk sweet and shrill and cold in the branches, and nobody cares to deviate from the asphalt path to the dewy grass: the houses beyond the green mass themselves gigantic, remote, dim, and the pulse of London beats low and inaudible, as if she feared the irresistible enemy that is drawing its lines invisibly and silently about her on every side. If a breeze arises it makes that sound of the dry curled leaves chafing along the pavement; at night they seem spies in the unguarded by-ways. But there are also days – and spring and summer days, too – when a quiet horror thicks and stills the air outside London.

The ridges of trees high in the mist are very grim. The isolated trees stand cloaked in conspiracies here and there about the fields. The houses, even whole villages, are translated into terms of unreality as if they were carved in air and could not be touched; they are empty and mournful as skulls or churches. There is no life visible; for the ploughmen and the cattle are figures of light dream. All is soft and grey. The land has drunken the opiate mist and is passing slowly and unreluctantly into perpetual sleep. Trees and houses are drowsed beyond awakening or farewell. The mind also is infected, and gains a sort of ease from the thought that an eternal and universal rest is at hand without any cry or any pain.

SUSSEX

The road skirts the marshland, the stream and the town, and goes through a gap in the Downs towards another range and more elms and farms at its feet. Stately walks the carter's boy with his perpendicular brass-bound whip, alongside four wagon-horses, while the carter rides. It is a pleasant thing to see them going to their work in the early gold of the morning, fresh, silent, their horses jingling, down the firm road. If they were leading their team to yoke them to the chariot of the sun they could not be more noble. They are the first men I have seen this morning, and truly they create for a little while the illusion that they are going to guide the world and that all will be well in the golden freshness under the blue.

The road now divides to go round the base of the Downs, but a farm track sets out to climb them. There, at the corner, is a church, on the very edge of the flat vale and its elms and ashes in the midst of meadows; a plain towered church, but with a rough churchyard, half graveyard and half orchard, its grass and parsley and nettle uncut under the knotty apple trees, splashed with silver and dull gold-green, dotted by silver buds among yellow-lichened branches that are matted densely as a magpie's nest. The dust from the high road powders the nettles and perfects the arresting melancholy of the desolation, so quiet, so austere, and withal as airy as a dream remembered. But above are the Downs, green and sweet with uplifting grass, and beyond them the sea, darkly gleaming under lustrous white cliffs and abrupt ledges of turf, in the south; in the south-east a procession of tufted trees going uphill in single file; in the south-west the dazzling slate roofs of a distant town, two straight sea walls and two steamers and their white wakes; northward the most beautiful minor range in all the downland, isolated by a river valley at the edge of which it ends in a gulf of white quarry, while on the other side it heaves and flows down almost to the plain, but rises again into a lesser hill with woods, and then slowly subsides. Within a few square miles it collects every beauty of the chalk hill; its central height is a dome of flawless grass only too tender to be majestic; and that is supported by lesser rounds and wavering lines of approach in concavity and convexity, playgrounds for the godlike shadows and lights, that prolong the descent of the spent wave of earth into the plain.

An uncertain path keeps to the highest ridge. The sides of the Downs are invaded by long stream-like gorse-sided coombes, of which the narrow floor is palest green grass. The highest points command much of earth, all of heaven. They are treeless, but occasionally the turf is over-arched by the hoops of a brier thicket, the new foliage pierced by upright dead grey grass. They are the haunt of the swift, the home of wheatear and lark and of whatsoever in the mind survives or is born in this pure kingdom of grass and sky. Ahead, they dip to a river and rise again, their sweep notched by a white road.

At the inland end of this river valley is an antique red-tiled large village or small town, a perfect group of human dwellings, as inevitable as the Downs, dominated by a mound and on it a windmill in ruin; mothered by a church at the river's edge. Under the sign of "Ye Olde — " is a room newly wainscoted in shining matchboard. Its altar – its little red sideboard – is symmetrically decorated by tiers and rows of lemonade, cherry cider and ginger ale bottles, many-coloured, and in the midst of these two syphons of soda-water. The doorways and windows

'The carter's boy.'

are draped in white muslin, the hearth filled by a crinkled blue paper fan; the mantelpiece supports a dozen small vases. The oilcloth is new and odorous and bright. There are pink geraniums in salmon-coloured bowls on the table; a canary in a suspended cage; and on the walls a picture of a girl teasing a dog with a toy mouse.

At the cross-roads is a group of old slated white farm buildings and a tiled farm-house of brick and flint; and above, at the top of a slope of down, is a grey spire and two orange roofs of cottages amidst a round cluster of trees; the sheep graze and their bells tittle-tattle. The seaward-going road alongside but above the river dips then under steep banks of blackthorn and parsley to a village of flint where another spire rises out of the old roofs of a farm-house and its family of barns and lodges; a nightingale sings at hand, a wheeling pewit cries and gleams over the blue ripples of the river. Across the water a shallow scoop has been carved by Nature out of the side of the down; it is traversed by two diverging paths which alone are green, for the rest of the surface is of gorse and, full in the face of the sun, forms a mossy cirrus over the mist of its own warm shade. The down beside the road is now all cowslips among its scattered bramble and thorn, until it is cloven by a tributary bay, a quarter of a mile in length, marshy at first and half-filled by elms and willows, but at its higher end occupied, behind ash trees and an orchard, by a farm-house, a circular doomed building and a barn, all having roofs of ochre tile, except the thatched barn, and grey stained walls; a straight road goes to the house along the edge of the marsh and elms. Grey plover whistle singly on the wet borders of the stream or make a concerted whimper of two or three.

A little beyond is a larger bay of the same kind, bordered by a long curving road entirely lined by elms dividing it from the broad meadow that has an elm rookery in a corner under the steep clean slope of down; at the end is a church singing to itself with all its bells in the solitude. And the hedges are full of strong young thrushes which there is no one to frighten – is there any prettier dress than the speckled feathers of their breasts and the cape of brown over their shoulders and backs, as they stir the dew in May?

Then the valley opens wide and the river doubles in gleaming azure about a narrow spit of grass, in sight of a sharp white fall of chalk, into the lucid quiet sea. At this bend a company of sycamores girds and is one with a group of tiled and thatched and gabled buildings, of ochre, brown and rose. The road crosses the river and a path leads near the sea, between mustard flower, lucerne, beans, corn and grass, in flint-walled fields, to a church and farm of flint, overtopped by embowering chestnuts, ilex and the elms of rooks; and below there is another valley and river, a green pathless marsh, at whose edge five noisy belching chimneys stand out of a white pit. The path, over turf, rises to the Downs, passing a lonely flint barn with rich dark roof and a few sycamores for mates. This is the cornland, and the corn bunting sings solitary and monotonous, and the linnets twitter still in flocks. Above and around, the furzy coombes are the homes of blackbirds that have a wilder song in this world of infinite corn below and grass above, and but one house. Violets and purple orchis (and its white buds) cloud the turf. On the other side the Downs sink to gently clustered and mounded woods and yet more corn surrounding a thatched flint barn, a granary and cart-lodge, and, again a farm under sycamores.

The soft-ribbed grey sky of after-sunset is slowly moving, kindly and promising rain. The air is still, the road dusty, but the hedges tender green, and the grasshopper lark sings under the wild parsley of the roadside and the sedge-warbler in the sallows.

Just beyond is the town by the beautiful domed hill, a town of steep lanes and wallflowers on old walls and such a date as 1577 modestly inscribed on a doorway; its long old street, sternly adapted to the needs of shopkeepers and gentry, looks only old-fashioned, its age being as much repressed as if it were a kind of sin or originality. This is that spirit which would quarrel with the stars for not being in straight lines like print, the spirit of one who, having been disturbed while shaving by the sight of a favourite cat in the midst of her lovers and behaving after the manner of her kind, gives orders during the long mid-day meal that she shall be drowned forthwith, or – no – to-morrow, which is Monday. This is that spirit which says:

> Nature is never stiff, and none recognizes this fact better than – & Son, and their now well-known and natural-looking rockeries have reclaimed many a dreary bit of landscape. At – they showed me photographs of various country seats where the natural-looking scenery has been evolved by their artistic taste and ingenuity out of the most ordinary efforts of Nature. Thus a dull old mill-stream has, with the aid of rockeries and appropriate vegetation, been converted into a wonderfully picturesque spot, an ordinary brook was transformed into a lovely woodland scene, with ferns, mosses, and lichens growing among the rockeries, and the shores of an uninteresting lake became undulating banks of beauty by the same means; while the beautiful rockeries in – Park were also the work of this firm. – & Son have other ways, too, of beautifying gardens and grounds by the judicious use of balustrades, fountains, quaint figures, etc., made of "– terra-cotta," or artificial stone, which is far more durable than real stone or marble, not so costly, and impervious to frost and all weathers, although it takes the vegetation in the same way, and after a year's exposure it can scarcely be distinguished from antique stone. In it the great *spécialité* here just now is "sundials," the latest craze; for without a sundial no ancient or up-to-date garden is considered complete.

Nevertheless the town smells heartily of cattle, sheep, and malt; a rookery and white orchard confront the railway station, and in the midst of the streets the long grass is rough and wet and full of jonquils round ancient masonry: seen from a height the town shares the sunlight equally with massy foliage and finds its place as a part of Nature, and the peregrine takes it in its sweep.

The turtle-doves have come and the oaks are budding bronze in the Weald. The steep roadside banks are cloaked in grass, violet, and primrose still, and robin-run-in-the-hedge and stitchwort and cuckoo flowers, and the white-throats talk in the hazel copses. A brooklet runs in a hollow that would almost hold the Thames, and crossing the road fills a rushy mill-pond deep below, and makes a field all golden and shining with marigold. Just beyond, a gnarled lime avenue leads to a grey many-windowed house of stone within a stately park. Opposite the gate an old woman sits on the grass, her feet in the dust at the edge of the road; motor-cars sprinkle her and turn her black to drab; she sits by the wayside eternally, expecting nothing.

Turn out of this main road, and by-ways that tempt neither cyclists nor motorists go almost as straight. Here is no famous house, not a single inn or church, but only the unspoilt Weald, and far away, a long viaduct that carries noiseless trains against the sky above hollow meadows. Bluebell, primrose, anemone – anemone, primrose, bluebell – star and cloud the lush banks and the roots of the blackthorns, hazels and maples of the hedge. A stream washes the roots of many oaks, and flows past flat fields of dusky grass, cuckoo flower and marigold – black pines at the verge. The light smoke of a roadside fire ascends into the new leaves of the hazels where two tramps are drying their clothes. Many oaks are down and lie pale and gleaming like mammoth bones among the bluebells in plantations roughened by old flint pits.

The faggots of oak tops and cords of twisted timber are being made up; the woodmen light a fire and the chips fly from the axes. It is only to these men that I am a stranger as I walk through the land. At first I admire the hardihood and simplicity of their necessary toil among the oaks, but they lift their dark eyes, and then – it is as strange as when I pass a white embowered house, and the road is muffled with straw, and I hear by chance that someone unknown is dying behind that open window through which goes the thrush's song and the children's homeward chatter. Neither townsman or countryman, I cannot know them. The countryman knows their trades and their speech, and is of their kind; the townsman's curiosity wins him a greeting. But in May at least I am content, in the steep little valley made by a tributary of the Medway, its sides wooded with oak and the flowers glad of the sun among the lately cleared undergrowth, and the cuckoo now in this oak and now in that, and the turtle-doves whose voices, in the soft lulls after rain, make the earth seem to lie out sleek in the sun, stretching itself to purr with eyes closed. The cuckoo is gone before we know what his cry is to tell us or to remind us of.

There are few things as pleasant as the thunder and lightning of May that comes in the late afternoon, when the air is as solid as the earth with stiff grey rain for an hour. There is no motion anywhere save of this perpendicular river, of the swaying rain-hit bough and quivering leaf. But through it all the thrushes sing, and jolly as their voices are the roars and echoes of the busy thunder quarrying the cliffs of heaven. And then the pleasure of being so wet that you may walk through streams and push through thickets and be none the wetter for it.

Before it is full night the light of the young moon falls for a moment out of a troubled but silent sky upon the young corn, and the tranquil bells are calling over the woods.

Then in the early morning the air is still and warm, but so moist that there is a soul of coolness in the heat, and never before were the leaves of the sorrel and wood sanicle and woodruff, and the grey-green foliage and pallid yellow flowers of the large celandine, so fair. The sudden wren's song is shrewd and sweet and banishes heaviness. The huge chestnut tree is flowering and full of bees. The parsley towers delicately in bloom. The beech boughs are encased in gliding crystal. The nettles, the millions of nettles in a bed, begin to smell of summer. In the calm and sweet air the turtle-doves murmur and the blackbirds sing – as if time were no more – over the mere.

The roads, nearly dry again, are now at their best, cool and yet luminous, and at their edges coloured rosy or golden brown by the sheddings of the beeches, those gloves out of which the leaves have forced their way, pinched and crumpled by the confinement. At the bend of a broad road descending under beeches these parallel lines of ruddy chaff give to two or three days in the year a special and exquisite loveliness, if the weather be alternately wet and bright and the long white roads and virgin beeches are a temptation. What quests they propose! They take us away to the thin air of the future or to the underworld of the past. This one takes us to the old English sweetness and robustness of an estate of large meadows, sound oak trees not too close together, and a noble house within an oak-paled park. A poet and a man lives there, one who recalls those other poets – they are not many – who please us over the gulf of time almost as much by the personal vigour and courage which we know to have been theirs or is suggested by their work, men like Chaucer, Sidney, Ben Jonson, Drayton, Byron, William Morris, and among the living – and – and – . I think we should miss their poems more than some greater men's if they were destroyed. They stand for their time more clearly than the greatest. For example, Chaucer's language, ideas and temper make it impossible for us to read his work, no matter in how remote a study or garden, shut out from time and change, without feeling that he and all those who rode and talked and were young with him are skeletons or less, though Catullus or Milton may be read with no such feeling. Chaucer seems to remind us of what once we were. His seems a golden age. He wrote before Villon had inaugurated modern literature with the cry:

Mais où sont les neiges d'antan?

before men appear to us to have learned how immense is the world and time. But we, looking back, with the help of this knowledge, see in the work of this man who filled a little nook of time and space with gaiety, something apart from us, an England, a happy island which his verses made. His gaiety bathes the land in the light of a golden age and the freshness of all the May days we can never recover. He "led a lusty life

in May": "in his lust present was all his thought." And the gaiety is no
less in the sorrowful passages than in the joyful; when, for example, he
compares the subjection of the fierce, proud Troilus to love, with the
whipping of a spirited horse; when he uses the apparent commonplace
about age creeping in "always as still as stone" upon fresh youth; when
he exclaims to the false Jason:

Have at thee, Jason! now thy horne is blowe;

or cries at the fate of Ugolino's children:

Alias, Fortune! it was greet crueltee
Swiche briddes for to putte in swich a cage!

Even in Griselda's piteous cry:

O tendre, O deere, O yonge children myne,

there is an intimation that in those words her sorrow is being spent and
that, though it will be renewed, it will be broken up by joyfulness many
times before her death.

For, as Chaucer's laughter is assuredly never completed by a sigh, so
there is something hearty in his tears that hints of laughter before and
after. His was a sharp surprising sorrow that came when he was forced
to see the suffering of lovely humanity. He is all gaiety; but it has two
moods. Sorrow never changes him more than shadow changes a merry
brook. In both moods he seems to speak of a day when men had not
only not so far outstripped the lark and nightingale as we have done,
but had moments when their joy was equal to the lark's above the grey
dew of May dawns. And thus, if we only had to thank Chaucer for the
gaiety which is left behind in his poems, as the straw of a long-past
harvest clings to the thorns of a narrow lane, we could never be thankful
enough.

I feel that Chaucer was the equal of those of whom he wrote, as
Homer was the equal of Achilles and Odysseus, just as Byron was the
peer of the noblest of the Doges and of the ruined Emperor whom he
addressed as:

Vain froward child of Empire! say
Are all thy playthings snatched away?

Byron is one of the few poets whose life it was ever necessary to write. His acts were representative; from his Harrow meditations on a tomb to his death on the superb pedestal of Missolonghi, they are symbolic. His life explains nearly everything in his poetry. The life and the poetry together make an incomparable whole. Most lives of poets stand to their work as a block of unhewn marble stands to the statue finished and unveiled; if the marble is not as much forgotten as was Pygmalion's when Galatea breathed and sighed. Byron's poetry without his life is not finished; but with it, it is like a statue by Michael Angelo or Rodin that is actually seen to grow out of the material. He was a man before he was a poet. Other poets may once have been men; they are not so now. We read their lives after their poetry and we forget them. It is by their poetry that they survive – blithe or pathetic of glorious, but dim, ghosts who are become a part of the silence of libraries and lovers' hearts. They are dead but for the mind that enjoys and the voice that utters their verse. I had not the smallest curiosity about Mr. Swinburne when he was alive and visible. When I think of him, I think of Rosamund speaking to Eleanor or Tristram to Isoud; he has given up his life to them. But with Byron it is different. If all record of him could be destroyed, more than half of him would be lost. For I think that it is upon the life and the portraits and the echoes that are still reverberating in Europe, that we found our belief that he is a great man. Without them he would be an interesting rhetorician, perhaps little more. There are finer poems than his "Mazeppa," but the poet is the equal of that wild lover and of the great king who slept while the tale was told.

And Shelley, too, is an immortal sentiment. Men may forget to repeat his verses; they can never be as if Shelley had never been. He is present wherever love and rapture are. He is a part of all high-spirited and pure audacity of the intellect and imagination, of all clean-handed rebellion, of all infinite endeavour and hope. The remembered splendour of his face is more to us than Parliaments; one strophe of his odes is more nourishing than a rich man's gold . . .

Under those oaks in May I could wish to see these men walking together, to see their gestures and brave ways. It is the poet there who all but creates them for me. But only one can I fairly see because I have seen him alive and speaking. Others have sent up their branches higher among the stars and plunged their roots deeper among the rocks and waters. But he and Chaucer and Jonson and Byron have obviously much plain humanity in their composition. They have a brawn and friendliness not necessarily connected with poetry. We use no ceremony – as we do with some other poets – with Morris when we read:

> The days have slain the days, and the seasons have gone by,
> And brought me the summer again; and here on the grass I lie,
> As erst I lay and was glad ere I meddled with right and with wrong.

Or the end of "Thunder in the Garden":

> Then we turned from the blossoms, and cold were they grown:
> In the trees the wind westering moved;
> Till over the threshold back fluttered her gown,
> And in the dark house was I loved.

There is a humanity of this world and moment in Morris's feeling for Nature with which no other poet's except Whitman's can be compared. Except in the greatest – the unaccomplished things – in "Leaves of Grass" there is no earth-feeling in the literature of our language so majestic and yet so tender as in "The Message of the March Wind." With him poetry was not, as it has tended more and more to be in recent times, a matter as exclusive as a caste. He was not half-angel or half-bird, but a man on close terms with life and toil, with the actual, troublous life of every day, with toil of the hands and brain together; in short, a many-sided citizen. He was one whom Skarphedin the son of Njal of Bergthorsknoll would not have disdained, and when he spoke he seemed indignant at the feebleness of words, one that should have used a sword and might have lamented with the still later poet:

The Spirit stands and looks on infamy,
And unashamed the faces of the pit
Snarl at their enemy;
Finding him wield no insupportable light,
And no whirled edge of blaze to hit
Backward their impudence, and hammer them to flight;
Although ready is he,
Wearing the same righteous steel
Upon his limbs, helmed as he was then
When he made olden war;
Yet cannot now with foulness fiercely deal.
There is no indignation among men,
The Spirit has no scimitar
Wilt thou not come again, thou godly sword,
Into the Spirit's hands?
That he may be a captain of the Lord
Again, and mow out of our lands
The crop of wicked men . . .
O for that anger in the hands
Of Spirit! To us, O righteous sword,
Come thou and clear our lands,
O fire, O indignation of the Lord!
(from *Poems and Interludes,* by Lascelles Abercrombie)

Bitter it is to think of that talk and laughter of shadows on the long lawns under those oaks; for though their shadows are even yet better than other men's bone or blood, never yet did dead mail lift up a hand to strike a blow or lay a brick. In a churchyard behind I saw the tombstone of one Robert Page, born in the year 1792 here in Sussex, and dead in 1822 – not in the Bay of Spezzia but in Sussex. He scared the crows, ploughed the clay, fought at Waterloo and lost an arm there, was well pleased with George the Fourth, and hoed the corn until he was dead. That is plain sense, and I wish I could write the life of this exact contemporary of Shelley.

That is quite probably his great-granddaughter, black-haired, of ruddy complexion, full lips, large white teeth, black speechless eyes, dressed in a white print dress and stooping in the fresh wind to take clean white linen out of a basket, and then rising straight as a hazel wand, on tiptoe, her head held back and slightly on one side while she pegs the clothes to the line and praises the weather to a passer-by. She is seventeen, and of such is the kingdom of earth.

Now at the coming on of night the wind has carried away all the noises of the world. The lucid air under the hazels of the lane is dark as if with dream, and the roadway leads glimmering straight on to a crystal planet low in the purple of the west. I cannot hear my footsteps, so full charged is the silence. I am no more in this tranquillity than one of the trees. The way seems paved that some fair spirit may pass down in perfect beauty and bliss and ease. The leaves will hail it and the blue sky lean down to bless, and the planet lend its beams for a path. Suddenly, the name of Mary is called by some one invisible. Mary! For a little while the cry is repeated more loudly but always sweetly; then the caller is entranced by the name, by the sound of her own voice and the silence into which it falls as into a well, and it grows less and less and ceases and is dead except in the brain of the hearer. I thought of all the music to ear and mind of that sound of "m." I suppose the depth of its appeal is due to its place at the beginning of the word "mother," or rather to the need of the soul which gave it that place; and it is a sound as dear to the animals as to us, since the ewe hears it first from her lamb and the cow from her calf as the woman from her child. It is the main sound in "music," "melody," "harmony," "measure," "metre," "rhythm," "minstrel," "madrigal." It endears even sadness by its presence in "melancholy," "moan" and "mourn." It makes melody on the lips of friends and lovers, in the names of "mistress," "comrade," "mate," "companion." It murmurs autumnally in all mellow sounds, in the music of wind and insect and instrument. To "me" and "mine" it owes a meaning as deep as to "mother". And this mild air could beat no more melodious burden than the name that floated upon it and sank into it, down, down, to reveal its infinite depth – Mary!

There are parks on both sides of the road, bounded by hedges or high brick walls, and the public road has all the decorum of a drive. For a mile the very ivy which is destined to adorn the goodly wall and spread into forms as grand as those at Godstow Nunnery is protected by wire netting. Doves croon in the oaks: underneath, hazel and birch flicker their new leaves over the pools of bluebells. The swallows fly low over every tuft of the roadside grass and glance into every bay of the wood, and then out above the white road, from which they rebound suddenly and turn, displaying the white rays of their tails. Now and then a gateway reveals the park. The ground undulates, but is ever smooth. It is of the mellow green of late afternoon. Bronzed oak woods bound the undulations, and here and there a solitary tree stands out on the grass and shows its poise and complexity with the added grace of new leaf. The cattle graze as on a painted lawn. A woman in a white dress goes indolent and stately towards the rhododendrons and rook-haunted elms.

The scene appears to have its own sun, mellow and serene, that knows not moorland or craggy coast or city. Only a thousand years of settled continuous government, of far-reaching laws, of armies and police, of roadmaking, of bloody tyranny and tyranny that poisons quietly without blows, could have wrought earth and sky into such a harmony. It is a thing as remote from me here on the dusty road as is the green evening sky and all its tranquillity of rose and white, and even more so because the man in the manor house behind the oaks is a puzzle to me, while the sky is always a mystery with which I am content. At such an hour the house and lawns and trees are more wonderfully fortified by the centuries of time than by the walls and gamekeepers. They weave an atmosphere about it. We bow the head and reverence the labour of time in smoothing the grass, mellowing the stone and the manners of the inhabitants, and yet an inevitable conflict ensues in the mind between this respect and the feeling that it is only a respect for surfaces, that a thousand years is a heavy price to pay for the maturing of park and house and gentleman, especially as he is most likely to be a well-meaning parasite on those who are concerned twenty-four hours a day about the difficulty of living and about what to do when they are alive.

No, it is the alien remote appearance of the house and land serene in the May evening light which creates this reverence in the mind. It is not

feudalism, or the old nobility and gentility, that we are bowing down to, but only to Nature without us and the dream within us. It is certainly not pure envy. Nor yet is it for the same reason as made Borrow reflect when he saw the good house at the end of an avenue of noble oaks near Llandovery

> . . . A plain but comfortable gentleman's seat with wings. It looked south down the dale. "With what satisfaction I could live fin that house," said I to myself, "if backed by a couple of thousand a year. With what gravity could I sign a warrant in its library, and with what dreamy comfort translate an ode of Lewis Glyn Cothi, my tankard of rich ale beside me. I wonder whether the proprietor is fond of the old bard and keeps good ale. Were I an Irishman instead of a Norfolk man I would go in and ask him."

Not if he were a Welshman, either. For I at least know that in no other man's house should I be better off than I am, and I lack the confidence to think I could make any use of his income. I would as soon envy a tramp because he has no possessions, or a navvy because he walks like a hero as he pushes a heavy trolley before him, his loose jacket fitting him as a mane fits a lion. To envy a man is to misunderstand him or yourself.

Nor yet is it pure admiration. That is what I feel for something external that can be described as right, as having absolute individuality and inevitableness of form. For example, I admire certain groups that are the result of what we call chance – an arrangement of fishing boats going out to sea, first one, then at a long interval two close together, a fourth a little behind, and then by ones and pairs and clusters at different intervals; or the four or five oaks left in a meadow that was once a copse; or the fruit fallen on autumn rime; or sunset clouds that pause darkly along the north-west in a way that will never be seen again; or of tragic figures at such a moment as when Polyxena, among the Grecian youths, gave her throat to the dagger of Neoptolemus, and fell beautiful in death.

No. Those houses are castles in Spain. They are fantastic architecture. We have made them out of our spirit stuff and have set our souls to roam their corridors and look out of their casements upon the sea or the mountains or the clouds. It is because they are accessible only to the everywhere wandering irresistible and immortal part of us that they are beautiful. There is no need for them to be large or costly or antique. The poorest house can do us a like service. In a town, for example, and in a suburb, I have had the same yearning when, on a fine still morning of May or June, in streets away from the traffic, I have seen through the open windows a cool white-curtained shadowy room, and in it a table with white cloths and gleaming metal and glass laid thereon, and nobody has yet come down to open the letters. It all seems to be the work of spirit hands. It is beautiful and calm and celestial, and is a profound pleasure – tinged by melancholy – to see. It gives a sense of fitness – for what? For something undivined, imperfectly known, guessed at, or hoped for, in ourselves; for a wider and less tainted beauty, for a greater grace. Or it may not be a house at all, but a hill-top five miles off, up which winds a white road in two long loops between a wood and the turf. The grass is smooth and warm and bright at the summit in the blue noon; or in the horizontal sunbeams each stem is lit so that the hill is transmuted into a glowing and insubstantial thing; and then, at noon or evening, something in me flies at the sight and desires to tread that holy ground. It is an odd world where everything is fleeting yet the soul desires permanence even for fancies so unprofitable as this.

And so these thoughts at the sight of the great houses mingle with the thoughts that grow at twilight and fade gradually away in the windless night when the sky is soft-ridged all over with white clouds and in the dark vales between them are the stars. Then, for it is Saturday, follows another pleasure of the umbrageous white country roads at night – the high contented voices of children talking to father and mother as they go home from the market town. The parents move dark-clothed, silent, laden; the children flit about them with white hats or pinafores. Their voices travel far and long after they are invisible in the mist that washes over the fields in long white firths, but die away as the misty night blots out the hills, the clouds, the stars, the trees, and everything but the branches overhead and the white parsley flowers floating along the hedge. There is no breath of wind. The owls are quiet. The air is full of the scent of holly flower and may and nettles and of the sound of a little stream among the leaves.

EIGHT

June

NOW DAY BY DAY, indoors and out of doors, the conquest of spring proceeds to the music of the conquerors. One evening the first chafer comes to the lamp, and his booming makes the ears tremble with dim apprehension. He climbs, six-legged and slow, up the curtain, supporting himself now and then by unfurling his wings, or if not he falls with a drunken moan, then begins to climb again, and at last blunders about the room like a ball that must strike something, the white ceiling, the white paper, the lamp, and when he falls he rests. In his painful climbing he looks human, as perhaps a man looks angelic to an angel; but there is nothing lovelier and more surprising than the unfurling of his pinions like a magic wind-blown cloak out of that hard mail.

Another day the far-off woods in a hot, moist air first attain their rich velvet mossiness, and even near at hand the gorse-bushes all smouldering with bloom are like clouds settled on the earth, having no solidity, but just colour and warmth and pleasantness.

The broad-backed chestnuts bloom. On the old cart-lodge tiles the vast carapace of the house-leek is green and rosy, and out of the midst of it grow dandelions and grass, and the mass of black mould which it has accumulated in a century bends down the roof.

The hawthorn-bloom is past before we are sure that it has reached its fulness. Day after day its warm and fragrant snow clouded the earth with light, and yet we waited, thinking surely to-morrow it will be fairer still, and it was, and the next day we thought the same and we were careless as in first love, and then one day it lay upon the grass, an empty shell, the vest of departed loveliness, and another year was over. The broad grass is full of buttercups' gold or it is sullen silvery under a burning afternoon sun, without wind, the horizon smoky, the blue sky and its white, still clouds almost veiled by heat; the red cattle are under the elms; the unrippled water slides under sullen silvery willows.

The night-haze peels off the hills and lets the sun in upon small tracts of wood – upon a group of walnuts in the bronze of their fine, small leaf – upon downland grass, and exposes blue sky and white cloud, but then returns and hides the land, except that the dewy ground-ash and the ivy and holly gleam; and two cuckoos go over crying and crying continually in the hollow vale.

Already the ash-keys hang in cool, thick bunches under the darker leaves. The chestnut-bloom is falling. The oak-apples are large and rosy. The wind is high, and the thunder is away somewhere behind the pink mountains in the southern sky or in the dark drifts overhead. And yet the blue of the massy hangers almost envelops the beechen green; the coombes and the beeches above and around their grassy slopes of juniper are soft and dim, and far withdrawn, and the nightjar's voice is heard as if the wind there were quiet. The rain will not come; the plunging wind in the trees has a sound of waterfalls all night, yet cannot trouble the sleep of the orange-tip butterfly on the leopard's-bane's dead flower.

Now the pine blooms in the sandy lands, above the dark-fronded brake and glaucous-fruited whortleberry, the foxgloves break into bell after bell under the oaks and birches. The yellow broom is flowering and scented, and the white lady's bedstraw sweetens the earth's breath. The careless variety of abundance and freshness makes every lane a bride. Suddenly, in the midst of the sand, deep meadows gleam, and the kingfisher paints the air with azure and emerald and rose above the massy water tumbling between aspens at the edge of a neat, shaven lawn, and, behind that, a white mill and miller's house with dark, alluring windows where no one stirs.

June puts bronze and crimson on many of her leaves. The maple-leaves and many of the leaves of thorn and bramble and dogwood are rosy; the hazel-leaves are rosy-brown; the herb-robert and parsley are rose-red; the leaves of ash and holly are dark lacquered. The copper beeches, opulently sombre under a faintly yellowed sky, seem to be the

'The kingfisher paints the air with azure and emerald and rose.'

sacred trees of the thunder that broods above. Presently the colour of the threat is changed to blue, which soiled white clouds pervade until the whole sky is woolly white and grey and moving north. There is no wind, but there is a roar as of a hurricane in the trees far off; soon it is louder, in the trees not so remote; and in a minute the rain has traversed half a mile of woods, and the distant combined roar is swallowed up by the nearer pattering on roof and pane and leaf, the dance of leaves, the sway of branches, the trembling of whole trees under the flood. The rain falls straight upon the hard road, and each drop seems to leap upward from it barbed. Great drops dive among the motionless, dusty nettles. The thunder unloads its ponderous burden upon the resonant floor of the sky; but the sounds of the myriad leaves and grass-blades drinking all but drowns the boom, the splitting roar, and the echo in the hills. When it is over it has put a final sweetness into the blackbird's voice and into the calm of the evening garden when the voice of a singer does but lay another tribute at the feet of the enormous silence. Frail is that voice as the ghost-moth dancing above the grass so faithfully that it seems a flower attached to a swaying stem, or as the one nettle-leaf that flutters in a draught of the hedge like a signalling hand while all the rest of the leaves are as if they could not move again, or as the full moon that is foundering on a white surf in the infinite violet sky. More large and more calm and emptier of familiar things grows the land as I pass through it, under the hoverings of the low-flying but swiftly-turning nightjar, until at midnight only a low white mist moves over the gentle desolation and warm silence. The mist wavers, and discloses a sky all strewn with white stars like the flowers of an immense jessamine. It closes up again, and day is born unawares in its pale arms, and earth is for the moment nothing but the tide of downs flowing west and the branch of red roses that hangs heavily laden and drowsed with its weight and beauty over my path, dipping its last spray in the dew of the grass.

The day is a Sunday, and no one is on foot or on wheel in the broad arable country that ripples in squares of green, or brown, or yellow, or grey, to the green Downs and their dark, high-perched woods. As if for some invisible beholder, the green elders and their yellow-green flower-buds make their harmony with the yellow-lichened barns against which they lean; the grass and the noble trees, the groups of wayside aspen, the line of horse-chestnuts, the wych-elms on both sides of the road, the one delicate sycamore before the inn and the company of sycamores above the cross – the spacious thatch and tiles of the farmyard quadrangle – the day newly painted in white and blue – the green so green in the hedges, and the white and purple so pure in the flowers – all seem to be meant for eyes that know nothing of Time and of what "brought death into the world and all our woe." And in this solitude the young birds are very happy. They have taken possession of the thick hedges, of the roadside grass, of the roads themselves. They flutter and run and stumble there; they splash in the pools and in the dust, which not a wheel nor a foot has marked. These at least are admitted into the kingdom along with that strange wildfowl that lives "to maintain the trade and mystery of typographers."

Such a day, in the unblemished summer land, invariably calls up thoughts of the Golden Age. As mankind has looked back to a golden age, so the individual, repeating the history of the race, looks back and finds one in his own past. Historians and archaeologists have indeed made it difficult for men of our time to look far back for a golden age. We are shown a skull with supraciliary prominences and are told that its owner, though able to survive the mammoth by means of tools of flint, lived like the Tasmanian of modern times; and his was no Golden Age. Then we look back to heroic ages which poetry and other arts have magnified – to the Greece of Homer or Pheidias, to the Ireland of Cuchulain, to the Wales of Arthur, to the England which built the great cathedrals or produced Chaucer, Sir Philip Sidney, Izaak Walton.

In the same way, few men can now look back to their childhood like Thomas Traherne and say that

All appeared new and strange at first, inexpressibly rare and delightful and beautiful. I was a little stranger which at my entrance into the world was saluted and surrounded with innumerable joys. My knowledge was Divine. I knew by intuition those things which since my Apostasy I collected again by the highest reason. My very ignorance was advantageous. I seemed as one brought into the Estate of Innocence. All things were spotless and pure and glorious; yea, and infinitely mine, and joyful and precious. I knew not that there were any sins or complaints or laws. I dreamed not of poverties, contentions, or vices. All tears and quarrels were hidden from mine eyes. Everything was at rest, free and immortal. I knew nothing of sickness or death or rents or exaction, either for tribute or bread . . . All Time was Eternity, and a perpetual Sabbath. Is it not strange, that an infant should be heir of the whole world and see those mysteries which the books of the learned never unfold?

(*Centuries of Meditation,* by Thomas Traherne (Dobell.)

We blink, deliberately or not, unpleasant facts in our own lives, as in the social life of Greece or the Middle Ages. Some have no need to do so; robustly or sensitively made, their childish surroundings have been such as to meet their utmost needs or to draw out their finest powers or to leave them free. Ambition, introspection, remorse had not begun. The vastness and splendour and gloom of a world not understood, but seen in its effects and hardly at all in its processes, made a theatre for their happiness which – especially when seen through a mist of years – glorify it exceedingly, and it becomes like a ridge of the far-off downs transfigured in golden light, so that we in the valley sigh at the thought that where we have often trod is heaven now. Such beauties of the earth, seen at a distance and inaccessibly serene, always recall the equally inaccessible happiness of childhood. Why have we such a melting mood for what we cannot reach? Why, as we are whirled past them in a train, does the sight of a man and child walking quietly beside a reedy pond, the child stooping for a flower and its gossip unheard – why should we tremble to reflect that we have never tasted just that cloistered balm?

Perhaps the happiest childhoods are those which pass completely away and leave whole tracts of years without a memory; those which are remembered are fullest of keen joy as of keen pain, and it is such that we desire for ourselves if we are capable of conceiving such fantastic desires. I confess to remembering little joy, but too much drowsy pleasure in the mere act of memory. I watch the past as I have seen workless, homeless men leaning over a bridge to watch the labours of a titanic crane and strange workers below in the ship running to and fro and feeding the crane. I recall green fields, one or two whom I loved in them, and though no trace of such happiness as I had remains, the incorruptible tranquillity of it all breeds fancies of great happiness. I recall many scenes: a church and churchyard and black pigs running down from them towards me in a rocky lane – ladslove and tall, crimson, bitter dahlias in a garden – the sweetness of large, moist yellow apples eaten out of doors – children: I do not recall happiness in them, yet the moment that I return to them in fancy I am happy. Something like this is true also of much later self-conscious years. I cannot – I am not tempted to – allow what then spoiled the mingling of the elements of joy to reappear when I look back. The reason, perhaps, is that only an inmost true self that desires and is in harmony with joy can perform these long journeys, and when it has set out upon them it sheds those gross incrustations which were our curse before.

Many are the scenes thus to be recalled without spot or stain. It is a May morning, warm and slightly breezy after midnight rain. In the beech woods the trees are unloading the dew, which drops from leaf to leaf and down on to the lemon-tinged leaves of dark dog's mercury. At the edge of the wood the privet branches arc bent down by the weight of raindrops of the size of peas. The dewy white stitchwort stars and the feathered grasses are curved over on the banks. The sainfoin is hoary and sparkling as I move. Already the sun is hot and the sky blue, with faint white clouds in whirls. And in the orchard-trees and drenched luxuriant hedges the garden-warbler sings a subdued note of rushing, bubbling liquidity as of some tiny brook that runs in quick pulsations among the fleshy-leaved water-plants. The bird's head is uplifted; its throat is throbbing; it moves restlessly from branch to branch, but always renews its song on the new perch; being leaf-like, it is not easily seen. And sometimes through this continuous jargon the small, wild song of the blackcap is heard, which is the utmost expression of moist warm dawns in May thickets of hawthorn-bloom and earliest roses. On such a dawn the very spirit bathes in the dew and nuzzles into the fragrance with delight; but it is no sooner left behind with May than it has developed within me into an hour and a scene of utmost grace and bliss, save that I am in it myself.

It is curious, too, how many different kinds of Eden or Golden Age Nature has in her gift, as if she silently recorded the backward dreams of each generation and reproduced them for us unexpectedly. It is, for instance, an early morning in July. The cows pour out from the milking-stalls and blot out the smell of dust with their breath in the white road between banks of hazel and thorn. The boy who is driving them to the morning's pasture calls to them monotonously, persuasively, in turn, as each is tempted to crop the roadside sward: "Wo, Cherry! Now, Dolly! Wo, Fancy! Strawberry! . . . Blanche! . . . Blossom! . . . Cowslip! . . . Rosy! Smut! . . . Come along, Handsome! . . . Wo, Snowdrop! . . . Lily! . . . Darky! . . . Roany! . . . Come along, Annie!" Here the road is pillowed with white aspen-down, there more fragrant than pines with the brown sheddings of yew, and here thick with the dry scent of nettle and cow-parsnip, or glorious in perfect mingling of harebell and foxglove among the bracken and popping gorse on the roadside. The cows turn into the aftermath of the sainfoin, and the long valley echoes to their lowing. After them, up the road, comes a gipsy-cart, and the boy hangs on the gate to see the men and women walking, black-haired, upright, bright-eyed, and on the name-board of the cart the words: "Naomi Sherwood, Burley, Hampshire." These things also propose to the roving, unhistoric mind an Eden, one still with us, one that is passing, not, let us hope, the very last.

Some of these scenes, whether often repeated or not, come to have a rich symbolical significance; they return persistently and, as it were, ceremoniously – on festal days – but meaning I know not what. For example, I never see the flowers and scarlet-stained foliage of herb-robert growing out of old stone-heaps by the wayside without a feeling of satisfaction not explained by a long memory of the contrast between the plant and the raw flint; so also with the drenched lilac-bloom leaning out over high walls of unknown gardens; and inland cliffs, covered with beech, jutting out westward into a bottomless valley in the mist of winter twilights, in silence and frost. Something in me belongs to these things, but I hardly think that the mere naming of them will mean anything except to those – many, perhaps – who have experienced the same. A great writer so uses the words of every day that they become a code of his own which the world is bound to learn and in the end take unto itself. But words are no longer symbols, and to say "hill" or "beech" is not to call up images of a hill or a beech-tree, since we have so long been in the habit of using the words for beautiful and mighty and noble things very much as a book-keeper uses figures without seeing gold and power. I can, therefore, only try to suggest what I mean by the significance of the plant in the stone-heap, the wet lilac, the misty cliff, by comparing it with that of scenes in books where we recognize some power beyond the particular and personal. All of Don Quixote's acts have this significance; so have the end of Mr. Conrad's story of *Youth* and the opening of Mr. Hudson's *El Ombu* – the old man sitting on a summer's day under the solitary tree to tell the history "of a house that had been." Malory's *Morte d'Arthur* is full of scenes like this. For ten centuries, from the battle of Badon to the writing of *Morte d'Arthur,* these stories were alive on the lips of many kinds of men and women in many lands, from Connemara to Calabria. Many of these men and women survive only in the turns which their passionate hearts gave to these ghostly, everlastingly wandering tales. Artists have worked upon them. Bards have sung them, and the sound of their harping is entangled in the words that have reached us to-day. This blending of many bloods is suggested by the Saracen in the *Morte d'Arthur* who was descended from Hector and Alexander and Joshua and Maccabæus; by Taliesin, whose "original country is the region of the summer stars," who was with Noah and Alexander and at the birth of Christ. And thus has the tale become so full in the ear of humanity, so rich in scenes designed to serve only an immediate purpose, yet destined by this grace to move all kinds of men in manifold ways. Such is the chess-playing in *The Dream of Rhonabwy*; the madness of Tristram when he ran naked in the woods many days, but was lured by the music of a damsel playing on his own harp; the speech of Arthur at the scattering of his knights in the Sangraal quest; Launcelot's fighting with the black knights against the white; Launcelot's adventures ending at the castle of Carbonek, where he put on all his arms and armour and went – "and the moon shone clear" – between the lions at the gate and forced open the door and saw the "Holy Vessel, covered with red samite, and many angels about it"; and Arthur and Guenevere watching the dead Elaine in the barge; and in the wars of Arthur and Launcelot, the scene opening with the words: "Then it befell upon a day in harvest-time, Sir Launcelot looked over the walls, and spake on high unto King Arthur and Sir Gawaine . . ."

No English writer has expressed as well as Traherne the spiritual glory of childhood, in which Wordsworth saw intimations of immortality. He speaks of "that divine light wherewith I was born" and of his "pure and virgin apprehensions," and recommends his friend to pray earnestly for these gifts: "They will make you angelical, and wholly celestial." It was by the "divine knowledge" that he saw all things in the peace of Eden:

The corn was orient and immortal wheat, which never should be reaped, nor was ever sown. I thought it had stood from everlasting to everlasting. The dust and stones of the street were as precious as gold; the gates were at first the end of the world. The green trees when I saw them first through one of the gates transported and ravished me; their sweetness and unusual beauty made my heart to leap and almost mad with ecstasy; they were such strange and wonderful things. The Men! O what venerable and reverend creatures did the aged seem! Immortal Cherubims! And young men glittering and sparkling angels, and maids strange seraphic pieces of life and beauty! Boys and girls tumbling in the street, and playing, were moving jewels. I knew not that they were born or should die; but all things abided eternally as they were in their proper places. Eternity was manifest in the light of the day, and something infinite behind everything appeared, which tallied with my expectation and moved my desire . . .

Yet was this light eclipsed. He was "with much ado" perverted by the world, by the temptation of men and worldly things and by "opinion and custom," not any "inward corruption or depravation of Nature."

For he tells us how he once entered a noble dining-room and was there alone "to see the gold and state and carved imagery," but wearied of it because it was dead, and had no motion. A little afterwards he saw it "full of lords and ladies and music and dancing," and now pleasure took the place of tediousness, and he perceived, long after, that "men and women are, when well understood, a principal part of our true felicity." Once again, "in a lowering and sad evening, being alone in the field, when all things were dead quiet," he had the same weariness, nay, even horror. "I was a weak and little child, and had forgotten there was a man alive in the earth." Nevertheless, hope and expectation came to him and comforted him, and taught him "that he was concerned in all the world." That he was "concerned in all the world" was the great source of comfort and joy which he found in life, and of that joy which his book pours out for us. Not only did he see that he was concerned in all the world, but that river and corn and herb and sand were so concerned. God, he says, "knoweth infinite excellencies" in each of these things; "He seeth how it relateth to angels and men." In this he anticipated Blake's *Auguries of Innocence*. He seems to see the patterns which all living things are for ever weaving. He would have men strive after this divine knowledge of things and of their place in the universe.

He came to believe that "all other creatures were such that God was Himself in their creation, that is, Almighty Power wholly exerted; and that every creature is indeed as it seemed in my infancy, not as it is commonly apprehended."

Yet he feels the superiority of man's soul to the things which it apprehends: "One soul in the immensity of its intelligence is greater and more excellent then the whole world." Even so Richard Jefferies prayed that his soul "might be more than the cosmos of life." The soul is greater than the whole world because it is capable of apprehending the whole world, because it is spiritual, and the spiritual nature is infinite. Thus Traherne was led to the splendid error of making the sun "a poor little dead thing." Or perhaps it was a figure of speech used to convince the multitude of his estimation of man's soul as above all visible things. In the same spirit he speaks of "this little Cottage of Heaven and Earth as too small a gift, though fair," for beings of whom he says: "Infinity we know and feel by our souls; and feel it so naturally, as if it were the very essence and being of the soul"; and again, with childlike simplicity and majesty:

"Man is a creature of such noble principles and severe expectations, that could he perceive the least defect to be in the Deity, it would infinitely displease him."

He could not well have thought of man except loftily, since he was himself one whom imagination never deserted – imagination the greatest power of the mind by which not poets only live and have their being:

"For God," says he, "hath made you able to create worlds in your own mind which are more precious unto Him than those which He created; and to give and offer up the world unto Him, which is very delightful in flowing from Him, but made more in returning to Him."

That power to create worlds in the mind is the imagination, and is the proof that the creature liveth and is divine. "Things unknown," he says, "have a secret influence on the soul," and "we love we know not what." The spirit can fill the whole world and the stars be your jewels: "You never enjoy the world aright, till the sea itself floweth in your veins, till you are clothed with the heavens, and crowned with the stars, and perceive yourself to be the sole heir of the whole world." And our inheritance is more than the world, "because men are in it who are every one sole heirs as well as you." It is a social mysticism. "The world," he says in another place, "does serve you, not only as it is the place and receptacle of all your joys, but as it is a great obligation laid upon all mankind, and upon every person in all ages, to love you as himself; as it also magnifieth all your companions." His is the true "public mind," as he calls it. "There is not," he says in another place – "there is not a man in the whole world that knows God, or himself, but he must honour you. Not only as an Angel or as a Cherubim, but as one redeemed by the blood of Christ, beloved by all Angels, Cherubims, and Men, the heir of the world, and as much greater than the Universe, as he that possesseth the house is greater than the house. O what a holy and blessed life would men lead, what joys and treasures would they be to each other, in what a sphere of excellency would every man move, how sublime and glorious would their estate be, how full of peace and quiet would the world be, yea, of joy and honour, order and beauty, did men perceive this of themselves, and had they this esteem for one another!"

Here, as in other passages, he seems to advance to the position of Whitman, whom some have blamed for making the word "divine" of no value because he would apply it to all, whereas to do so is no more than to lay down that rule of veneration for men – and the other animals – which has produced and will produce the greatest revolutions.

This conception of universal divinity sprang from his doctrine of Love. By love we can be at one with the divine power which he calls God. "Love," he says, "is the true means by which the world is enjoyed: our love to others, and others' love to us." Why, even the love of riches he excuses, since "we love to be rich . . . that we thereby might be more greatly delightful." And just as Richard Jefferies says that Felise loved before ever she loved a man, so Traherne says: "That violence wherewith a man sometimes doteth upon one creature is but a little spark of that love, even toward all, which lurketh in his nature . . . When we dote upon the perfections and beauties of some one creature, we do not love that too much, but other things too little." It is this love by which alone the commonwealth of all forms of life can be truly known, and men are like God when they are "all life and mettle and vigour and love to everything," and "concerned and happy" in all things. His feeling of the interdependence of all the world is thus inseparable from his doctrine of love; love inspires it; by love alone can it be real and endure. "He that is in all and with all can never be desolate." And, nevertheless, he cannot always be thinking of the universe – he thought that the sun went round the earth – and just as he regards man as superior to other forms of life, so, perhaps, he has a filial love of "this cottage of Heaven and Earth," the brown land and blue sky, and one of the most beautiful of his meditations is where he says:

When I came into the country, and being seated among silent trees, and meads, and hills, had all my time in mine own hands, I resolved to spend it all, whatever it cost me, in the search of happiness, and to satiate that burning thirst which Nature had enkindled in me from my youth. In which I was so resolute, that I chose rather to live upon ten pounds a year, and go in leather clothes, and feed upon bread and water, so that I might have all my time clearly to myself, than to keep many thousands per annum in an estate of life where my time would be devoured in care and labour. And God was so pleased to accept of that desire, that from that time to this, I have had all things plentifully provided for me, without any care at all, my very study of Felicity making me more to prosper, than all the care in the whole world. So that through His blessing I live a free and a kingly life as if the world were turned again into Eden, or much more, as it is at this day.

Traherne is remarkable in many ways, but for nothing more than for his mingling of man and nature in the celestial light of infancy. He begins, indeed, with the corn – the "orient and immortal wheat" – but he goes on to the dust and stones and gates of the town, and then to the old men and the young men and the children. But it was only on "some gilded cloud or flower" that Vaughan saw "some shadows of eternity"; he longs to travel back to his childish time and to a city of the soul, but a shady city of palm-trees. Wordsworth, though he says that "every common spirit" was "apparell'd in celestial light" in his early childhood, only mentions "meadow, grove and stream"; it is a tree, a single field, a flower, that reminds him of his loss; it is the fountains, meadows, hills and groves which he is anxious to assure of his lasting love. Perhaps many people's memories in this kind are of Nature more than of men. Even the social Lamb is at his deepest in recalling the child who was solitary in the great house and garden at Blakesmoor. With some the reason for this priority of Nature is that her solitudes are the most rich. The presence of other children and of adults is comparatively commonplace, and in becoming, permanently or temporarily, part of a community, the spirit makes some sacrifice. Provided, then, that a child is happy and at ease in the solitude of Nature, it is more open than in company to what is afterwards regarded as spiritual intercourse. But above all, our memories of Nature are seldom or never flawed by the seeming triviality, the dislikes, the disgusts, the misunderstandings which give to memories of human society something of dulness and the commonplace. Thinking of ourselves and other children, we may also think of things which make idealization impossible. Thinking of ourselves in a great wood or field of flowers ever so long ago, it is hard not to exaggerate whatever give-and-take there was between the spirit of the child and the vast pure forces of the sun and the wind. In those days we did not see a tree as a column of a dark stony substance supporting a number of green wafers that live scarcely half a year, and grown for the manufacture of furniture, gates, and many other things; but we saw something quite unlike ourselves, large, gentle, of foreign tongue, without locomotion, yet full of the life and movement and sound of the leaves themselves, and also of the light, of the birds, and of the insects; and they were givers of a clear, deep joy that cannot be expressed. The brooding mind easily exalts this joy with the help of the disillusions and the knowledge and the folly and the thought of later years. A little time ago I heard of the death of one whom I had once seemed to know well, had roamed and talked and been silent with him, and I should have gone on doing so had he not gone far away and died. And when I heard of his death I kept on recalling his face and figure to my mind under familiar conditions, in the old rooms, by the same river, under the same elms. As before, I saw him in the clothes which he used to wear, smiling or laughing or perhaps grim. But wherever he was and whatever his look, there was always something – the shadow of a shadow, but awful – in his face which made me feel that had I only seen it (and I felt that I ought to have seen it), in those days, I should have known he was to die early, with ambitions unfulfilled, far away.

And in this same way will the brain work in musing of earlier times.

All that has come after deepens that candid brow of the child as a legend will darken a bright brook.

I once saw a girl of seven or eight years walking alone down a long grassy path in an old garden. On one hand rose a peaceful long slope of down; on the other, beyond the filberts, a high hedge shut out all but the pale blue sky, with white clouds resting on its lower mist like water-lilies on a still pool. Turning her back to the gabled house and its attendant beeches, she walked upon the narrow level path of perfect grass. The late afternoon sun fell full upon her, upon her brown head and her blue tunic, and upon the flowers of the borders at either side, the lowly white arabis foaming wild, the pansy, the white narcissus, the yellow jonquil and daffodil, the darker smouldering wallflowers, the tall yellow leopard's-bane, the tufts of honesty among the still dewy leaves of larkspur and columbine. But here and there, as she walked, the light was dimmed by the clusters of cool white humming cherry-blossom hanging out of the hot sky. In front of her the cherry trees seemed to meet and make a corridor of dark stems on either hand, paved green and white and gold, and roofed by milky white clouds that embowered the clear, wild warble of blackcaps. Farther on, the flowers ceased and the grass was shadowed by new-leaved beeches, and at length involved in an uncertain mist of trees and shadows of trees, and there the cuckoo cried. For the child there was no end to the path.

She walked slowly, at first picking a narcissus or two, or stooping to smell a flower and letting her hair fall over it to the ground; but soon she was content only to brush the tips of the flowers with her outstretched hands, or, rising on tiptoe, to force her head up amongst the lowest branches of cherry-bloom. Then she did nothing at all but gravely walk on into the shadow and into Eternity, dimly foreknowing her life's days. She looked forward as one day she would look back over a broad sea of years, and in a drowsy, haunted gloom, full of the cuckoo's note, saw herself going always on and on among the interlacing shadows of tree trunks and branches and joys and pleasures and pains and sorrows that must have an end, she knew not how. She stopped, not venturing into that strange future under the beeches. She stared into the mist, where hovered the phantoms of the big girl, the young woman, the lover . . . which in turn she was to become. Under the last cherry tree something went out of her into the shadow, and those phantoms fed upon her blood as she stood still. But presently in the long beech corridors the gloom began to lighten and move and change to a glinting blue that approached her. "Pee-oi," shouted the peacock, now close at hand; "pee-oi . . . pee-oi, as he passed her by, and turning, she also shouted "pee-oi," frightening the cuckoo from the beeches, as she ran back among the flowers to the house.

What is to come of our Nature-teaching in schools? What does it aim at? Whence does it arise? In part, no doubt, it is due to our desire to implant information. It is all very well for the poet to laugh –

> When Science has discovered something more
> We shall be happier than we were before;

but that is the road we are on at a high rate of speed. If we are fortunate we shall complete our inventory of the contents of heaven and earth by the time when the last man or woman wearing the last pair of spectacles has decided that, after all, it is a very good world and one which it is quite possible to live in. That, however, is an end which would not in itself be a sufficient inducement to push on towards it; still less can such a vision have set us upon the road.

Three things, perhaps, have more particularly persuaded us to pay our fare and mount for somewhere – three things which are really not to be sharply distinguished, though it is convenient to consider them separately. First, the literary and philosophical movement imperfectly described as the romantic revival and return to Nature of the eighteenth and nineteenth centuries. Poets and philosophers need private incomes, State porridge and what not, but literature and philosophy is a force, and for a century it has followed a course which was entered in the period of the French Revolution. This literature shows man in something like his true position in an infinite universe, and shows him particularly in his physical environment of sea, sky, mountain, rivers, woods, and other animals. Second, the enormous, astonishing, perhaps excessive, growth of towns, from which the only immediate relief is the pure air and sun of the country, a relief which is sought by the urban multitudes in large but insufficient numbers and for too short a time. Third, the triumph of science, of systematized observation. Helped, no doubt, by the force of industrialism – to which it gave help in return – science has had a great triumph. At one time it was supposed to have fatally undermined poetry, romance, religion, because it had confused the minds of some poets and critics.

These three things considered, Nature-study is inevitable. Literature sends us to Nature principally for joy, joy of the senses, of the whole frame, of the contemplative mind, and of the soul, joy which if it is found complete in these several ways might be called religious. Science sends us to Nature for knowledge. Industrialism and the great towns send us to Nature for health, that we may go on manufacturing efficiently, or, if we think right and have the power, that we may escape from it. But it would be absurd to separate joy, knowledge and health, except as we separate for convenience those things which have sent us out to seek for them; and Nature-teaching, if it is good, will never overlook one of these three. Joy, through knowledge, on a foundation of health, is what we appear to seek.

There is no longer any need to hesitate in speaking of joy in connection with schools, yet might we not still complain, as Thomas Traherne did two hundred and fifty years ago:

> There was never a tutor that did professly teach Felicity, though that be the mistress of all other sciences. Nor did any of us study these things but as aliena, which we ought to have studied as our enjoyments. We studied to inform our Knowledge, but knew not for what end we so studied. And for lack of aiming at a certain end we erred in the manner.

If we cannot somehow have a professor of Felicity we are undone. Perhaps Nature herself will aid. Her presence will certainly make for felicity by enlarging her pupil for a time from the cloistered life which modern towns and their infinite conveniences and servitudes encourage. Tolstoy has said that in the open air "new relations are formed between pupil and teacher: freer, simpler and more trustful"; and certainly his walk on a winter night with his pupils, chattering and telling tales (see *The School at Yasnaya Polyana*, by Leo Tolstoy), leaves an impression of electrical activity and felicity in the young and old minds of that party which is hardly to be surpassed. And how more than by Nature's noble and uncontaminated forms can a sense of beauty be nourished? Then, too, the reading of great poetry might well be associated with the study of Nature, since there is no great poetry which can be dissevered from Nature, while modern poets have all dipped their pens in the sunlight and wind and great waters, and appeal most to those who most resemble them in their loves. The great religious books, handed down to us by people who lived in closer intercourse with Nature than many of us, cannot be understood by indoor children and adults. Whether connected with this or that form of religion or not, whether taken as "intimations of immortality" or not, the most profound and longest remembered feelings are often those derived from the contact of Nature with the child's mind.

Of health, though there are exactly as many physicians as patients, it is unnecessary to say anything, except that one of the pieces of knowledge – I do not speak of information – which science has left to us is that movement and the working of the brain in pure air and sunlight is good for body and soul, especially if joy is aiding.

Knowledge aids joy by discipline, by increasing the sphere of enjoyment, by showing us in animals, in plants, for example, what life is, how our own is related to theirs, showing us, in fact, our position, responsibilities and debts among the other inhabitants of the earth. Pursued out of doors where those creatures, moving and still, have their life and their beauty, knowledge is real. The senses are invited there to the subtlest and most delightful training, and have before them an immeasurable fresh field, not a field like that of books, full of old opinions, but one with which every eye and brain can have new vital intercourse. It is open to all to make discoveries as to the forms and habits of things, and care should be taken to preserve the child from the most verbose part of modern literature, that which repeats in multiplied ill-chosen words stale descriptions of birds and flowers, etc., coupled with trivial fancies and insincere inventions. Let us not take the study, the lamp and the ink out of doors, as we used to take wild life – having killed it and placed it in spirits of wine – indoors. Let us also be careful to have knowledge as well as enthusiasm in our masters. Enthusiasm alone is not enthusiasm. There must, at some stage, be some anatomy, classification, pure brain-work; the teacher must be the equal in training of the mathematician, and he must be alive, which I never heard was a necessity for mathematicians. But not anatomy for all, perhaps; for some it might be impossible, and a study of colours, curves, perfumes, voices – a thousand things – might be substituted for it. Yet Nature-study is not designed to produce naturalists, any more than music is taught in order to make musicians. If you produce nothing but naturalists you fail, and you will produce very few. The aim of study is to widen the culture of child and man, to do systematically what Mark Pattison tells us in his dry way he did for himself, by walking and outdoor sports, then – at the late age of seventeen – by collecting and reading such books as *The Natural History of Selborne,* and finally by a slow process of transition from natural history into "the more abstract poetic emotion . . . a conscious and declared poetical sentiment and a devoted reading of the poets." Geology did not come for another ten years, "to complete the cycle of thought, and to give that intellectual foundation which is required to make the testimony of the eye, roaming over an undulating surface, fruitful and satisfying. When I came in after years to read *The Prelude* I recognized, as if it were my own history which was being told, the steps by which the love of the country boy for his hills and moors grew into poetical susceptibility for all imaginative presentations of beauty in every direction." The botany, etc., would naturally be related to the neighbourhood of school or h o m e; for there is no parish or district of which it might not be said, as Jefferies and Thoreau each said of his own, that it is a microcosm. By this means the natural history may easily be linked to a preliminary study of hill and valley and stream, the positions of houses, mills and villages, and the reasons for them, and the food supply, and so on, and this in turn leads on to – nay, involves – all that is most real in geography and history. The landscape retains the most permanent marks of the past, and a wise examination of it should evoke the beginnings of the majestic sentiment of our oneness with the future and the past, just as natural history should help to give the child a sense of oneness with all forms of life. To put it at its lowest, some such cycle of knowledge is needed if a generation that insists more and more on living in the country, or spending many weeks there, is not to be bored or to be compelled to entrench itself behind the imported amusements of the town.

NINE

History and the Parish

SOME DAY there will be a history of England written from the point of view of one parish, or town, or great house. Not until there is such a history will all our accumulations of information be justified. It will begin with a geological picture, something large, clear, architectural, not a mass of insignificant names. It must be imaginative: it might, perhaps, lean sometimes upon Mr. Doughty's *Dawn in Britain*. The peculiar combination of soil and woodland and water determines the direction and position and importance of the ancient trackways; it will determine also the position and size of the human settlements. The early marks of these – the old flint and metal implements, the tombs, the signs of agriculture, the encampments, the dwellings – will have to be clearly described and interpreted. Folk-lore, legend, place-names must be learnedly, but bravely and humanly used, so that the historian who has not the extensive sympathy and imagination of a great novelist will have no chance of success. What endless opportunities will he have for really giving life to past times in such matters as the line made by the edge of an old wood with the cultivated land, the shapes of the fields, with their borders of streams or hedge or copse or pond or wall or road, the purpose and interweaving of the roads and footpaths that suggest the great permanent thoughts and the lesser thoughts and dreams of the brain . . . As the historic centuries are reached, the action of great events, battles, laws, roads, invasions, upon the parish – and of the parish upon them – must be shown. Architecture, with many of its local characteristics still to be traced, will speak as a voice out of the stones of castle, church, manor, farm, barn and bridge. The birds and beasts cannot be left out. The names of the local families – gentle and simple – what histories are in them, in the curt parish registers, in tombstones, in the names of fields and houses and woods. Better a thousand errors so long as they

are human than a thousand truths lying like broken snail-shells round
the anvil of a thrush. If only those poems which are place-names could
be translated at last, the pretty, the odd, the romantic, the racy names
of copse and field and lane and house. What a flavour there is about
the Bassetts, the Boughtons, the Worthys, the Tarrants, Winterbournes,
Deverills, Manningfords, the Suttons: what goodly names of the South
Country – Woodmansterne, Hollingbourne, Horsmonden, Wolstanbury,
Brockenhurst, Caburn, Lydiard Tregoze, Lydiard Millicent, Clevancy,
Amesbury, Amberley (I once tried to make a beautiful name and in the
end it was Amberley, in which Time had forestalled me); what sweet
names Penshurst, Frensham, Firle, Nutley, Appleshaw, Hambledon,
Cranbrook, Fordingbridge, Melksham, Lambourn, Draycot, Buscot,
Kelmscot, Yatton, Yalding, Downe, Cowden, Iping, Cowfold, Ashe, Liss
. . . Then there are the histories of roads. Every traveller in Hampshire
remembers the road that sways with airy motion and bird-like curves
down from the high land of clay and flint through the chalk to the sand
and the river. It doubles round the head of a coombe, and the whole
descent is through beech woods uninterrupted and all but impenetrable
to the eye above or below except where once or twice it looks through an
arrow slit to the blue vale and the castled promontory of Chanctonbury
twenty miles south-east. As the road is a mere ledge on the side of a
very steep hill the woods below it hurry down to a precipitous pit full
of the glimmering, trembling and murmuring of innumerable leaves and
no sight or sound of men. It is said to have been made more than half
a century ago to take the place of the rash straight coach road which
now enters it near its base. A deeply-worn, narrow and disused track
joining it more than half-way down suggests that the lower part was
made by the widening of an old road; but much of the upper half is
new. Certainly the road as it now is, broad and gently bending round
the steep coombe, is new, and it was made at the expense of the last of a
family which had long owned the manor house near the entrance of the
coombe. His were all the hanging beech woods – huge as the sky – upon
the hill, and through them the road-makers conducted this noble and
pleasant way. But near the top they deviated by a few yards into another

estate. The owner would not give way. A lawsuit was begun, and it was not over when the day came for the road to be open for traffic according to the contract or, if not, to pass out of the defaulter's hands. The day passed; the contract was broken; the speculation had failed, and the tolls would never fill the pockets of the lord of the manor. He was ruined, and left his long white house by the rivulet and its chain of pools, his farms and cottages, his high fruit walls, his uncounted beeches, the home of a hundred owls, his Spanish chestnuts above the rocky lane, his horse-chestnut and sycamore stately in groups, his mighty wych-elms, his apple trees and all their mistletoe, his walnut trees, and the long bay of sky that was framed by his tall woods east and north and west.

There are many places which nobody can look upon without being consciously influenced by a sense of their history. It is a battlefield, and the earth shows the scars of its old wounds; or a castle or cathedral of distinct renown rises among the oaks; or a manor house or cottage, or tomb or woodland walk that speaks of a dead poet or soldier. Then, according to the extent or care of our reading and the clearness of our imagination, we can pour into the groves or on the turf tumultuous or silent armies, or solitary man or woman. It is a deeply-worn coast; the spring tide gnaws the yellow cliff, and the wind files it with unceasing hiss, and the relics of every age, skull and weapon and shroudpin and coin and carven stone, are spread out upon the clean, untrodden sand, and the learned, the imaginative, the fanciful, the utterly unhistoric and merely human man exercises his spirit upon them, and responds, if only for a moment. In some places history has wrought like an earthquake, in others like an ant or mole; everywhere, permanently; so that if we but knew or cared, every swelling of the grass, every wavering line of hedge or path or road were an inscription, brief as an epitaph, in many languages and characters. But most of us know only a few of these unspoken languages of the past, and only a few words in each. Wars and parliaments are but dim, soundless, and formless happenings in the brain; toil and passion of generations produce only an enriching of the light within the glades, and a solemnizing of the shadows.

Out of a whole century or age we remember nothing vividly and in a manner that appeals to the eye, except some such picture as that which Gerald of Wales gives of a Welsh prince, Cyneuric, son of Rhys. He was tall and handsome, fair-complexioned, his hair curled; his dress was a thin cloak, and under that a shirt, his legs and feet being bare, regardless of thistle and brier; a man to whom nature and not art had given his beauty and comely bearing. Outside Wales, and in ages far removed from the twelfth century, this figure of a man will follow us, and help to animate any wild scene that is coloured by antiquity. It is some such man, his fair hair perhaps exchanged for black, and his nobility more animal and clothed in skins, that we see, if we see a man at all, when we muse deeply upon the old road worn deep into the chalk, among burial mound and encampment; we feel rather than see the innumerable companies of men like this, following their small cattle to the stream or the dew-pond, wearing out the hard earth with their naked feet and trailing ash staves. Going up such a road, between steep banks of chalk and the roots and projecting bases of beeches whose foliage meets overhead – a road worn twenty feet deep, and now scarce ever used as a footpath except by fox and hare – we may be half-conscious that we have climbed that way before during the furrowing of the road, and we move as in a dream between this age and that dim one which we vainly strive to recover.

But because we are imperfectly versed in history, we are not therefore blind to the past. The eye that sees the things of to-day, and the ear that hears, the mind that contemplates or dreams, is itself an instrument of an antiquity equal to whatever it is called upon to apprehend. We are not merely twentieth-century Londoners or Kentish men or Welshmen. We belong to the days of Wordsworth, of Elizabeth, of Richard Plantagenet, of Harold, of the earliest bards. We, too, like Taliesin, have borne a banner before Alexander, have been with our Lord in the manger of the ass, have been in India, and with the "remnant of Troia," and with Noah in the ark, and our original country is "the region of the summer stars." And of these many folds in our nature the face of the earth reminds us, and perhaps, even where there are no more marks visible upon the land than there were in Eden, we are aware of the passing of time in ways too difficult and strange for the explanation of historian and zoologist and philosopher. It is this manifold nature that responds with such indescribable depth and variety to the appeals of many landscapes.

We come to a huge, flat-bottomed, grassy coombe, smooth as a racecourse, that winds out of the cornland into the heart of the Downs. It is like the bed of a river of great depth. At its entrance beeches clothe either side; but presently they cease, and up the steep juniper slopes go the paths of hares, of the herds and flocks of earliest ages and of the men and women and children also, whose children's children's children have forgotten them though not perhaps their philosophy. The grass of the slope is mingled with small sweet herbage, the salad burnet rosy-stemmed, the orange bird's-foot trefoil, the purple thyme, the fine white flax, the delicatest golden hawk-bit, and basil and marjoram, and rosettes of crimson thistles, all sunny warm and fragrant, glittering and glowing or melting into a simmering haze, musical with grasshoppers and a-flutter with blue butterflies, so that the earth seems to be a thick-furred, genial animal. At length the windings shut out the plain, and the coombe is a green hall roofed by the hot blue sky. Its walls are steeper than ever, and the burrowings of the rabbits have streaked the grasses with long splashes – like those made by sea-birds on rocks – of white chalk. The curves of these walls are like those of the flight of the swifts that dive overhead. Here there are no human paths, no sign of house, of grave, of herd, of cultivation. It is the world's end, and the rabbits race up and down as in a dream of solitude.

Yet the mind is not discontented and unfed. This is no boundless solitude of ocean where one may take a kind of pleasure

> To float for ever with a careless course
> And think himself the only being alive.

It is not an end but a beginning that we have reached. These are the elements – pure earth and wind and sunlight – out of which beauty and joy arise, original and ancient, for ever young. Their presence restores us not to the Middle Ages, not to the days of Mr. Doughty's heroic princes and princesses of Britain (*The Dawn in Britain,* by Charles Doughty), not to any dim archaeologist's world of reeking marsh and wood, of mammoth and brutish men, but to a region out of space and out of time in which life and thought and physical health are in harmony with sun and earth, fragrant as the flowers in the grass, blithe as the grasshopper, swift as the hares, divine; and out of it all arises a vision of the man who will embody this thought, a man whom human infelicity, discontented with the past, has placed in a golden age still farther back, for the sufficient reason that in every age he has been a dream, and our dreaming is of the dawn or the night, always disappointed but undaunted by the day that follows. And so no storied valley or hillside is richer in humanity than this coombe. It is one of the countless Edens where we are in contact not with the soldier and ploughman and mason that change the surface of the earth but with prophet and poet who have ever lived to trace to Nature and to the early ages the health and vigour of men. There is the greatest antiquity of all, peace and purity and simplicity, and in the midst is the mother Earth, the young mother of the world, with a face like Ceres before she had lost Persephone in the underworld. In fact, so blessed is this solitary hall that after climbing out it is mournful to see the rabbit-worn tunnels and the Roman camp on the ridge.

CORNWALL

In Cornwall, where the wrinkles and angles of the earth's age are left to show, antiquity plays a giant's part on every hand. What a curious effect have those ruins, all but invisible among the sands, the sea-blue scabious, the tamarisk and rush, though at night they seem not inaudible when the wild air is full of crying! Some that are not nearly as old are almost as magical. One there is that stands near a great water, cut off from a little town and from the world by a round green hill and touched by no road but only by a wandering path. At the foot of this hill, among yellow mounds of sand, under blue sky, the church is dark and alone. It is not very old – not five centuries – and is of plainest masonry: its blunt short spire of slate slabs that leans slightly to one side, with the smallest of perforated slate windows at the base, has a look of age and rusticity.

In the churchyard is a rough grey cross of stone – a disk supported by a pillar. It is surrounded by the waving noiseless tamarisk. It looks northward over the sandhills at a blue bay, guarded on the west by tall grey cliffs which a white column surmounts.

For a time the nearer sandhills have rested and clothed themselves in bird's-foot trefoil, thyme, eyebright and short turf: but once the church was buried beneath them. Between the round hill and the church a tiny stream sidles along through a level hiding-place of flags and yellow flag flowers, of purple figwort and purple orchis and green grass.

A cormorant flies low across the sky – that sable bird which seems to belong to the old time, the time of badger and beaver, of ancient men who rose up out of the crags of this coast. To them, when the cuckoo first called one April, came over the blue sea a small brown ship, followed by three seals, and out of it descended a Christian from Ireland, black-haired, blue-eyed, with ready red lips and deep sweet voice and spoke to them, all alone. He told them of a power that ruled the blue waters and shifting sands, who could move the round green hill to the rock of the white gulls; taller and grimmer than the cloven headland yet sweet and gentle as the fennel above; deep-voiced as the Atlantic storm, tender also as the sedge-warbler in the flags below the hill; whose palace was loftier than the blue to which the lark was now soaring, milder and richer than the meadows in May and everlasting; and his attendants were more numerous and bright than the herring under a moon of frost. The milk-pails should be fuller and the grass deeper and the corn heavier in the ear if they believed in this; the pilchards should be as water boiling in the bay; and they should have wings as of the white birds that lounged about the precipices of the coast. And all the time the three seals lay with their heads and backs above the shallows and watched. Perhaps the men believed his word; perhaps they dropped him over the precipice to see whether he also flew like a gull: but here is the church named after him.

All along the coast (and especially where it is lofty and houseless, and on the ledges of the crags the young grey gulls, unable to fly, bob their heads seaward and try to scream like their parents who wheel far and near with double yodelling cry), there are many rounded barrows looking out to sea. And there are some amidst the sand-hills, bare and corrugated by the wind and heaved up like a feather-bed, their edges golden against the blue sky or mangily covered by drab marram grass that whistles wintrily; and near by the blue sea, slightly roughened as by a harrow, sleeps calm but foamy among cinder-coloured isles; donkeys graze on the brown turf, larks rise and fall and curlews go by; a cuckoo sings among the deserted mines. But the barrows are most noble on the high heather and grass. The lonely turf is full of lilac scabious flowers and crimson knapweed among the solid mounds of gorse. The brown-green-grey of the dry summer grass reveals myriads of the flowers of thyme, of stonecrop yellow and white, of pearly eyebright, of golden lady's fingers, and the white or grey clover with its purest and earthiest of all fragrances. Here and there steep tracks descend slantwise among the thrift-grown crags to the sea, or promise to descend but end abruptly in precipices. On the barrows themselves; which are either isolated or in a group of two or three, grow thistle and gorse. They command mile upon mile of cliff and sea. In their sight the great headlands run out to sea and sinking seem to rise again a few miles out in a sheer island, so that they resemble couchant beasts with backs under water but heads and haunches upreared. The cliffs are cleft many times by steep-sided coves, some with broad sand and shallow water among purple rocks, the outlet of a rivulet; others ending precipitously so that the stream suddenly plunges into the black sea among a huddle of sunless boulders. Near such a stream there will be a grey farm amid grey outbuildings – with a carved wooden eagle from the wreckage of the cove, or a mermaid, once a figure-head with fair long hair and round bosom, built into the wall of a barn. Or there is a briny hamlet grouped steeply on either side of the stream which gurgles among the pebbles down to the feet of the bearded fisherman and the ships a-gleam. Or perhaps there is no stream at all, and bramble and gorse come down dry and hot to the lips of the emerald and purple pools. Deep roads from the sea to the cliff-top have been worn by smuggler and fisherman and miner, climbing and descending. Inland shows a solitary pinnacled church tower, rosy in the warm evening – thin line of trees, long bare stems and dark foliage matted – and farther still the ridges of misty granite, rough as the back of a perch.

Of all the rocky land, of the sapphire sea white with quiet foam, the barrows are masters. The breaking away of the rock has brought them nearer to the sea as it has annihilated some and cut off the cliff-ways in mid-career. They stand in the unenclosed waste and are removed from all human uses and from most wayfaring. Thus they share the sublimity of beacons and are about to show that tombs also have their deaths. Linnet and stonechat and pipit seem to attend upon them, with pretty voices and motions and a certain ghastliness, as of shadows, given to their cheerful and sudden flittings by the solemn neighbourhood. But most of their hold upon the spirit they owe to their powerful suggestion that here upon the high sea border was once lived a bold proud life, like that of Beowulf, whose words, when he was dying from the wounds of his last victory, were: "Bid the warriors raise a funeral mound to flash with fire on a promontory above the sea, that it may stand high and be a memorial by which my people shall remember me, and seafarers driving their tall ships through the mist of the sea shall say: 'Beowulf's Mound.'"

In Cornwall as in Wales, these monuments are the more impressive, because the earth, wasting with them and showing her bones, takes their part. There are days when the age of the Downs, strewn with tumuli and the remnants of camp and village, is incredible; or rather they seem in the course of long time to have grown smooth and soft and kind, and to be, like a rounded languid cloud, an expression of Earth's summer bliss of afternoon. But granite and slate and sandstone jut out, and in whatsoever weather speak rather of the cold, drear, hard, windy dawn. Nothing can soften the lines of Trendreen or Brown Willy or Carn Galver against the sky. The small stone-hedged ploughlands amidst brake and gorse do but accentuate the wildness of the land from which they have been won. The deserted mines are frozen cries of despair as if they had perished in conflict with the waste; and in a few years their chimneys standing amidst rotted woodwork, the falling masonry, the engine rusty, huge and still (the abode of rabbits, and all overgrown with bedstraw, the stern thistle and wizard henbane) are in keeping with the miles of barren land, littered with rough silvered stones among heather and furze, whose many barrows are deep in fern and bramble and foxglove. The cotten grass raises its pure nodding white. The old roads dive among still more furze and bracken and bramble and foxglove, and on every side the land grows no such crop as that of grey stones. Even in the midst of occasional cornfield or weedless pasture a long grey upright stone speaks of the past. In many places men have set up these stones, roughly squaring some of them, in the form of a circle or in groups of circles – and over them beats the buzzard in slow hesitating and swerving flight. In one place the work of Nature might be mistaken for that of man. On a natural hillock stands what appears to be the ruin of an irregularly heaped wall of grey rock, roughened by dark-grey lichen, built of enormous angular fragments like the masonry of a giant's child. Near at hand, bracken, pink stonecrop, heather and bright gold tormentil soften it; but at a distance it stands black against the summer sky, touched with the pathos of man's handiwork overthrown, yet certainly an accident of Nature. It commands Cape Cornwall and the harsh sea, and St. Just with its horned church tower. On every hand lie cromlech, camp, circle, hut and tumulus of the unwritten years. They are confused and mingled with the natural litter of a barren land. It is a silent Bedlam of history, a senseless cemetery or museum, amidst which we walk as animals must do when they see those valleys full of skeletons where their kind are said to go punctually to die. There are enough of the dead; they outnumber the living; and there those trite truths burst with life and drum upon the tympanum with ambiguous fatal voices. At the end of this many-barrowed moor, yet not in it, there is a solitary circle of grey stones, where the cry of the past is less vociferous, less bewildering, than on the moor itself, but more intense. Nineteen tall, grey stones stand round a taller, pointed one that is heavily bowed, amidst long grass and bracken and furze. A track passes close by, but does not enter the circle; the grass is unbent except by the weight of its bloom. It bears a name that connects it with the assembling and rivalry of the bards of Britain. Here, under the sky, they met, leaning upon the stones, tall, fair men of peace, but half-warriors, whose songs could change ploughshare into sword. Here they met, and the growth of the grass, the perfection of the stones (except that one stoops as with age), and the silence, suggests that since the last bard left it, in robe of blue or white or green – the colours of sky and cloud and grass upon this fair day – the circle has been unmolested, and the law obeyed which forbade any but a bard to enter it. Sky-blue was the colour of a chief bard's robe, emblematic of peace and heavenly calm, and of unchangeableness. White, the colour of the Druid's dress, was the emblem of light, and of its correlatives, purity of conduct, wisdom, and piety. Green was the colour of the youthful ovate's robe, for it was the emblem of growth. Their uniformity of colour signified perfect truth. And the inscription upon the chair of the bards of Beisgawen was, "Nothing is that is not for ever and ever." Blue and white and green, peace and light and growth – "Nothing is that is not for ever and ever" – these things and the blue sky, the white, cloudy hall of the sun, and the green bough and grass, hallowed the ancient stones, and clearer than any vision of tall bards in the morning of the world was the tranquil delight of being thus "teased out of time" in the presence of this ancientness.

It is strange to pass from these monumental moors straight to the sea which records the moments, not the years or the centuries. In fine weather especially its colour – when, for example, it is faintly corrugated and of a blue that melts towards the horizon into such a hue that it is indistinguishable from the violet wall of dawn – is a perpetual astonishment on account of its unearthliness and evanescence. The mind does not at once accept the fact that here underneath our eyes is, as it were, another sky. The physical act of looking up induces a special mood of solemnity and veneration, and during the act the eyes meet with a fitting object in the stainless heavens. Looking down we are used to seeing the earth, the road, the footpath, the floor, the hearth; but when, instead, it is the sea and not any of these things, although our feet are on firm land, the solemnity is of another kind. In its anger the sea becomes humanized or animalized: we see resemblances to familiar things. There is, for instance, an hour sometimes after sunset, when the grey sky coldly lights the lines of white plumes on a steely sea, and they have an inevitable likeness to a trampling chivalry that charges upon a foe. But a calm sea is incomparable except to moods of the mind. It is then as remote from the earth and earthly things as the sky, and the remoteness is the more astonishing because it is almost within our grasp. It is no wonder that a great idea was expressed by the fortunate islands in the sea. The youthfulness, the incorruptibility of the sea, continually renewing itself, the same from generation to generation, prepares it as a fit sanctuary of the immortal dead. So at least we are apt to think at certain times, coming from the heavy, scarred, tormented earth to that immense aery plain of peacock blue. And yet at other times that same unearthliness will suggest quite other thoughts. It has not changed and shrunken and grown like the earth; it is not sun-warmed: it is a monster that has lain unmoved by time, sleeping and moaning outside the gates within which men and animals have become what they are. Actually that cold fatal element and its myriad population without a sound brings a wistfulness into the mind as if it could feel back and dimly recall the dawn of time when the sea was incomprehensible and impassable, when the earth had but lately risen out of the waters and was yet again to descend beneath: it becomes a type of the waste where everything is unknown or uncertain except death, pouring into the brain the thoughts that men have had on looking out over untrodden mountain, forest, swamp, in the drizzling dawn of the world. The sea is exactly what it was when mountain, forest, swamp were inperturbable enemies, and the sight of it restores the ancient fear. I remember one dawn above all others when this restoration was complete. When it was yet dark the wind rose gustily under a low grey sky and a lark sang amidst the moan of gorse and the creek of gates and the deeply-taken breath of the tide at the full. Nor was it yet light when the gulls began to wheel and wind and float with a motion like foam on a whirlpool or inter-woven snow. They wheeled about the masts of fishing-boats that nodded and kissed and crossed in a steep cove of crags whose black edges were slavered by the foam of the dark sea; and there were no men among the boats or about the grey houses that looked past the walls of the cove to the grim staircase and sea-doors of a black headland, whose perpendicular rocks stood up far out of the reach of the wings fashioned in the likeness of gigantic idols. The higher crags were bushy and scaly with lichen, and they were cushioned upon thrift and bird's-foot trefoil and white bladder campion. It was a bristling sea, not in the least stormy, but bristling, dark and cold through the slow colourless dawn, dark and cold and immense; and at the edge of it the earth knelt, offering up the music of a small flitting bird and the beauty of small flowers, white and gold, to those idols. They were terrible enough. But the sea was more terrible; for it was the god of whom those rocks were the poor childish images, and it seemed that the god had just then disclosed his true nature and hence the pitiful loveliness of the flowers, the pitiful sweetness of the bird that sang among the rocks at the margin of the kind earth.

Now and then the sea will startle by some resemblance to the earth. Thus I have come unexpectedly in sight of it on a strange coast and have not known that it was the sea. A gale from the north-east was blowing, and it was late afternoon in midwinter. The land was sandy moorland, treeless and dark with iron-coloured heather. A mile away I saw rising up into the sky what seemed a peaty mountain in Cardiganshire, as it would be in a tempest of rain, and it was only when I was near the cliff and could see the three long walls of white waves towards the shore that I knew it was the sea. More common is the calm dark-blue sea in midsummer, over which go criss-cross bands of lighter hue, like pale moorland paths winding about a moor.

In a stern land like Cornwall that so often refuses the consolations of grass and herb and tree, the relentings are the more gracious. These are to be found in a whole valley where there are sloping fields of corn and grass divided by green hedges, and woods rich and misty and warm, and the bones of the land are buried away until it ends in a bay where high and cavernous dark rocks stand on either side of blue water and level sand. Often all the sweetness of the country round seems to have run into one great roadside hedge as dewdrops collect in the bosom of a leaf. The stones of the original wall are themselves deeply hidden in turf, or from the crevices ferns descend and the pale blooms of pennywort rise up; the lichen is furry and the yellow or pink stonecrop is neat and dense; ivy climbs closely up and hangs down in loose array. Up from the top of the wall or mound rise bramble and gorse and woodbine over them, or brier and thorn and woodbine again; and the tallest and massiest of foxgloves cleave through these with their bells, half a hundred of them in rows five deep already open and as many more yet in bud, dense as grapes, dewy, murmurous; and below the foxgloves are slender parsleys, rough wood sage and poppies. At the foot of the wall, between it and the road, is a grassy strip, where the yarrow grows feathery with gilded cinquefoil and tormentil – or above nettles as dense as corn rise large disks of white hog parsnip flower, a coarse and often dirty flower that has a dry smell of summer – or bramble and brier arch this way and that their green and rosy and purple stems, bright leaves, flowers pink and white. Only the shin-breaking Cornish stiles of stone, interrupting the hedge and giving a view of barren hills or craggy-sided sea, destroy the illusion created by this exuberance of herb and bush and the perfume of woodbine and rose.

Nowhere is the stateliness or grace or privacy of trees more conspicuous than about the Cornish towns and farms. The tall round-topped elms above Padstow, for example, would be natural and acceptable unconsciously elsewhere; but above those crossing lines of roof they have an indescribable benevolence. The farm-houses are usually square, dry and grey, being built of slate with grey-slated roofs painted by lichen; some are white-washed; in some, indeed, the stones are of many greys and blues, with yellowish and reddish tinges, hard, but warm in the sun and comforting to look at when close to the sea and some ruinous promontory; few are screened by ivy or climbing rose. The farm buildings are of the same kind, relieved by yellow straw, the many hues of hay, the purple bracken stacks, the dark peat. The gates are coarse and mean, of iron or of cheap or rough wood, lightly made, patched, held together by string, and owing their only charm to the chance use of the curved ribs of ships as gate-posts. But to many of the buildings sycamore and ash and apple trees bent above tall grass lend their beauty of line, of mass, of colour, of shade, of sound and of many motions. I can never forget the rows of ash trees, the breezy sycamores and the tamarisks by ancient Harlyn, with its barrows on the hill, its ruins of chapel and church among rushes and poppies, its little oak wood by the sandy river mouth where the men of old time buried their dead, the poppied corn, the white gulls and their black shadows wheeling over sunny turf. The file of lean woods seen between Perranporth and St. Agnes inland. The sycamores above the farm near Towan cross where the road dips and the deep furrow of a little valley winds, with hay upon its slopes, out to sea. The green wood, long and beautiful, below the gentle brown slopes of Hudder Down. The several companies of trees in the valley by the Red River, and the white farm of Reskajeage near by, under ash and elm, sycamore and wych-elm and lime, a rough orchard of apples and a gnarled squat medlar to one side – the trees grouped as human figures are when they begin to move after some tense episode. The wych-elm, sycamore and ash round the tower of Gwithian church and in amongst the few thatched cottages alongside the yellow towans and violet sea. In a land of deserted roofless houses with solid chimneys that no man wants, the narrow copse of small spindly oaks upholding with bare crooked steins as of stone a screen of leaves, above a brooklet that runs to the sea through dense rush and foxglove and thistle where the sedge-warbler sings. The long low mound of green wood nearest to Land's End. Between Tregothal and Bosfranken, the wet copse in a narrow valley, where red campion and bracken and bramble are unpenetrated among flowery elders, sallows, thorns and sycamores. A farm that has a water-mill and water gloomy and crystal under sycamore and ash. The thin halting procession of almost branchless trees on the ridge of the Beacon above Sancreed – a procession that seems even at midday to move in another world, in the world and in the age of the stone circles and cairns and cromlechs of the moor beyond. The sycamore and elder that surround and tower above Tregonebris near Boscawen Un. The avenue of ash and elm and wych-elm and sycamore, very close together, leading from grey Nancothan mill, where the dark-brown water mingles its noise with the rustling trees. The wych-elms and golden-fruited sycamores about the roads near St. Hilary, and the long avenue of ash up to the church itself, and the elms through which the evening music floats, amidst the smell of hay, in a misty mountained sunset.

Under the flaming fleeces of a precipitous sky, in a windless hush and at low tide, I descended to a narrow distinct valley just where a stream ran clear and slow through level sands to a bay, between headlands of rocks and of caves among the rocks. The sides of the valley near the sea were high and steep and of grass until their abrupt end in a low but perpendicular wall of rock just above the river sands. Inland the valley began to wind and at the bend trees came darkly trooping down the slopes to the water. Immediately opposite the ford – the wet sands being unscathed by any foot or hoof or wheel – a tributary ran into the river through a gorge of its own. It was a gorge not above a hundred feet across, and its floor was of sand save where the brook was running down, and this floor was all in shadow because the banks were clothed in thick underwood and in ash, sycamore, wych-elm and oak meeting overhead. And in these sands also there was no footprint save of the retreated sea. There was no house, nor wall, nor road. And there was no sound in the caverns of foliage except one call of a cuckoo as I entered and the warbling of a blackbird that mused in the oaks and then laughed and was silent and mused again and filled the mind with the fairest images of solitude – solitude where a maid, thinking of naught, un-thought of, unseen, combs out her yellow hair and lets her spirit slip down into the tresses – where a man fearful of his kind ascends out of the deeps of himself so that his eyes look bravely and his face unstiffens and unwrinkles and his motion and gesture is fast and free – where a child walks and stops and runs and sings in careless joy that takes him winding far out into abysses of eternity and makes him free of them, so that years afterward the hour and place and sky return, and the eternity on which they opened as a casement, but not the child, not the joy.

I like trees for the cool evening voices of their many leaves, for their cloudy forms linked to earth by stately stems – or the pale lifting of the sycamore leaves in breezes and also their drooping, hushed and massed repose, for the myriad division of the light ash leaves – for their straight pillars and for the twisted branch work, for their still shade and their rippling or calm shimmering or dimly glowing light, for the quicksilver drip of dawn, for their solemnity and their dancing, for all their sounds and motions – their slow-heaved sighs, their nocturnal murmurs, their fitful fingerings at thunder time, their swishing and tossing and hissing in violent rain, the roar of their congregations before the south-west wind when it seems that they must lift up the land and fly away with it, for their rustlings of welcome in harvest heat – or their kindliness and their serene remoteness and inhumanity, and especially the massiest of the trees that have also the glory of motion, the sycamores, which are the chief tree of Cornwall, as the beeches and yews are of the Downs, the oaks of the Weald, the elms of the Wiltshire vales.

Before I part from trees I should like to mention those of mid-Somerset – and above all, the elms. I am thinking of them as they are at noon on the hottest days of haymaking at the end of June. The sky is hot, its pale blue without pity and changing to a yellow of mist near the horizon. The land is level and all of grass, and where the hay is not spread in swathes the grass is almost invisible for the daises on its motionless surface. Here and there the mower whirrs and seems natural music, like the grasshopper's, of the burning earth. Through the levels wind the heavy-topped grey willows of a hidden stream. In the hedges and in the wide fields and about the still, silent farm-houses of stone there are many elms. They are tall and slender despite their full mounded summits. They cast no shade. In the great heat their green is all but grey, and their leaves are lost in the mist which their mingling creates. Grey-hooded, grey-mantled, they seem to be stealing away over the fields to the sanctuary of the dark-wooded hills, low and round and lapped entirely in leaves, which stand in the mist at the edge of the plain – to be leaving that plain to the possession of the whirring mower and the sun of almighty summer.

Sycamores solemnized the Cornish farm in the twilight, where I asked the farmer's wife if she could let us have two beds for the night. She stood in the doorway, hands on hips, watching her grandchildren's last excited minutes of play in the rickyard.

"He's the master," she replied, pointing to the farmer who was talking to his carter, between the rickyard and the door, under the sycamores.

"Two beds?"

"That is what we should like," said my friend and I.

"What do you want with two beds?" he asked with a tinge of scorn as well as of pity in his frank amusement. "My missus and I have only had one bed these forty years."

Here he laughed so gaily that he could not have embarrassed the very devil of puritanism, and turning to his man he called forth a deep bass laughter and from his wife a peal that shook her arms so that she raised them to the sides of the porch for better support; the children also turned their laughter our way.

"But perhaps one of you kicks in his sleep? . . . We don't . . . Come inside. I dare say you are tired . . . Good-night, John. Now, children, up with you."

I think they were the most excellent pair of man and woman I ever saw. Both were of a splendid physical type, she the more energetic, black-haired, black-eyed, plump and tall and straight; he the more enduring, fair-haired and bearded, blue-eyed, hardly her equal in height, certainly not in words. In forty years neither had overpowered the other. They had not even agreed to take separate paths, but like two schoolboys, new friends, they could afford to contend together in opinions without fear of damage or a lazy truce. He had ploughed and sowed and reaped: she had borne him seven children, had baked and churned and stitched. They had loved sweet things together, and, with curses at times, their children and the land. Physical strength and purity – that were in them the whole of morality – seemed to have given them that equality with the conditions of life which philosophy has done nothing but talk about. They of all men and women had perhaps jarred least upon the music of the spheres. They had the right and power to live, and the end was laughter.

In all those years they had been separated but once. Until four years ago she had not been out of Cornwall except to bury her mother, who had suddenly died in London. Two hundred pounds fell to her share on that death and the money arrived one morning after the harvest thanksgiving. For a week she continued to go about her work in the old way save that she sent rather hurriedly for a daughter who had just left her place as cook in Exeter. At the end of the week, having stored the apples and shown her daughter how to use the separator, she walked in to Penzance in her best clothes but without even a handbag; her husband was out with his gun. By the next day she was at Liverpool. She sent off a picture postcard, with a little note written by the shopkeeper, saying that she would be back by Christmas, and telling her husband to sell the old bull. Then she sailed for New York. She saw Niagara; she visited her nephew, John Davy, at Cincinnati; she spent two weeks in railway travelling west and south, and saw the Indians. Four days before Christmas she was back in the rickyard, driving before her a young bull and carrying in her hand a bunch of maize.

"Well, Ann, you're back before your time," said her husband, after praising the beast.

"Yes, Samuel, and I feel as if I could whitewash the dairy, that I do," said she.

"Suppose you wait till to-morrow," proposed Sam Davy.

"I think I will, for I can hear that Mary is behind with the separator."

"She's a good girl, but she hasn't got your patience, my dear."

"Oh, here, Sam, here's the change," she said, giving him the bunch of maize.

In Cornwall many of the women looked less English than the men. The noticeable men were fair-haired and of fair complexion, blue-eyed and rather small-headed, upright and of good bearing. The noticeable women had black hair, pale, seldom swarthy, faces, very dark eyes. Perhaps the eyes were more foreign than anything else in them: they were singularly immobile and seldom changed in expression with their voices. Several of the dark-eyed, black-haired women had a beauty of a fearless character like gipsy women, in their movement and expression. But the wives of small farmers and miners on piecework look old very soon and are puckered and shadowy in the face. Some of these middle-aged and old women suggested an early and barbarous generation. The eyes were small and deep-set, and the face narrowed forward like an animal's; which gave the whole a peering expression of suspicion and even alarm. The eyes of most human beings are causes of bewilderment and dismay if curiously looked at; but the strangest I ever saw were in an old Cornish woman. They were black and round as a child's, with a cold brightness that made them seem not of the substance of other eyes, but like a stone. They were set in a narrow, bony face of parchment among grey hair crisp and disarrayed. I saw them only for a few minutes while I asked a few questions about the way, and it was as much as I could do to keep up the conversation, so much did those motionless eyes invite me to plunge into an abyss of human personality – such intense loneliness and strangeness did they create, since they proclaimed shrilly and clearly that beyond a desire to be fed and clothed we had nothing in common. Had they peered up at me out of a cromlech or hut at Bosporthennis I could not have been more puzzled and surprised.

Men and women were hospitable and ready to smile as the Welsh are; and they have an alluring naïveté as well as some righteousness. One family was excessively virtuous or had a wish to appear so: I do not know which alternative to like the less, since it was in a matter of game. They rented land on a large estate and had a right to the rabbits: the hares were sacred to the great landowner. The farmer's wife assured me that one of her sons had lately brought in a lame hare and proposed to put it out of its pain, but that she had said: "No, take it out and let it die outside anywhere. The best thing is to be afraid in things of this kind and then you won't go wrong." Doing much the same kind or quantity of manual work as their husbands and being much out of doors, the women's manners were confident and free. Their speech was as a rule fluent and grammatical and clearly delivered, with less accent than in any part of England. Coming into a mining village one day and wanting tea, I asked a woman who was drawing water from a farmyard well if she could make me some, thinking she was the farmer's wife. She said she would, but took me to one of a small row of cottages over the way, where her husband was half-naked in the midst of his Saturday wash. Taking no notice of him she led me into the sitting-room and, with a huge loaf held like a violin, began buttering and cutting thin slices while she talked to me, to the little children and to her husband, from the adjacent kitchen. She was tall, straight as a pillar, black-haired, with clear untanned but slightly swarthy skin, black eyes, kindly gleaming cheeks and red lips smiling above her broad breast and hips. Her clothes were black but in rags that hardly clung to her shoulders and waist. She was barely five and twenty, but had six young children about her, one in a cradle by the hearth and another still crawling at her feet. Her only embarrassment came when I asked to pay for my tea – she began adding up the cost, a pennyworth of bread and butter, a halfpennyworth of tea, etc.! The kitchen consisted simply of a large grate and baking oven, plain tables and chairs on a flagged floor. But the sitting-room was a museum – with photographs of a volunteer corps, of friends and relations on the wall over the fire; foxgloves in jam-pots surrounded by green crinkled paper in the fireplace; on the mantelpiece, cheap little vases and scraps of ore and more photographs. On the walls were three pictures: one of two well-dressed children being timidly inspected by fallow deer; another of a grandmother showing a book to a child whose attention is diverted by the frolics of two kittens at her side; and a third of Jesus, bleeding and crowned with thorns, high on a cross over a marble city beneath a romantic forest ridge, behind which was the conflagration of a crimson sunset.

Other sitting-rooms were similarly adorned, with the addition of a picture of John Wesley as a child escaping from the window of a burning house, with many anxious men holding up their hands from below. The smell of flowers and of sun-warmed furniture and old upholstery mingles in such rooms.

But the kitchens are often as charming as in Wales. I remember one especially near Carn Galver. The farm-house was of whitened stone under a steep thatch. In front were fuchsia trees in the corner of a stony yard; to one side, the haystacks and piles of furze and bracken and peat. The farmer's wife was carrying peat on an iron hook into the kitchen and I followed her. A pan of yellow scalded cream stood inside. The fireplace was a little room in itself, with seats at each side and a little fire of wood and three upright turves in one corner of the great stone hearth: over the fire the kettle boiled. Horse ornaments of polished brass surmounted the fireplace. The wallpaper had given up its pattern long since to a smoky uneven gold; nailed to it were calendars and lists of fairs and sales; against it were two small tables, one to support a Bible and an almanac, the other spread with a white cloth on which was a plate and a bowl of cream. Behind the door and between it and the fire was a high-backed settle of dark wood, with elbow-rests. The floor was flagged and sanded. The light came in through a little square window on to the Bible by the opposite wall, and through the open door on to the figure of the housewife, a woman of forty. A delicate white face shone beneath a broad untrimmed straw hat that was tied tightly under her chin so as to hide her ears and most of her black hair. Her black skirt was kilted up behind; a white apron contrasted with black shoes, black stockings and black clothes. At first her face was hardly seen, not only because but a part of it emerged from the shell of her hat, but because the spirit that emanated from it was more than the colour and features and so much in harmony with the sea and crag and moor and dolmen of her land. It is evading an insuperable difficulty to say that this spirit was not so much human as fay. It was the spirit of which her milky complexion, the bright black eyes, white teeth and fine red lips of her readily smiling and naïvely watching fearless face, her slender form, her light and rapid movements upon small feet, were only the more obvious expressions. Her spirit danced before her – not quite visibly, not quite audibly – as she moved or spoke or merely smiled; if it could have been seen it would have been a little singing white flame changing to blue and crimson in its perpetual flickering. It was a spirit of laughter, of laughter unquenchable since the beginning of time, of laughter in spite of and because of all things, the laughter of life like a jewel in desolate places. It was a spirit most ancient and yet childlike, birdlike: it belonged to a world outside any which other human beings ever seemed to touch, but the laughter in it made it friendly, for it was far deeper than humour, it

was gaiety of heart. Her goings to and fro on those light feet had the
grace, quickness, suddenness of a bird, of a wren that slips from twig
to twig and jets out its needle of song, of a moorhen flicking its tail and
hooting sharply. Her laugh startled and delighted like the laugh of the
woodpecker as it leaps across the glades – like the whistling of birds up
amongst the dark clouds and the moon. But most of all she called to
mind the meadow pipit of her own crags, that rises from green ledges
out over the sea and then, falling slantwise with body curved like a
crescent, utters his passionate pulsating song, so rapid and passionate
that it seems impossible and unfit that it should end except in death, yet
suddenly ceasing as it lands again upon the samphire or the thrift. The
spirit was as quicksilver in the corners of her eyes, as quicksilver in the
heart. Such a maid she must have been as the bard would have thought
to send out the thrush to woo for him, when he heard the bird of ermine
breast singing from the new-leaved hazel at dawn, on the edge of a brook
among the steep woods – singing artfully with a voice like a silver bell –
solemnly, too, so as to seem to be performing a sacrifice – and amorously,
bringing balm to lovers' hearts and inspiring the bard to send by him a
message to the sun of all maidens that she, white as the snow of the first
winter night, should come out to the green woods to him. She had lived
for generations on the moor, for generations upon generations, and this
was what she had gained from heather and furze and crag and seawind
and sunshine tempered by no trees – inextinguishable laughter. But she
was inarticulate. She milked the cows, made butter, baked bread, kept
the peat fire burning and tended her children. When she talked, I asked
for more cream. Perhaps after several more generations have passed she
will be a poet and astonish the world with a moorland laughter of words
that endure.

Everything in that house was old or smooth and bright with use, and
the hollowed threshold of the doorway in the sun put me in mind of a
hundred old things and of their goodliness to mortal eyes – the wrecked
ship's ribs, their bolt-holes rusty, that stand among nettles as gate-posts
– the worn dark stones that rock to the tread among the ripples of an

umbrageous ford – many a polished stile and gate – the group of rigid but still gracious bowery thorns dotted with crimson haws in the middle of a meadow, their boles and lower branches rubbed hard and smooth and ruddy like iron by the cows – the ash staff beginning to bend like its master, the old man upon the roads who once wore scarlet and wound the horn for Mr. —'s hounds. Odd it is how old use sanctifies a little thing. There was once a hut where a good man, but a poor and a weak and unwise, stayed all one fair summer and talked of English roads – he was a lord of the roads, at least of South Country roads – and of ships, which he knew. Now on the first night of his stay, needing a candlestick he kicked off the top of a pointed wooden paling, so as to make a five-angled piece on which he stuck the candle in its own grease. All through his stay he used the candlestick, when he read the *Divina Commedia* and *Pantagruel* and *Henry Brocken* and recollected airs of Italy and Spain, amidst the sound of nightjars and two leafy streams: the light flickered out as he mused about the open sea, calm but boundless and without known harbour, on which he was drifting cheerfully, regardless of Time, pied with nights and days. The hut was burnt and the man went – to drown a little afterwards with a hundred unlike himself in the sea – but among nettle and dock the candlestick was picked up safe. It had broken off straight and the simple shape was pleasant; it was dark with age; along with the mound and little pillar of wax remaining it had the shape of a natural thing; and it was his.

Animate as well as inanimate things are open to this sanctification by age or use. I am not here thinking of ceremonious use – for which I have small natural respect, so that I have been denied the power of appreciating either a great religious pomp or the dancing of Mademoiselle Genée. But some men, particularly sailors and field labourers, but also navvies and others who work heavily with their hands, have this glory of use. Their faces, their clothes, their natures all appear to act and speak harmoniously, so that they cause a strong impression of personality which is to be deeply enjoyed in a world of masks, especially of black clerical masks. One of the best examples of this kind was a gamekeeper who daily preceded me by twenty or thirty yards in a morning walk up through a steep wood of beeches. He was a short, stiffly-built and stoutish man who wore a cap, thick skirted coat and breeches, leather gaiters and heavy boots, all patched and stained, all of nearly the same colour as his lightish-brown hair and weathered skin, but not so dark as the gun over his shoulder. The shades of this colour were countless and made up like the colour of a field of ripe wheat, which they would have resembled had they not been liberally dusted all over, just as his brown beard was grizzled. He went slowly up, swinging slightly at the shoulders and always smoking a pipe of strong shag tobacco of which the fumes hovered in the moist air with inexpressible sweetness and a good brown savour: if I may say so, the fit emanation of the brown woodland man who, when he stood still, looked like the stump of a tree.

TEN

Summer

SUSSEX

FAR UP ON THE Downs the air of day and night is flavoured by honeysuckle and new hay. It is good to walk, it is good to lie still; the rain is good and so is the sun; and whether the windy or the quiet air be the better let us leave to a December judgment to decide. One day the rain falls and there is no wind, and all the movement is in the chaos of the dark sky; and thus is made the celestial fairness of an earth that is brighter than the heavens; for the green and lilac of the grasses and the yellow of the goat's-beard flowers glow, and the ripening corn is airy light. But next day the sun is early hot. The wet hay steams and is sweet. The beams pour into a southward coombe of the hills and the dense yew is warm as a fruit-wall, so that the utmost of fragrance is extracted from the marjoram and thyme and fanned by the coming and going of butterflies; and in contrast with this gold and purple heat on flower and wing, through the blue sky and along the hill-top moist clouds are trooping, of the grey colour of melting snow. The great shadows of the clouds brood long over the hay, and in the darker hollows the wind rustles the dripping thickets until mid-day. On another morning after night rain the blue sky is rippled and crimped with high thin white clouds by several opposing breezes. Vast forces seem but now to have ceased their feud. The battle is over, and there are all the signs of it plain to be seen; but they have laid down their arms, and peace is broad and white in the sky, but of many colours on the earth – or there is blue of harebell and purple of rose-bay among the bracken and popping gorse, and heather and foxglove are purple above the sand, and the mint is hoary lilac, the meadow-sweet is foam, there is rose of willow-herb and yellow of flea-bane at the edge of the water, and purple of gentian

and cistus yellow on the Downs, and infinite greens in those little dense
Edens which nettle and cow-parsnip and bramble and elder make every
summer on the banks of the deep lanes. A thousand swifts wheel as
if in a fierce wind over the highest places of the hills, over the great
seaward-looking camp and its three graves and antique thorns, down to
the chestnuts that stand about the rick-yards in the cornland below.

These are the hours that seem to entice and entrap the airy inhabitants
of some land beyond the cloud mountains that rise farther than the
farthest of downs. Legend has it that long ago strange children were
caught upon the earth, and being asked how they had come there, they
said that one day as they were herding their sheep in a far country they
chanced on a cave; and within they heard music as of heavenly bells,
which lured them on and on through the corridors of that cave until they
reached our earth; and here their eyes, used only to a twilight between
a sun that had set for ever and a night that had never fallen, were dazed
by the August glow, and lying bemused they were caught before they
could find the earthly entrance to their cave. Small wonder would this
adventure be from a region no matter how blessed, when the earth is
wearing the best white wild roses or when August is at its height.

The last hay-wagon has hardly rolled between the elms before the
reaper and the reaping-machines begin to work. The oats and wheat
are in tents over all the land. Then, then it is hard not to walk over the
brown in the green of August grass. There is a roving spirit everywhere.
The very tents of the corn suggest a bivouac. The white clouds coming
up out of the yellow corn and journeying over the blue have set their
faces to some goal. The traveller's-joy is tangled over the hazels and
over the faces of the small chalk-pits. The white beam and the poplar
and the sycamore fluttering show the silver sides of their leaves and
rustle farewells. The perfect road that goes without hedges under elms
and through the corn says, "Leave all and follow." How the bridges
overleap the streams at one leap, or at three, in arches like those of
running hounds! The far-scattered, placid sunsets pave the feet of the
spirit with many a road to joy; the huge, vacant halls of dawn give a
sense of godlike power.

But it is hard to make anything like a truce between these two incompatible desires, the one for going on and on over the earth, the other that would settle for ever, in one place as in a grave and have nothing to do with change. Suppose a man to receive notice of death, it would be hard to decide whether to walk or sail until the end, seeing no man, or none but strangers; or to sit – alone – and by thinking or not thinking to make the change to come as little as is permitted. The two desires will often painfully alternate. Even on these harvest days there is a temptation to take root for ever in some corner of a field or on some hill from which the world and the clouds can be seen at a distance. For the wheat is as red as the most red sand, and up above it tower the elms, dark prophets persuading to silence and a stillness like their own. Away on the lesser Downs the fields of pale oats are liquid within their border of dark woods; they also propose deep draughts of oblivion and rest. Then, again, there is the field – the many fields – where a regiment of shocks of oats are ranked under the white moon between rows of elms on the level Sussex land not far from the sea. The contrast of the airy matter underfoot and the thin moon over head, with the massy dark trees, as it were suspended between; the numbers and the order of the sheaves; their inviolability, though protected but by the gateway through which they are seen – all satisfy the soul as they can never satisfy the frame. Then there are the mists before heat which make us think of autumn or not, according to our tempers. All night the aspens have been shivering and the owls exulting under a clear full moon and above the silver of a great dew. You climb the steep chalk slope, through the privet and dog-wood coppice; among the scattered junipers – in this thick haze as in darkness they group themselves so as to make fantastic likenesses of mounted men, animals, monsters; over the dead earth in the shade of the broad yews, and thence suddenly under lightsome sprays of guelder-rose and their cherry-coloured berries; over the tufted turf; and then through the massed beeches, cold and dark as a church and silent; and so out to the level waste cornland at the top, to the flints and the clay. There a myriad oriflammes of ragwort are borne up on tall stems of equal height, straight and motionless, and near at hand quite clear, but farther away forming a green mist until, farther yet, all but the flowery surface is invisible, and that is but a glow. The stillness of the green and golden multitudes under the grey mist, perfectly still though a wind flutters the high tops of the beech, has an immortal beauty, and that they should ever change does not enter the mind which is thus for the moment lured happily into a strange confidence and ease. But the sun gains power in the south-east. It changes the mist into a fleeting garment, not of cold or of warm grey, but of diaphanous gold. There is a sea-like moan of wind in the half-visible trees, a wavering of the mist to and fro until it is dispersed far and wide as part of the very light, of the blue shade, of the colour of cloud and wood and down. As the mist is unwoven the ghostly moon is disclosed, and a bank of dead white clouds where the Downs should be. Under the very eye of the veiled sun a golden light and warmth begins to nestle among the mounds of foliage at the surface of the low woods. The beeches close by have got a new voice in their crisp, cool leaves, of which every one is doing something – cool, though the air itself is warm. Wood-pigeons coo. The white cloud-bank gives way to an immeasurable half-moon of Downs, some bare, some saddle-backed with woods, and far away and below, out of the ocean of countless trees in the southern veil, a spire. It is a spire which at this hour is doubtless moving a thousand men with a thousand thoughts and hopes and memories of men and causes, but moves me with the thought alone that just a hundred years ago was buried underneath it a child, a little child whose mother's mother was at the pains to inscribe a tablet saying to all who pass by that he was once "an amiable and most endearing child."

And what nights there are on the hills. The ash-sprays break up the low full moon into a flower of many sparks. The Downs are heaved up into the lighted sky – surely they heave in their tranquillity as with a slowly taken breath. The moon is half-way up the sky and exactly over the centre of the long curve of Downs; just above them lies a long terrace of white cloud, and at their feet gleams a broad pond, the rest of the valley being utterly dark and undistinguishable, save a few scattered lamps and one near meadow that catches the moonlight so as to be transmuted to a lake. But every rainy leaf upon the hill is brighter than any of the few stars above, and from many leaves and blades hang drops as large and bright as the glowworms in their recesses. Larger by a little, but not brighter, are the threes and fours of lights at windows in the valley. The wind has fallen, but a mile of woods unlading the rain from their leaves make a sound of wind, while each separate drop can be heard from the nearest branches, a noise of rapt content, as if they were telling over again the kisses of the shower. The air itself is heavy as mead with the scent of yew and juniper and thyme.

ELEVEN

An Umbrella Man

HAMPSHIRE

A BEGGAR is a rich man on some of these August days, especially one I know, whom first I met some Augusts ago now. A fine Sunday afternoon had sprinkled the quiet and thinly-peopled land with black-dressed men and white-dressed women, the older married couples and their trains of children keeping chiefly to the roads and most straightforward paths, the younger, with one child or none, choosing rather the green lanes, while the lovers and the boys found out tall hedge-sides and the footpaths across which more than one year's growth of hazel had spread, so that the shortest of the maids must stoop. Many showers following a dry season made miles of the country as clean and fragrant as a garden. Honeysuckle and privet were in every hedge with flowers that bring a thrill of summer bridals on their scent. The brisk wind was thymy from the Downs. The ragwort was in its glory; it rose tall as a man in one straight leap of dark-foliaged stem, and then crowned itself in the boldest and most splendid yellows derived from a dark golden disk, and almost lemon rays; it was as if Apollo had come down to keep the flocks of a farmer on these chalk hills and his pomp had followed him out of the sky. A few birds still sang; one lark now and then, a cirl-bunting among the topmost haws of a thorn, chiffchaffs in the bittersweet and hazel of the little copses. There was apparently comfort, abundance and quiet everywhere. They were seen in the rickyards where grand haystacks, newly thatched, stood around ancient walnut trees. Even the beeches had a decorous look in their smooth boles and perfect lavish foliage. The little patches of flowery turf by the roadside and at corners were brighter and warmer than ever, as the black bees and the tawny skipper butterflies flew from bloom to bloom

A cirl-bunting

of the crimson knapweed. Amplest and most unctuous of all in their expression of the ceremonious leisure of the day and the maturity of the season were the cart-horses. They leaned their large heads benignly over the rails or gates; their roan or chestnut flanks were firm and polished; manes, tails and fetlocks spotless; now and then they lifted up their feet and pressed their toes into the ground, showing their enormous shoes that shone and were of girth sufficient to make a girdle for the lightest of the maids passing by.

Sunday with not too strict a rod of black and white ruled the land and made it all but tedious except in the longest of the green lanes, which dipped steeply under oaks to a brook muffled in leaves and rose steeply again, a track so wet in spring – and full of the modest golden green of saxifrage flowers – that only the hottest Sunday ever saw it disturbed except by carter and horses. In a hundred yards the oak-hidden windings gave the traveller a feeling of reclusion as if he were coiled in a spool; very soon a feeling of possession ripened into one of armed tyranny if another's steps clattered on the stones above. Sometimes in a goodly garden a straight alley of shadows leads away from the bright frequented borders to – we know not quite whither, and perhaps, too much delighted with half-sad reverie, never learn, smother even the guesses of fancy, lest they should bring some old unpleasant truth in their train; but if the fancy will thread the alley and pass the last of the shadows it is into some such lane as this that it would gladly emerge, to come at last upon the pure wild. It seemed that I had come upon the pure wild in this lane, for in a bay of turf alongside the track, just large enough for a hut and thickly sheltered by an oak, though the south-west sun crept in, was a camp. Under the oak and at the edge of the tangled bramble and brier and bracken was a low purple light from those woodside flowers, self-heal and wood betony. A perambulator with a cabbage in it stood at one corner; leaning against it was an ebony-handled umbrella and two or three umbrella-frames; underneath it an old postman's bag containing a hammer and other tools. Close by stood half a loaf on a newspaper, several bottles of bright water, a black pot of potatoes ready for boiling, a tin of water steaming against a small fire of hazel twigs. Out on the sunny grass two shirts were drying. In the midst was the proprietor, his name revealed in fresh chalk, on the side of his perambulator: "John Clark, Hampshire."

He had spent his last pence on potatoes and had been given the cabbage. No one would give him work on a Sunday. He had no home, no relations. Being deaf, he did not look for company. So he stood up, to get dry and to think, think, think, his hands on his hips, while he puffed at an empty pipe. During his meditation a snail had crawled half-way up his trousers, and was now all but down again. He was of middle height and build, the crookedest of men, yet upright, like a branch of oak which comes straight with all its twistings. His head was small and round, almost covered by bristly grey hair like lichen, through which peered quiet blue eyes; the face was irregular, almost shapeless, like dough being kneaded, worn by travel, passion, pain, and not a few blows; where the skin was visible at all through the hair it was like red sandstone; his teeth were white and strong and short like an old dog's. His rough neck descended into a striped half-open shirt, to which was added a loose black waistcoat divided into thin perpendicular stripes by ribs of faded gold; his trousers, loose and patched and short, approached the colour of a hen pheasant; his bare feet were partly hidden by old black boots. His voice was hoarse and, for one of his enduring look, surprisingly small, and produced with an effort and a slight jerk of the head.

He was a Sussex man, born in the year 1831, on June the twenty-first (it seemed a foppery to him to remember the day, and it was impossible to imagine with what ceremony he had remembered it year by year, during half a century or near it, on the roads of Sussex, Kent, Surrey, and Hampshire). His mother was a Wild – there were several of them buried not far away under the carved double-headed tombstones by the old church with the lancet windows and the four yews. He was a labourer's son, and he had already had a long life of hoeing and reaping and fagging when he enlisted at Chatham. He had kept his musket bright, slept hard and wet, and starved on thirteenpence a day, moving from camp to camp every two years. He had lost his youth in battle, for a bullet went through his knee; he lay four months in hospital, and they took eighteen pieces of bone out of his wound – he was still indignant because he was described as only "slightly wounded" when he was discharged after a "short service" of thirteen years. He showed his gnarled knee to explain his crookedness. Little he could tell of the battle except the sobbing of the soldier next to him – "a London chap from Haggerston way. Lord! he called for his mother and his God and me to save him, and the noise he made was worse than the firing and the groaning of the horses, and I was just thinking how I could stop his mouth for him when a bullet hits me, and down I goes like a baby."

He had been on the road forty years. For a short time after his discharge he worked on the land and lived in a cottage with his wife and one child. The church bells were beginning to ring, and I asked him if he was going to church. At first he said nothing, but looked down at his striped waistcoat and patched trousers; then, with a quick violent gesture of scorn, he lifted up his head and even threw it back before he spoke. "Besides," he said, "I remember how it was my little girl died – My little girl, says I, but she would have been a big handsome woman now, forty-eight years old on the first of May that is gone. She was lying in bed with a little bit of a cough, and she was gone as white as a lily, and I went in to her when I came home from reaping. I saw she looked bad and quiet-like – like a fish in a hedge – and something came over me, and I caught hold of both her hands in both of mine and held them tight, and put my head close up to hers and said; 'Now look here, Polly, you've got to get well. Your mother and me can't stand losing you. And you aren't meant to die; such a one as you be for a lark.' And I squeezed her little hands, and all my nature seemed to rise up and try to make her get well. Polly she looked whiter than ever and afraid; I suppose I was a bit rough and dirty and sunburnt, for 'twas a hot harvest and 'twas the end of the second week of it, and I was that fierce I felt I ought to have had my way . . . All that night I thought I had done a wrong thing trying to keep her from dying that way, and I tell you I cried in case I had done any harm by it . . . That very night she died without our knowing it. She was a bonny maid, that fond of flowers. The night she was taken ill she was coming home with me from the Thirteen Acre, where I'd been hoeing the mangolds, and she had picked a rose for her mother. All of a sudden she looks at it and says, 'It's gone, it's broke, it's gone, it's gone, gone, gone,' and she kept on, 'It's broke it's gone, it's gone,' and when she got home she ran up to her mother, crying, 'The wild rose is broke, mother; broke, gone, gone,' she says, just like that," said the old man, in a high finical voice more like that of a bird than a child . . .

"Then my old woman – well, she was only a bit of a wench too; seventeen when we were married – she took ill and died within a week after . . . There was a purpose in it . . . I t was then the end of harvest. I spent all my wages down at the 'Fighting Cocks,' and then I set out to walk to Mildenhall in Wiltshire, where my wife came from. On the way I met a chap I had quarrelled with in Egypt, and he says to me, 'Hullo, Scrammy-handed Jack,' with a sort of look, and I, not thinking what I did, I set about him, and before I knew it he was lying there as might be dead, and I went and gave myself up, and I don't mind saying that I wished I might be hanged for it. However, I did six months. That was how I came to be in the umbrella line. I took up with a chap who did a bit of tinkering and umbrella-mending and grinding in the roving way, and a job of hoeing or mowing now and then. He died not so very long after in the year of the siege of Paris, and I have been alone ever since. Nor I haven't been to church since, any more than a blackbird would go and perch on the shoulder of one of those ladies with feathers and wings and a bit of a fox in their hats."

Labourer, soldier, labourer, tinker, umbrella man, he had always wandered, and knew the South Country between Fordingbridge and Dover as a man knows his garden. Every village, almost every farm-house, especially if there were hops on the land, he knew, and could see with his blue eyes as he remembered them and spoke their names. I never met a man who knew England as he did. As he talked of places his eyes were alight and turned in their direction, and his arm stretched out to point, moving as he went through his itinerary, so that verily, wherever he was, he seemed to carry in his head the relative positions of all the other places where he had laboured and drunk and lit his solitary fire. "Was you ever at H—? " he said, pointing to the Downs, through which he seemed to see H— itself. "General—, that commanded us, lived there. He died there three years ago at the age of eighty-eight, and till he died I was always sure of a half-crown if I called there on a Christmas Eve, as I generally managed to do." Of any place mentioned he could presently remember something significant – the words of a farmer, a song, a signboard, a wonderful crop, the good ale – the fact that forty-nine years ago the squire used to go to church in a smock frock. All the time his face was moved with free and broad expressions as he thought and remembered, like an animal's face. Living alone and never having to fit himself into human society, he had not learnt to keep his face in a vice. He was returning – if the grave was not too near at the age of seventy-seven – to a primeval wildness and simplicity. It was a pleasure to see him smoke – to note how it eased his chest – to see him spit and be the better for it. The outdoor life had brought him rheumatism, but a clear brain also and a wild purity, a physical cleanliness too, and it was like being with a well-kept horse to stand beside him; and this his house was full of the scent of the bracken growing under the oaks. Earth had not been a kind but a stern mother, like some brawny full-bosomed housewife with many children, who spends all her long days baking and washing, and making clothes, and tending the sick one, and cutting bread and pouring out tea, and cuffing one and cuddling another and listening to one's tale, and hushing their unanimous chatter with a shout or a bang of her enormous elbow on the table. The blows of such a one are shrewd, but they are not as the sweetness of her nursing voice for enduring in the memory of bearded men and many-childed women.

Once or twice again I met him in later summers near the same place. The last time he had been in the infirmary, and was much older. His fire was under the dense shelf of a spruce bough in a green deserted road worn deep in the chalk, blocked at both ends, and trodden by few mortal feet. Only a few yards away, under another spruce, lay a most ancient sheep who had apparently been turned into the lane to browse at peace. She was lame in one leg, and often fed as she knelt. Her head was dark grey and wise, her eyes pearly green and iridescent with an oblong pupil of blackish-blue, quiet, yet full of fear; her wool was dense but short and of a cinder grey; her dark horny feet were overgrown from lack of use. She would not budge even when a dog sniffed at her, but only bowed her head and threatened vainly to butt. She was huge and heavy and content, though always all alone. As she lay there, her wool glistening with rain, I had often wondered what those eyes were aware of, what part she played in the summer harmonies of night and day, the full night heavens and cloudless noon, storm and dawn, and the long moist heat of dewy mornings. She was now shorn, and the old man watched her as he drank the liquor in which a cabbage and a piece of bacon had been boiled. "I often thinks," he said, "that I be something like that sheep . . . 'slightly wounded' . . . but not ' short service' now . . . haha! . . . left alone in this here lane to browse a bit while the weather's fine and folks are kind . . . But I don't know but what she is better off. Look there," he said, pointing to a wound which the shearer had made in one of her nipples, where flies clustered like a hideous flower of crape, "I have been spending this hour and more flicking the flies off her . . . Nobody won't do that for me – unless I come in for five shillings a week Old Age Pension. But I reckon that won't be for a roving body like me without a letter-box." In the neighbouring field a cart-horse shook herself with a noise of far-off thunder and laughed shrilly and threw up her heels and raced along the hedge. A bee could be seen going in and out of the transparent white flowers of convolvulus. The horse had her youth and strength and a workless day before her; the bee its business, in which was its life, among sunbeams and flowers; and they were glad. The old man smacked his lips as he drained the salty broth, tried three times to light his empty pipe and then knocked out the ashes and spat vigorously, and took a turn up the lane alone in the scent of the bracken.

TWELVE
Children of Earth

A T THE END OF the lane, at the head of one of the beechen chalky coombes, just where the beeches cease and the flinty clay begins, stands a thatched cottage under five tall ash trees. A grassy lane runs by, but on three sides the place is surrounded by huge naked concave sweeps of grey ploughland which take the February sunshine and cloud shadow as delicately as beaten silver. The walls are of grey-white soft stone, but only a little of them is visible, because the steep thatch sweeps almost to the ground and overhangs the gables, in each of which is a small window and under one a door. In hot summer or windy winter, if the field happens to be without a crop, the earth is of the same colour as the thatch, and the cottage looks as if it were the work – like a mole-hill – of some creature that has worked underground and risen up just there and rested, peering out of the two dark windows upon the world. It is impossible to find any point of view from which any house can be seen along with this, except one – the ash trees, the tall hazels of the lane, or the swelling fields hide them away. But the pewits loop their flight every spring over and round about the cottage, and the dark eyes under the thatch can always see a hare, and often half a dozen. Whether the ashes are purple in spring, yellow in autumn or grey in winter, whether the surrounding fields are bare, or green with turnips, or yellow with charlock, or empurpled gold with ripe wheat, the cottage is always the same stubborn, dull, simple mound raised up out of the earth. The one other house is not so high; nor has it eyes; nor do an old man and a girl and two children go in and out of it; it is, in fact, not a house of the living, but of the dead, a round tumulus at the edge of the hill.

The grey mound of the dead and the grey house of the living are at their best in the midst of winter and in the midst of summer. Standing upon the tumulus in the north-west wind, the cottage could be seen huddled under the lashing trees. Many a thousand beech trees on the steep slopes below gave out a roar, and it was a majestic position to be up there, seeing and feeling that the strong wind was scouring the world with a stream miles deep and miles wide. Far underneath, two beechen promontories with bald white brows projected into the vast valley; not really much lower than the hill of the tumulus, but seeming so in that more than Amazonian stream of air. Beyond these promontories the broad land was washed bright and clear. Nearer at hand the thrice cleaned traveller's joy was as silken foam surging upon the surface of black yews and olive hazels. The kestrel swayed and lunged in his flight. Branches gleamed, hard and nervously moving. Rain-pools glittered, and each brittle stem and flower of a dead plant, each grass-blade and brown lock of beech or oak-leaf, gave out its little noise to join the oceanic murmur of the earth. Now and then a dead leaf took flight, rose high and went out over the valley till it was invisible, never descending, in search of the moon. Near the horizon a loose white drift went rapidly just over the summits of the highest woods; but in the upper air were the finest flowers of the wind – hard white flowers of cloud, flowers and mad tresses and heaven-wide drapery of gods, and some small and white like traveller's joy, as if up there also they travelled and knew the houseless joy along the undulating highway of the deep wind. And the little house was as a watch-tower planted in the middle swirl of the current that was scouring valley and wood and sky and water and, as far as it could, the dull eyes and duller brains of men.

In summer I saw it at the end of one of those days of sun and wind and perfectly clear air when the earth appears immensely heavy and great and strong – so that for a moment it is possible to know the majesty of its course in space – and the sheep very light, like mere down, as they crawl in a flock over the grass. Swathes and wisps of white cloud were strewn over the high blue sky as if by haymakers. But the lanes were deep, and for miles at a time nearly shut out the sky, and all the day the lanes were empty and wholly mine. Here the high banks were thickly grown with wild parsnip, and its umbels of small yellow-green flowers, fragrant and a little over-sweet, were alive and, as it were, boiling over with bees and the sunniest flies. There the hazel was laced with white bryony, whose leaves and pale tendrils went hovering and swimming and floating over the hedge. In one place an elder tree stood out of the hedge, stiff, with few branches, and every leaf upon them red as a rose. Wherever there was a waste strip beside the road the tall yellow ragwort grew densely, each of the nearer flowers as hard and clear as brass, the farther ones dimly glowing and half lost in the green mist of their leaves and the haze of the brightness of their multitudes. Where the road changed into an unused lane the grass was tall, and under the hazels, yet fully seen, were the wild basil and marjoram and centaury and knapweed and wood betony, and over them hung moths of green crimson-spotted silk. There, too, were the plants that smell most of the dry summer – the white parsleys and the white or rosy cow-parsnip, the bedstraws white and yellow, the yellow mug-wort. Now and then the hedges gave way and on either hand was open turf; sloping steep and rough on one side, grooved by ancient paths of men and cattle, dotted by thorns, with the freshly flowering traveller's joy over them, ash trees at the top; on the other side, level, skirted by cloudy wych-elms and having at one corner a white inn half shadowed by a walnut, and two sycamores and cattle below them; and at another, a stately autumnal house veiled by the cedars and straight yews on its darkly glowing lawn.

All these things I saw as if they had been my own, as if I were going again slowly through old treasures long hidden away, so that they were memoried and yet unexpected. Nothing was too small to be seen, and ascending the chalk hill among the beeches every white flint was clear on the sward, each in its different shape – many chipped as the most cunning chisel would be proud to chip them; one, for example, carved by the loss of two exquisitely curved and balanced flakes into the likeness of a moth's expanded upper wings.

A dark beech alley, paved with the gold and green of moss and walled by crumbling chalk, brought me to the tumulus. There lay the old house in shadow, its ash crest lighted yellow by horizontal beams that caught here the summit of a wood, and there the polished grass stems on a rising field. It was the one house, and at that hour it gathered to itself all that can be connected with a home. It was alone, but its high cool thatch was full of protection and privacy, sufficient against sun or rain or wind or frost, yet impregnated with free air and light. Its ash trees communed with the heavens and the setting sun. The wheat glowed at its gates. The dark masses of the lower woods enhanced by a touch of primeval gloom and savagery the welcoming expression of the house. Slowly the light died out of the ash-tops and the wheat turned to a mist. The wood seemed to creep up close and lay its shadows over the house. But, stronger than the wood and the oncoming tide of night that enveloped it, the spirits of roof and wall and hearth were weaving a spell about the house to guard it, so that it looked a living, breathing, dreaming thing. Nimble, elvish, half-human but wholly kind small spirits I fancied them, creeping from corners in stone and thatch and rafter, at war with those that dwelt in lonely and dark places, that knew not fire and lamp and human voices save as invaders. For a little while there was a pause, a suspense, a hesitation – Could the small spirits win? – Were not the woods older and more mighty? – Was not that long black bar of cloud across the cold west something sinister, already engulfing the frail white moon? But suddenly, as if the life of the house had found a powerful voice, one eye in the nearer gable was lit by a small lamp and a figure could be guessed behind it. The first Promethean spark of fire stolen from the gods was hardly a more signal victory than that at which the house and I rejoiced when the white light glimmered across the corn. It seemed the birth of light.

*   *   *   *   *

The man who lives under that roof and was born there seventy years ago is like his house. He is short and immensely broad, black-haired, with shaved but never clean-shaven face creased by a wide mouth and long narrow black eyes – black with a blackness as of cold, deep water that had never known the sun but only the candle light of discoverers. His once grey corduroys and once white slop are stained and patched to something like the colour of the moist, channelled thatch and crumbling "crunch" of the stone walls. He wears a soft felt hat with hanging broad brim of darker earthy hues; it might have been drawn over his face and ears in his emergence from his native clay and flint. Only rarely does his eye – one eye at a time – gloom out from underneath, always accompanied by a smile that slowly puckers the wrinkled oak-bark of his stiff cheeks. His fingers, his limbs, his face, his silence, suggest crooked oak timber or the gnarled stoles of the many times polled ash. It is barely credible that he grew out of a child, the son of a woman, and not out of the earth itself, like the great flints that work upwards and out on to the surface of the fields. Doubtless he did, but like many a ruined castle, like his own house, he has been worn to a part of the earth itself. That house he will never give up except by force, to go to workhouse or grave. They want him to go out for a few days that it may be made more weather-tight; but he fears the chances and prefers a rickety floor and draughty wall. He is half cowman, half odd-job man – at eight shillings a week – in his last days, mending hedges, cleaning ditches, and carrying a sack of wheat down the steep hill on a back that cannot be bent any farther. Up to his knees in the February ditch, or cutting ash-poles in the copse, he is clearly half converted into the element to which he must return. When the underwood is for sale it is a pleasure to read the notices fixed to the doors of barn and shed, with the names of the copses and woods. At Penshurst lately, for example, I saw these names:

Black Hoath Wood.
Heronry Pond.
Marlpit Field.
Tapner's Wood.
Ashour Farm.
Sidney's Coppice.
Weir Field.
Well Place.

I was back in Sidney's time, remembering that genial poem of Ben Jonson's, "To Penshurst," and especially the lines

Thy copse too, named of Gamage, thou hast there,
That never fails to serve thee season'd deer,
When thou wouldst feed or exercise thy friends.
The lower land, that to the river bends,
Thy sheep, thy bullocks, kine, and calves do feed;
The middle grounds thy mares and horses breed.
Each bank doth yield thee conies; and the tops
Fertile of wood, Ashore and Sidney's copps,
To crown thy open table, doth provide
The purple pheasant with the speckled side, . . .

And so onward to that opulence and ease three centuries old

Then hath thy orchard fruit, thy garden flowers,
Fresh as the air, and new as are the hours.
The early cherry, with the later plum,
Fig, grape, and quince, each in his time doth come;
The blushing apricot and woolly peach
Hang on thy walls, that every child may reach.
And though thy walls be of the country stone,
They're reared with no man's ruin, no man's groan;
There's none, that dwell about them, wish them down;
But all come in, the farmer and the clown;
And no one empty handed, to salute
Thy lord and lady, though they have no suit.
Some bring a capon, some a rural cake,
Some nuts, some apples; some that think they make
The better cheeses, bring them; or else send
By their ripe daughters, whom they would commend
This way to husbands; and whose baskets bear
An emblem of themselves, in plum or pear . . .

Almost to such a time as that does the old man carry back the thoughts.
His old master was the fifth in the direct line to work one farm in the
vale; he left money in his will to pay for new smocks, all of the best
linen, to be worn by the labourers who should carry him to the grave.

The old man has three companions under that roof. The hand that
lit the lamp is his daughter's, the youngest by the second wife, whom
he married when he was fifty. The other two are her children, and she

is unmarried. She earns no money except by keeping a few fowls and bees. When the younger child was born – the old man having to go six miles out at midnight for the parish doctor – the married women commented: "There's forgiveness for the first, but not for the second; no": for the first showed indiscretion, carelessness, youth; the second, helplessness. The old man can hardly leave the children, and though he is deaf he will, when he is told that the baby is crying, go to the room and listen carefully for the pleasure of the infant voice. That voice means colder winter nights for him and less cheer of meat and ale. But for all young life he has a passion equal to a mother's, so he laces up his boots and does not grieve. See him in the dim outlying barn with the sick heifer which is sure to die. The wet killed several in the open field; this one is to die on dry hay. She lies with stiff, high-ridged back, patient and motionless, except that her ears move now and then like birds – they alone seem alive. There is a deep blue gleam in her eyes. Her head is stretched forward upon the ground. She is alone. Through the open door the sunlight falls, and the swallows fly in and out or hang twittering at the dark beams over her head. Twice a day the cowman comes to the door and salutes her with deep, slow voice, hearty and blithe: "Hoho! Cowslip; how's Cowslip?" He pulls away the foul hay from under her and puts in fresh, talking now in a high falsetto voice as to a child; he raises her head that she may lap the bucket of gruel, still talking unintelligible baby talk interlarded with her pretty name. She holds up her head for a minute or two, heartened by her moist lips and full stomach and that friend's voice. He stands in the doorway watching and silent now, as her head slowly sinks down, and she sighs while her limbs find their position of least pain. "She's going to die," he mutters in the deep voice as he goes.

A very different earth child, an artist, used to live in a cottage at the foot of the opposite Downs. The village itself, whether you saw it from its own street or from the higher land, was wrought into such a rightness of form as few other artists than Time ever achieve; it made a music to which the hands unconsciously beat time. But though apparently complete in itself, it was as part of a huge and gentle harmony of sky, down and forest that the village was most fascinating. Like all beautiful things in their great moments the whole scene was symbolic, not only in the larger sense by expressing in an outward and visible way an inward grace, but in the sense that it gathered up into itself the meaning which many other scenes only partly and in a scattered way expressed.

Two roads of a serpentining form that was perpetually alluring from afar climbed the Down from the village and, skirting the forest, ended in the white mountains of the moon. At the tail of one of these roads the artist lived. His work still further enlarged the harmony of sky and down and village. For a short time I used to wonder why it was that when I entered his studio the harmony was prolonged into something even more huge and gentle than seemed to have been designed. How came it that he could safely hang his pictures on the wall of the Down, as practically they were hung?

It is not enough to say merely that it was because they did not, as some landscapes seem to do, enter into competition with Nature. The spirit that raised and sculptured the Downs, that entered the beech and made a melody of its silent towering and branching, that kept the sky above alive and beautiful with the massiveness of mountains and the evanescence of foam, was also in this man's fingers. He was a great lover of these things, and to his love for them combined the ecstasy of courtship with the understanding of marriage. But he loved them too well to draw and paint them. He was not of those who tear themselves from a mistress to write a sonnet on her face. No. He painted the images which they implanted – such was their love of him and his of them – in his brain. There many a metamorphosis as wonderful as Ovid's was made. The beech trees mingled with the fantasies of the brain and brought forth boles that are almost human forms, branches that are thoughts and roots that are more than wood. Often, I think, he hardly looked at Nature as he walked, except to take a careless pleasure in the thymy winds, in the drama of light and shade on the woods and hills, in the sound of leaves and birds and water. Within him these things lived a new life until they reached forms as different from their beginnings as we are from Palaeolithic man. They attained to that beauty of which, as

I have said, Nature was so little jealous, by this evolution. Some of his pictures of the leaf-dappled branch-work of beeches always remind me of the efflorescence of frost on a window-pane, and the comparison is not purely fantastic but has a real significance.

And yet the landscapes of this metamorphosis are not, as might have been expected, decorations that have lost all smell of earth and light of sun and breath of breeze. Decorative they certainly are, and I know few pictures which are less open to the accusation of beings scraps from Nature, which it is more impossible to think of extending beyond the limits of the frame. But such is the personality of the artist that all this refinement only made more powerful then ever the spirit of the motionless things, the trees, the pools, the hills, the clouds. Frankly, there is a deep fund of what must narrowly, and for the moment only, be called inhumanity in the artist, or he could not thus have reinforced or intensified the inhumanity of Nature. Consider, for example, his "Song of the Nightingale." Those woods are untrodden woods as lonely as the sky. They are made for the nightingale's song to rule in solitude under the crescent moon. No lovers walk there. Mortal who enters there must either a poet or a madman be.

Look again at his "Castle in Spain," how it is perched up above that might of forest, like a child that has climbed whence it can never descend. And the little house at the edge of the high, dark wood – in "The Farm under the Hill" – is as frail and timid as if it heard the roaring of wild beasts, and the little white road winds into the darkness as to death. So, too, with the children who make a pretence of playing hoops at the edge of just such another wood, though mortal has never come out of it since the beginning of the world. The ship in the "Fall of the Leaf" is subdued to the spirit of autumn as is the poet subdued to the immense scenes of "Alastor." To introduce an elvish figure, as he has done, in "Will o' the Wisp" was an unnecessary aid to the elvishness of the scene itself. Indeed, his human fantastic figures seem to be sometimes as much out of place as a Yankee at the court of King Arthur, though there are two notable exceptions – "The Sower" and "The Weed Burner" – both figures towards which idolatry might be excusable, so nobly do they represent labour in the field. And even in "The Weed Burner" the boy seems bemused by the motion and savour of the smoke that curdles up through the autumn air. The picture of a forest pool is magical, but it repudiates the fairy altogether. Nothing would be more out of place here than the kind of sucking harlequin or columbine which is commonly foisted upon us as a fairy; for here is something more desirable, the very forces which begot the fairies upon a different age from ours. Even when he draws a house it is, I think, for the house's sake, for the sake of whatever soul it has acquired, which men cannot take away. Was there ever such an inn as "The Wispers"? The landlord is dead, the casks are dry, a rat has littered on the top stair of the cellar, and the landlord says:

" 'Tis late and cold, stir up the fire:
Sit close, and draw the table nigher;
Be merry, and drink wine that's old,
A hearty medicine 'gainst a cold:
Your beds of wanton down the best,
Where you shall tumble to your rest;
I could wish you wenches too,
But I am dead, and cannot do.
Call for the best the house may ring,
Sack, white, and claret let them bring,
And drink apace, while breath you have;
You'll find but cold drink in the grave:
Plover, partridge, for your dinner,
And a capon for the sinner,
You shall find ready when you're up,
And your horse shall have his sup:
Welcome, welcome, shall fly round,
And I shall smile, though underground."

I like the inn, but the spider loves it, and his webs bar the door against all but ghostly travellers. The barn, again, with its doorway opening upon the summer night, has a life of its own. The two figures at the door are utterly dwarfed by its ancientness, its space, and the infinite silence without.

The picture in which there is most humanity is that of a high wall, ruinous and overgrown. The deep gap in it is tragical. But even here I am not sure that it is a wall that was raised by hand of mason, and as to the inhabitants who left it desolate I feel more doubtful still, I believe it was built in a dream, long ago lost in some victory gained by the forest over men, and quite forgotten until this artist thought it would be a happy lair for a faun. He has not shown us the faun – I wish he had; he ought to know what it was like – but that gap is its gateway out from the forest into the dew of the river lawns.

It induces an awful sense of the infinite variety of human character to think of the love of earth first in this man and then in that cowman old. I wonder tolerance is not deeper as well as wider than it is.

THIRTEEN

Going Westward

RAIN BEGINS as I set out and mount under the beeches. The sky is dark as a ploughed field, but the leaves overhead are full of light like precious stones. The rain keeps the eyes down so that they see one by one the little things of the wayside, the strings of the grey-green and of the scarlet bryony berries, the stony bark of the young ash unveiled by the moving leaves, the million tall straight shoots which the strong nature of ash and hazel has soared into since the spring. Then follows field after field of corn, of sheep among hurdled squares, of mustard in flower, of grass, interrupted now and then by the massed laurels and rhododendrons and the avenues of monkey puzzles that announce the pleasure grounds of the rich. It is a high land of too level clay, chiefly blest in that it beholds the Downs, their saddles of woodland, and, through the deepest passes, the sea and an island rising out of it like an iceberg; and that it is traversed by the Pilgrims' Way, which gathers to itself canterbury-bells and marjoram under its hazels, and pours traveller's joy cloudily over the ash and brier that overhang the side of an old chalk pit, long, straight and even like a wall. Just here are many grassy lanes between hazel and blackthorn hedges. An old farm-house with ivied chimneys and ten blind windows in front stands bereaved with weedy garden, but for miles the air sounds with poultry and the building of bungalows in deal and iron for strangers. It is not a stranger that rides by. I think his fathers must have been in this land when Wolf Hanger was not a strange name for the beeches over the hill. He is a tall straight man with long narrow face, clear, not too irregular features, sallow complexion, black hair and black drooping moustache, and flashing eyes as dark as privet berries in autumn dews.

Now it is a woodland country, of broad wooded common and low undulating Downs crowned or fringed by woods: this is "Swineherd's

County" according to the gipsies. Houses are few and stand either well off the road or with scarcely a dividing line between their gardens and the commons from which they have been filched. Their linen and red flannel flap under enormous beeches where an old track makes its way betwixt them. The children living here, the generations of them who have been bred in the little flint house, are children of the woods, their minds half made by the majestic but dark and deep-voiced trees that stand over them day and night and by the echoes – you may hear them summoning the echoes at evening out of the glades and see them pause as if dazed by the wild reply. Opposite the door is a close untrodden tangle of brier and thorn and bramble under oaks where the dead leaves of many autumns lie untouched even by the wind – so dense is the underwood – that sighs continually in the topmost boughs: at the edge nettles with translucent leaves waver and nod above mossy banks. Not far off is a Woodland Farm, a group of houses and barns and sheds built of flint and wood and thatched, aloof. A man enters one of the cavernous sheds with a pail; a thick, bent, knotty man, with bushy dark hair and beard and bright black eyes, a farmer, the son's son of one who rebuilt the house when the woods were darker and huger still. Life is a dark simple matter for him; three-quarters of his living is done for him by the dead; merely to look at him is to see a man five generations thick, so to speak, and neither Nature nor the trumpery modern man can easily disturb a human character of that density. As I watch him going to and fro I lose sight of everything away from his rude house and the tall woods, because they and he are so powerful – he has the trees as well as his ancestors at his back – and it is no flight of fancy to see him actually cut off from all the world except the house and woods, and yet holding his own, able to keep his fire burning, his larder full, his back covered and his house dry. I feel but a wraith as I pass by. I wonder what there is worth knowing that he does not know, with his bright eyes, bright long teeth, stiff limbs capable of unceasing toil, and that look of harmony with day and night. I see him looking on as the wounded trooper – two hundred and fifty years, a trifle, ago – drains the water just lifted from the well; look at his gallant face, his delicate ardour as of another race, bright dress, restless blue eyes, his helplessness after the defeat in a cavalry fight about nothing at all. The cornet rides away and the woodland fellow puts all his nature into the felling of a beech as into an object worthy of cold steel, and as he plies his axe he smiles at the thought of that brave, that silly face and sleek hair. He smiles to-day as he sees a youth go by with proud looks of command, incapable, as he well understands, of commanding anything except perhaps a wife or a groom or a regiment of townsmen – yet his landlord.

Rough grass and scattered thorns and lofty groups of mossy-pedestalled beeches lie on either side of the road, and grassy tracks lead to thatched cottages in the woods.

A grey-clouded silver sky moves overhead. Along the road the telegraph wires go humming the one shrill note in this great harmony of men and woods and sky. Beyond, a broad champaign of corn and grey grass heaves from the woodland edge. The road is gay with red polished fruit and equally red soft leaves, with darkest purple and bronze and wine-red and green berries and leaves, and beam foliage still pure green and white. So high now are the unkempt hedges that the land is hid and only the sky appears above the coloured trees: except at a meeting of ways when a triangular patch of turf is sacred to burdock, ragwort and thistle and – touching the dust of the road – the lowly silverweed; an oak overhangs, yet the little open space admits a vision of the elephantine Downs going west in the rain. In a moment the world is once again this narrow one of the high-hedged lane, where I see and touch with the eye and enjoy the shapes of each bole and branch in turn, their bone-like shapes, their many colours of the wood itself, wrinkled and grooved, or overlaid by pale green mould, silver lichen or dark green moss. Each bend in the road is different. At one all the leaves are yellow but green-veined, the bramble, the hazel, the elder; and there is a little chalk pit below, fresh white and overhung by yew and the dark purple elder berries, small but distinct: at another there is a maple of exquisite small leaves and numerous accordingly, a fair-built tree in a lovely attitude and surmounted by a plume, only a small plume, of traveller's joy. In Swineherd's County they call it "Angel's hair."

Suddenly there is a village of thatched roofs, phlox in the gardens, good spaces of green and of sycamore trees between one house and the next, and a green-weeded crystal river pervading all with its flash and sound. The anvil rings and the fire glows in the black smithy. The wheelwright's timber leans outside his thatched shed against an ancient elder, etherealized by lucent yellow leaves. Before the inn a jolly ostler with bow legs and purple neck washes the wheels of a cart, ever and anon filling his pail from the stream and swishing the bright water over the wheels as they spin. A decent white-haired old man stands and watches, leaning on his stick held almost at arm's length so as to make an archway underneath which a spaniel sprawls in the sun. The men are all at the corn and he does not know what to do. Can he read? asks the ostler, knowing the answer very well. No! We all read now, chuckles the ostler as he flings a pailful over the wheel. The old man is proud at least to have lived into such a notable day: "Yes, man reads now almost as well as master – quite as well. They used to be dummies, the working class people, yes, that they was. You can't tell what will happen now." Meantime the ostler fills his pail and the old man having too many thoughts to say any more, lays his blackthorn on the bench and calls for his glass of fourpenny ale.

Close by there is an entrance to the more open Downs. The uncut hedges are so thick that the lane seems a cutting through a wood, and soon it becomes a grassy track of great breadth under ash trees and amidst purple dogwood and crimson-hearted traveller's joy, and finally it is a long broad field full of wild carrot and scabious through which many paths meander side by side until the last gate gives a view, under oak and hazel sprays, on to the green undulations of hill and coombe, their sides studded with juniper and thorn, with something of oceanic breadth in the whole, as far as the utmost bound, leagues away, where a line of small trees stands against the sky in the manner of ships. The hedges in this downland are low or broken. A few ricks stand at the borders of stubble and grass. Sheep munch together in square pens. There is no house, and the rain has wiped out everything that moved save its own perpendicular fringes waving along the hills. This solitude of grey and brown is completed by the owner's notice, on a frail and tottering post: "Trespassers will be prosecuted with the utmost rigour of the law." Towards the farther verge compact copses of beech begin to saddle the ridges and invade the hollows so as to form cliffy dark sides to the friths of pale stubble or turf amongst them. And then the green way runs into a Roman road, and in the twilight and rain I can see many other narrow ancient tracks winding into the white road as straight as a sword, losing themselves in it like children in a dragon's mouth. The turf alongside is mounded by tumuli; and against the hedge a gipsy family pretend to shelter from the windy rain; the man stands moody, holding the pony, the women crouch with chins upon knees, the children laugh and will not be still. They belong to the little roads that are dying out: they hate the sword-like shelterless road, the booming cars that go straight to the city in the vale below. They are less at home there than the swallows that hunt the leeward sides of the sycamores, ever rushing up towards the trees and ever beaten back, like children playing "I'm the king of the castle," at the verge of the city. There, by the inn piano, soldiers and their friends and women sing with vague pathos songs about "Mother" and "Dear Love" and "Farewell" and "Love is all" and "The girls," while the streets glitter and gurgle with rain. Just before night the sky clears. It is littered with small dark clouds upon rose, like rocks on a wild and solitary coast of after-tempest calm, and it is infinitely remote and infinitely alluring. Those clouds are the Islands of the Blest. Even so alluring might be this life itself, this world, if I were out of it. For a moment I fancy how I might lean and watch it all, being dead. For a moment only, since the poverty of death is such that we cannot hope from it such a gift of contemplation from afar, cannot hope even that once out of the world we may turn round and look at it and feel that we are not of it any more, nor hope that we shall know ourselves to be dead and be satisfied. Rain shrouds the islands of the sky: the singers find them in their song.

In the morning the ground is beautiful with blue light from one white-clouded pane of sky that will not be hidden by the tumultuous rain. Outside the city the new thatch of the ricks shines pale in the sodden land, which presently gives way to a great water with leaning masts and a majestic shadowy sweep of trees down to the flat shore, to level green marsh and bridges crossing the streams that are announced by ripples in the sun, by swishing sedge, by willows blenching. Beyond is forest again. First, scattered cottages and little yellow apples beaming pale on crooked trees; then solitudes of heather and bracken, traversed and lighted by blue waters, ponds and streams among flats of rushes; and beyond, at either hand, woods on low and high land endlessly changing from brightness to gloom under windy clouds. The roads are yellow, and oaks and beeches hang over them in whispering companies. The wind reigns, in the high magnificent onset of the clouds, in the surging trees, in the wings of rooks and daws, in bowing sedges and cotton grass, in quivering heather and grass, in rippling water, in wildly flying linen; yet in the open there is a strange silence because the roar in my ears as I walk deafens me to all sound.

White ponies graze by dark waters and stir the fragrance of the bog myrtle. The rises of the heathery moor are scarred yellow where the gravel is exposed. Sometimes great beeches, plated with green lichen and grey, wave their stiffening foliage overhead; or there is a group of old hollies encircled by coeval ivy whose embraces make them one, and both seem of stone. Sometimes the yellow road runs green-edged among heather and gorse, shadowed by pines that shake and plunge in the wind but are mute. A white fungus shines damp in the purple moor. There are a myriad berried hawthorns here, more gorse, more heather and bracken. The tiny pools beneath are blown into ripples like a swarming of bees, but the infuriate streams cannot trouble the dark water and broad lily leaves in their bays. Other pools again are tranquil and lucid brown over submerged moss and pennywort and fallen leaves, worlds to themselves with a spirit indwelling in the pure element. Presently, denser trees hold back the wind save in their tempestuous crests, and now the road is carpeted with pine needles and nothing can be seen or felt but the engulfing sound of wind and rain. The pines are interrupted by tall bracken, hollies, and thorns, by necks of turf and isolated hawthorns thereon; and far away the light after rain billows grandly over the mounded forest. Many a golden stream pours through the dark trees. Oaks succeed, closing in lichened multitudes about a grassy-rutted ferny road, but suddenly giving way to beeches pallid and huge. One lies prone across the road, still green of leaf, having torn up a mound of earth and bracken and bramble as large as a house in its upheaval. Others have lost great branches, and the mossy earth is ploughed by their fall. They seem to have fought in the night and to be slumbering with dreams of battle to come; and their titanic passions keep far away the influence of the blue sky and silver clouds that laugh out unconcerned after the rain.

After them birches and birchlings grow out of the heather backed by a solid wall of oaks. And again there are many beeches over mossy golden turf, and one tree of symmetrical rounded foliage makes a circle of shade where nothing grows, but all about it a crowd of dwarf brackens twinkle and look like listeners at an oracle. Beyond, countless pillars of dark pines tower above green grass. Then the road forks; a shapely oak, still holding up dead arms through clouds of greenery, stands at one side; at the other a green road wanders away under beeches in stately attitudes and at ceremonious distance from one another: straight ahead, open low meadows surround a reedy water where coot and moorhen cry to each other among willow islets and the reflex of a bright and windy heaven. And yet once more the road pierces the dense woodland roar, form and colour buried as it were in sound, except where a space of smoothest turf expands from the road, and out of the crimson berries of an old thorn comes the voice of a robin singing persistently; and past that, inevitably, is a cottage among the beeches. More cottages are set in the moorland that rolls to a horizon of ridgy oak away from small green meadows behind the cottages. These give way to treeless undulations like gigantic long barrows, coloured by sand, by burnt gorse and by bracken; farther away a wooded hump all dark under threatening of storm; and farthest of all, the Downs, serene and pale. The plough begins to invade the forest. The undulations sink to rest in a land of corn and cloud, of dark green levels, of windy whitened abeles, and a shining flood gilded by a lofty western sky of gold and grey. Beside the darkling waters couches an old town with many windows looking under thatch and tile upon grave streets, ending in a spread of the river where great horses wading lift their knees high as they splash under a long avenue of aspens and alarm the moorhens. Beautiful looks the running river under the night's hunting of the clouds and the few bright stars, and beautiful again, broad blue, or streaked, or shadowy, or glittering, or reed-reflecting, beside a white mill or company of willows, under the breezes and pearl of dawn; and I wish there were a form for saluting a new country's gods and the *adhuc ignota . . . flumina.*

Two roads go northward against the stream; the main road straight or in long curves on one side of the river the other on the opposite bank in a string of fragments zigzagging east and west and north. These fragments connect houses or groups of houses with one another, and it looks as if only by accident they had made the whole which now connects two towns. Their chief business is to serve the wheels and feet of those bound upon domestic or hamlet but not urban business. Seen upon the map the road sets out straight for a town far north; but in two miles the hospitality of a great house seems to draw it aside, then of "The Plough"; emerging again it wanders awhile before returning to its northward line; and this it does time after time, and as often as it pauses a lesser road runs out of it to the great road across the river. There are scores of such parallel roads – sometimes the lesser is in part, or entirely, a footpath – in England, and in avoiding the dust, the smell, the noise, the insolence of the new traffic, the lesser are an invaluable aid. This one proceeds without rise or fall through the green river levels, but looks up to a ridge of white-scarred purple moor away from the stream, with oak and thatched cottages below the heather. It creeps in and out like an old cottage woman at a fair and sees everything. It sees all the farms and barns. It sees the portly brick house and its gardens bounded by high fruit walls and its walnut trees in front, on the bank of a golden brook that sings under elms and sallows; the twenty-four long white windows, the decent white porch, the large lawns, the pond and its waterfowl sounding in the reeds, the oaks and acacias, the horse mowing the lawn lazily, the dogs barking behind the Elizabethan stables. It sees the broad grassy borders – for this is not a road cut by a skimping tailor – and the woods of oak and ash and hazel which the squirrel owns, chiding, clucking and angrily flirting his tail at those who would like to share his nuts. At every crossing road these grassy borders, which are in places as broad as meadows so that cattle graze under their elms, spread out into a green; and round about are yellow thatched cottages with gardens full of scarlet bean flowers and yellow dahlias; and a pond reflects the blue and white sky, wagtails flutter at the edge and geese launch themselves as if for a voyage. The only sound upon the road is made by the baker's cart carrying a fragrant load.

After ten miles the road crosses the river and wanders even farther from the highway. Here there are more woods of hazel and oak, and borders where sloe and blackberry shine, polished by rain, among herbage of yellow ragwort and flea-bane, purple knapweed, yellowing leaves. The gateways show steep meadows between the woods. One shows two lovers of sixteen years old gathering nuts in the warm sun, the silence, the solitude. The boy bends down and she steps quickly and carelessly upon his back to reach a cluster of six, and then descending looks away for a little while and turns her left cheek to him, softly smiling wordless things to herself, so that her lover could not but lean forward and kiss her golden skin where it is most beautiful beneath her ear and her looped black hair. There is a maid whose ways are so wonderful and desirable that it would not be more wonderful and desirable if Helen had never grown old and Demeter had kept Persephone.

For a day white-throated convolvulus hides all the nettles of life. Of all the delicate passing things I have seen and heard – the slow, languid, gracious closing and unclosing of a pewit's rounded wings as it chooses a clod to alight on; the sound of poplar leaves striving with the sound of rain in a windy summer shower; the glow of elms where an autumn rainbow sets a foot amongst them; the first fire of September lighted among men and books and flowers – not one survives to compare with this gateway vision of a moment on a road I shall never travel again. To rescue such scenes from time is one of the most blessed offices of books, and it is a book that I remember now as I think of that maiden smiling, a book, (*The Heifer of the Dawn*, by F. W. Bain) which says:

> And I could tell thee stories that would make thee laugh at all thy trouble, and
> take thee to a land of which thou hast never dreamed. Where the trees have ever
> blossoms, and are noisy with the humming of intoxicated bees. Where by day
> the suns are never burning and by night the moonstones ooze with nectar in the
> rays of the camphor-laden moon. Where the blue lakes are filled with rows of
> silver swans, and where, on steps of lapis lazuli, the peacocks dance in agitation
> at the murmur of the thunder in the hills. Where the lightning flashes without
> harming, to light the way to women, stealing in the darkness to meetings with
> their lovers, and the rainbow hangs for ever like an opal on the dark blue
> curtain of the clouds. Where, on the moonlit roofs of crystal palaces, pairs of
> lovers laugh at the reflection of each other's lovesick faces in goblets of red wine,
> breathing as they drink air heavy with the fragrance of the sandal, wafted from
> the mountain of the south. Where they play and pelt each other with emeralds
> and rubies, fetched at the churning of the ocean from the bottom of the sea.
> Where rivers, whose sands are always golden, flow slowly past long lines of
> silent cranes that hunt for silver fishes in the rushes on their banks. Where men
> are true, and maidens love for ever, and the lotus never fades . . .

The great old books do the same a hundred times. Take *The Arabian Nights* for example. They are full of persons, places, and events depicted with so strong an appeal to our eyes and to that part of our intelligence which by its swiftness and simplicity corresponds to our eyes, that no conceivable malversation by a translator can matter much. They are proof against it, just as our tables and chairs and walking-sticks are proof against the man who tears our books and cracks our glass cases of artificial grapes or stuffed kingfishers when we move to a new house. This group of women is beyond the reach of time or an indifferent style:

> Ten female slaves approached with a graceful and conceited gait, resembling
> moons, dazzling the sight, and confounding the imagination, They stood in
> ranks, looking like the black-eyed damsels of Paradise; and after them came ten
> other female slaves, with lutes in their hands, and other instruments of diversion
> and mirth; and they saluted the two guests, and played upon the lutes, and sang
> verses; and every one of them was a temptation to the servants of God . . .

A hundred others flock to my mind, competing for mention like a

'A pond . . . wagtails flutter at the edge'

company of doves for a mere pinch of seed – Rose-in-Bloom sitting at a lattice to watch the young men playing at ball, and throwing an apple to Ansal Wajoud, "bright in countenance, with laughing teeth, generous, wide-shouldered"; or that same girl letting herself down from her prison and escaping over the desert in her most magnificent apparel and a necklace of jewels on her neck; Sinbad returning home rich from every voyage, and as often, in the midst of the luxuries of his rest, going down to the river by Bagdad and seeing a fair new ship and embarking for the sake of profit and of beholding the countries and islands of the world.

These clear appeals come into the tales like white statues suddenly carven to our sight among green branches. But they are also something more than a satisfaction to our love of what is large, bright, coloured, in high relief. Every one knows how, at a passage like that in the *Æneid*, when the exiled Æneas sees upon the new walls of the remote city of Carthage pictures of that strife about Troy in which he was a great part, or at a verse in a ballad like:

> It was na in the ha', the ha';
> It was na in the painted bower;
> But it was in the good greenwood,
> Amang the lily flower.

– how the cheek flushes and the heart leaps up with a pleasure which the incidents themselves hardly justify. We seem to recognize in them symbols or images of ideas which are important to mortal minds. They are of a significance beyond allegories. They are as powerful, and usually as mysterious in their power, as the landscape at sight of which the gazer sighs in his joy, he knows not why. In such passages the *Nights* abound.

One of the finest is in *Seifelmolouk* and *Bedia Eljemal*. The hero and his memlooks were captured by a gigantic Ethiopian king. Some were eaten. The survivors so pleased the king by the sweetness of their voices while they were crying and lamenting that they were hung up in cages for the king to hear them. *Seifelmolouk* and three of his companions the king gave to his daughter, and when the youth sat thinking of the happy past, and crying over it, she was overjoyed at the singing of her little captive. Perhaps more pleasing still is the door in the grass which was only to be removed to discover a splendid subterranean palace and a "woman whose aspect banished from the heart all anxiety and grief and affliction", even when the finder is the son of a king cutting wood in a forest, far from his lost home and from those who know him as the son of a king. The incognito appearances of the great caliph make scenes of the same class. A young man sits with his mistress, and the sound of her lovely singing draws four darwishes to the door; he descends and lets them in; they promise to do him an immense and undreamed-of service:

"Now these darwishes," says the tale, "were the Khalifeh Harun Er-Rashid, and the Wezir Ja'far El-Barmeki, and Abu-Nuwas El-Hasan, the son of Hani, and Mesrur the Executioner."

Then there is that page where Nimeh and the Persian sage open a shop in Damascus, and stock it with costly things, and the sage sits with the astrolabe before him, "in the apparel of sages and physicians" – to wait for Nimeh's lover, or some one who has news of her, to appear. Of a more subtly appealing charm is a sentence in the story of "Ala-ed-din," where a man tells the father of one who is supposed to have been executed that another was actually slain in his stead, "for I ransomed him, by substituting another, from among such as deserved to be put to death." A good book might be made of the stories of such poor unknown men in famous books as this prisoner who was of those that deserved to die.

Lofty, strange, and infinite in its suggestiveness is the tale of Kamar-ez-Zeman and the Princess Budur. Two demons, an Efrit and an Efritch, contend as to the superiority in beauty of a youth and a girl whom they watch asleep in widely remote parts of the earth; and they carry them through the midnight sky and lay the two side by side to judge. On the morrow, the youth longs for the girl and the girl for the youth. Of their dreams, the king, the father of the youth, says: "Probably it was a confused dream that thou sawest in sleep," and the father of the girl chains her up as mad. But in the end, after many wanderings and impediments, they transcend the separation of space and are married. Noblest of all, perhaps, is one of the short "Anecdotes" about the discovery of a terrestrial paradise.

Abd-allah went out to seek a straying camel, and chanced upon a superb and high-walled city lying silent in the desert. And when the caliph inquired about that city, a learned man told him that it was built by Sheddad, the king. This prince was fond of ancient books, and took delight in nothing so much as in descriptions of Paradise, so that his heart enticed him to make one like it on the earth. Under him were a hundred thousand kings, and under each of them were a hundred thousand soldiers, and he furnished them with the measurements and set them to collect the materials of gold and silver and ruby and pearl and chrysolite. For twenty years they collected. Then he sought a fit place among rivers on a vast open plain. In twenty years they built the city and finished its impregnable fortifications. For twenty years he laboured in equipping himself, his viziers, his harem and his troops for the occupation of this Paradise. Then when he was rejoicing on his way, "God sent down upon him and upon the obstinate infidels who accompanied him a loud cry from the Heaven of His power, and it destroyed them all by the vehemence of its sound. Neither Sheddad nor any of those who were with him arrived at the city or came in sight of it, and God obliterated the traces of the road that led to it; but the city remaineth as it was in its place until the hour of the judgment." . . .

Beyond the gateway the Downland and the corn begins, and with it the rain, so that the great yellow-banded bee hangs long pensive on the lilac flower of the scabious. Hereby is a farm with a wise look in its narrow window on either side of the white door under the porch; the walls of the garden and the farmyard are topped with thatch; opposite rises up a medlar tree, russet-fruited: and those two eyes of the little farm peep out at the stranger. From the next hill-top the land spreads out suddenly – an immense grey hedgeless land of pasture and ploughland and stubble with broadcast shadows of clouds and lines, and clumps of dark-blue trees a league apart. These woods are of pine and thorn and elder and beam, and some yew and juniper, haunted by the hare and the kestrel, by white butterflies going in and out, by the dandelion's down. Sometimes under the pines a tumulus whispers a gentle *siste viator* and the robin sings beside. Far away, white rounds of cloud bursting with sunlight are lifted up out of the ground; born of earth they pause a little upon the ridge and then take flight into the blue profound, their trains of shadow moving over the corn sheaves, over the ploughs working along brown bands of soil, the furzy spaces, the deeply cloven grassy undulations, the lines of yews and of corn-stacks. Slowly a spire like a lance-head is thrust up through the Downs into the sky.

Beyond the spire a huge woody mound rises up from the low flowing land, huge and carved all round by an entrenchment as if by the weight of a crown that it had worn for ages. Certainly it wears no crown to-day. Not a human being lives there; they have all fled to the riverside and the spire, leaving their ancient home to the triumphs of the wide-flowering traveller's joy, to the play of children on the sward within its walls, and to the archaeologist: and very sad and very noble it looks at night when it and the surrounding Downs lift up their dark domes of wood among the mountains of the sky, and the great silence hammers upon the ears.

Then a hedgeless road traverses without interrupting the long Downs. One after another, lines of trees thin and dark and old come out against the pale bright sky of late afternoon and file away, beyond the green turf and roots and the grey or yellow stubble. As the sun sets, dull crimson, at the foot of a muslin of grey and gold which his course has crimsoned, the low clouds on the horizon in the north become a deathly blue white belonging neither to day nor to night, while overhead the light-combed cloudlets are touched faintly with flame. Now the glory and the power of the colour in the west, and now the pallid north, fill the brain to overflowing with the mingling of distance, of sublime motion, and of hue, and intoxicate it and give it wings, until at last when the west is crossed by long sloping strata as of lava long cooled they seem the bars of a cage impassable. But even they are at last worn away and the sky is as nothing compared with earth. For there, as I move, the infinite greys and yellows of the crops, the grass, the bare earth, the clumps of firs, the

lines of beeches and oaks, play together in the twilight, and the hills meet
and lose their lines and flow into one another and build up beautiful
lines anew, the outward and visible signs of a great thought. Out of
the darkness in which they are submerged starts a crying of pewits and
partridges; and overhead and close together the wild duck fly west into
the cold gilded blue.

At dawn a shallow crystal river runs over stones and waves green hair
past ancient walls of flint, tall towers and many windows, with vines
about the mullions, past desolate grass of old elmy meads, high-gated, and
umbrageous roads winding white by carven gateways, under sycamore
and elm and ash and many alders and haughty avenues of limes, past an
old great church, past a park where elms and oaks and bushy limes hide
a ruin among nettles and almost hide a large stone house from which
peacocks shout, past a white farm, red-tiled, that stands with a village
of its own thatched barns, cart-lodges and sheds under walnut and elm,
enclosed within a circuit of old brick with a tower that looks along the
waters. It is a place where man has known how to aid his own stateliness
by that of Nature. The trees are grand and innumerable, but they stand
about in aristocratic ways; the bright young water does not flout the
old walls but takes the shadow of antiquity from them and lends them
dew-dropping verdure in return. The pebbles under the waves are half
of them fallen from the walls; the curves round which they bend are of
masonry; so that it is unapparent and indifferent whether the masonry
has been made to fit the stream or the stream persuaded to admit the
masonry. As I look, I think of it as Statius thought of the Surrentine villa
when he prayed that Earth would be kind to it and not throw off that
ennobling yoke. Everywhere the river rushes and shines, or roars unseen
behind trees. The sun is warm and the golden light hangs as if it were
fruit among the leaves over the ripples.

Above the stream the elms open apart and disclose a wandering grey
land and clumps of beeches, a grey windy land and a grey windy sky in
which the dark clumps are islanded. Flocks of sheep move to and fro,
and with them the swallows. Two shepherds, their heavy grey overcoats
slung about their shoulders and the sleeves dangling, their flat rush

baskets on their backs, stand twenty yards apart to talk, leaning on their sticks, while their swallow-haunted flocks go more slowly and their two dogs converse and walk round one another.

The oats have been trampled by rain, and two men are reaping it by hand. They are not men of the farm, but rovers who take their chance and have done other things than reaping in their time. One is a Hampshire man, but fought with the Wiltshires against "Johnny Boer" – he liked the Boers . . . "they were very much like a lot of working men . . . We never beat 'em . . . No, we never beat 'em." He is a man of heroic build; tall, lean, rather deep-chested than broad-shouldered, narrow in the loins, with goodly calves which his old riding breeches perfectly display; his head is small, his hair short and crisp and fair, his cheeks and neck darkly tanned, his eye bright blue and quick-moving, his features strong and good, except his mouth, which is over large and loose; very ready to talk, which he does continually in a great proud male voice, however hard he is working. A man as lean and hard and bright as his reaping-hook. First he snicks off a dozen straws and lays them on the ground for a bond, then he slashes fast along the edge of the corn for two or three yards, gathers up what is cut into his hook and lays it across the straws: when a dozen sheaves are prepared in the same way he binds them with the bonds and builds them into a stook of two rows leaning together. It is impossible to work faster and harder than he does in cutting and binding; only at the end of each dozen sheaves does he stand at his full height, straight as an ash and laugh, and round off what he has been saying even more vigorously than he began it. Then crouching again he slays twelve other sheaves. Then he goes over to the four-and-a-half-gallon cask in the hedge: it is a fuel that he likes, and he pays for it himself. In his walk and attitude and talk – except in his accent – there is little of the countryman. He is a citizen of the world, without wife or home or any tie except to toil – and after that pleasure – and toil again. A loose bold liver – and lover – there can be no doubt. The spirit of life is strong in him, in limbs and chest and eyes and brain, the spirit which compels one man to paint a picture, one to sacrifice his life for another, one to endure poverty for an idea, another to commit a murder. What is there for him – to be the mark for a bullet, to contract a ravenous disease, to bend slowly under the increasing pile of years, of work, of pleasures? He does not care. He is always seeing "a bit of life" from town to town, from county to county, a peerless fleshly man casting himself away as carelessly as Nature cast him forth into the world. His father before him was the same, ploughboy, circus rider, brickmaker, and day labourer again on the land, one who always "looked for a policeman when he had had a quart." He set out on his travels again and disappeared. His wife went another way, and she is still to be met with in the summer weather, not looking as if she had ever borne such a son as this reaper. As she grows older she seems to stretch out a connecting hand to long-vanished generations, to the men and women who raised the huge earthen walls of the camps on these hills. She has a trembling small face, wrinkled and yellow like old newspaper, above a windy bunch of rags, chiefly black rags. A Welshwoman who has been in England fifty years, she remembers or thinks of chiefly those Welsh years when, as a girl, she rode a pony into Neath market. She hums a Welsh tune and still laughs at it because she heard it first in those days from one then poor and old and abject – she herself tall and willful – and the words of it were: "O, my dear boy, don't get married." She would like once again to lie in her warm bed and hear the steady rain falling in the black night upon the mountain. She feels the sharp flint against the sole of her foot and appears not to be annoyed or indignant or resolved to be rid of the pain, but only puzzled by the flintiness of God as she travels, in the long pageant of those who go on living, the lonely downland road among the gorse and the foxgloves, in the hot but still misty morning when the grey and the chestnut horses, patient and huge and shining among the sheaves, wait for the reaping-machine to be uncovered and the days' work to begin.

Through the grey land goes a narrow and flat vale of grass and of thatched cottages. The river winds among willows and makes a green world, out of which the Downs rise suddenly with their wheat. Here stands a farm with dormers in its high yellow roof and a square of beeches round about. There a village, even its walls thatched, flutters white linen and blue smoke against a huge chalk scoop in the Downs behind. For miles only the cherry-coloured clusters of the guelder rose break through the rain and the gently changing grey of the cornland and green of the valley, until several farms of thatched brick gather together under elms and mellowing chestnuts and make a crooked hamlet. Or at a bend in the road a barn like a diminutive down stands among ricks and under elms; behind is a red farm and church tower embowered; in front, the threshing-machine booms and smokes and an old drenched woman stands bent aloft receiving the sheaves in her blue stiff claws. Close by, a man leads a horse away from a field and its companion looks over the gate with longing, and turns away and again returning almost jumps it, but failing through fearfulness at seeing the other so near the bend in the road, races down the hedge and back and stands listening to the other's whinny, and then scattering the turf dashes into an orchard beyond and whinnies as he gallops.

In majesty, rigid and black, the steam ploughs are working up against the treeless sky; and, just seen in the rain, the white horse carved upon the hill seems a living thing, but of mist.

Now, as if for the sake of the evening bells and the gleaners, the rain withholds itself, and over the drenching stubble the women and children, in black and grey and dirty white, crawl, doubled up, careless of the bells and of the soft moist gold of the sun that envelops them, as of the rain and wind that after a little while cover up the gold upon the field and the green and rose of the sky.

And so to the inn. Why do not inns have a regular tariff for the poorish man without a motor-car? Let inn-keepers bleed the rich, by all means, but why should they charge me one shilling and ninepence for a cod steak or a chop or the uneatable cold roast beef of new England, and then charge the same sum for the best part of a duckling and cheese and a pint of ale? I once asked the most enterprising publisher in London whether he would print a book that should tell the sober truth about some of our English inns, and he said that he dared not do anything so horrible. For fear of ruining my publisher I will not mention names, but simply say that at nine inns out of ten the charges are incalculable and excessive unless the traveller makes a point of asking beforehand what they are going to be, a course that provokes discomfort in his relation to the host outweighing what is saved. The tea room, on the other hand, is inexpensive. It lies behind a shop and there is a slaughter-house adjacent – even now the butcher can be heard parting the warm hide from the flesh. Inside, the room is green and the little light and the rain also come sickly through windows of stained glass and fall upon a piano, a bicycle, an embroidered deck chair, vases of dead grass on a marble-topped table, a screen pasted over with scraps from the newspapers, and, upon walls, a calendar from the butcher depicting a well-dressed love scene, a text or two, pictures of well-dresssed children and their animals, and upon the floor, oilcloth odorous and wet. Here, as at the inns, the adornments are dictated by a taste begotten by the union of peasant taste and town taste, and are entirely pretentious and unrelated to the needs of the host or of the guests.

FOURTEEN

An Old House and a Book

THE COUNTRY is deserted in the rain, and I have the world to myself, a world of frenzied rain among the elms of the lowland, an avenue of elms up to a great house, hidden sheep tinkling and bleating, shepherds muffled, huge slopes of grass and pearled clover above a coombe where a grey heron sails and clanks alone, a farm desolate among elder and ash at the highest part of the hills, and then miles of pathless pasture and stubble descending past an old camp and a tumulus to the submerged vale, where yellow elms tremble about a church tower, a cluster of red cottages and bowed yellow dahlias and chrysanthemums, and a house standing aloof. This house is some way from the Downs themselves, but just at the foot of a lesser slope, a fair golden hill – golden with cowslips in May – that rises on one side with a swift, short ascent and then shoots forward, as if with the impetus, almost level until, after crowning itself with beeches, it descends in a lazy curve to a field, roughened by the foundations of a vanished house, at one corner of which the chimneys join with another group of elms in the haze of rain.

Hanging from the wall in rags, too wet even to flap, are the remains of an auctioneer's announcement of a sale at the house behind. Mahogany – oak chests – certain ounces of silver – two thousand books – portraits and landscapes and pictures of horses and game – of all these and how much else has the red house been disembowelled? It is all shadowy within, behind the windows, like the eyes of a corpse, and without sound, or form, or light, and it is for no one that the creeper magnificently arrays itself in bediamonded crimson and gold that throbs and wavers in the downpour. The martins are still there, and their play up and down before the twenty windows is a senseless thing, like the play of children outside a chamber of agony or grief. They seem to be machines going on and on

when their master and purpose are dead. But then, too, there is gradually
a consolation, a restfulness, a deceit, a forgetting, in the continuity of
their movement and their unchanged voices. The two hundred autumns
perpetuated in the tones of the bricks are in vain. Strangers will come,
no doubt – hope they will not – and be pleased, actually proud, at this
mellowness, which ought to have died with the last of the family that
built the house.

The tall horse-chestnuts throw down their fruit out of the crisp, rusty
foliage and it rolls darkly burnished out of the pods white as mushrooms
in the rain, and where it falls it lies, and no child gathers it, and the
harvest wagons have crushed a thousand under their wheels. The moss
is beginning to encrust the gravel for the soft feet of the ghosts, of the old
men and the mothers and the maids and the schoolboys and tottering
babes that have trodden it once. Now that they are all gone, every one,
they seem always to have been ghosts, with loud, happy voices and wails
of sorrow, with smiles, dark looks, passionate splendours, bright hair,
the bright brown hair as of red deer in the men, the long, heavy coils
of living odorous gold in the women, but flitting to and fro, footless,
unconfined, like the swallows, returning and wandering up and down,
as if they had left something behind in their home.

When I first entered the house by an accident in passing that way,
a great-grandfather, a granddaughter and her son were alone in the
house, with two servants. The mother, early widowed, had come with
her child to minister to the last days of the ancient man. The house was
by then full of the reports of death. In almost every room there had been
a deathbed. For it had always been full of life; there was never such a
house for calling back its children; the sons of it brought their wives,
and the daughters their husbands, and often an excuse was made for one
pair to stay on indefinitely; and thus it came to be full also of death. This
granddaughter, however, had stayed, as she wished to believe, against
her will, because the old man was so fond of his great-grandchild. She
was a beautiful, strong woman, with the dark, lustrous skin, gold hair,
perfect clear features, proud step and prouder voice, of all the family;
she had shone before a thousand eyes; and yet she stayed on and on,

obsessed by the multitudinous memories of the house alone under the Downs. ·

Her grandfather would talk of nothing but his father and his grandfather, the lawyers, the captains, the scholars, whose bones were under the churchyard elms, and his sons and their sons, all of them also now dead. He had their childish ways by heart, the childish ways of men who were white-haired at his birth as well as of those who went golden-haired but yesterday into the grave; and all their names, their stately, their out-of-the-way names, and those which recorded the maiden names of their mothers; their nicknames, too, a whole book of them; the legends about the most conspicuous, their memorable speeches and acts, down to the names of their very dolls, and their legends also, which, of course, recurred again and again in the family fantasy. Every tree and field and gate and room was connected with some one of the dear and beauteous or brave dead, with their birth, their deeds, their ends.

The portraits of many of them, at least one to every generation, hung on the walls, and it was curious to notice, what never any one of them could see, except the granddaughter, the progress and the decline from generation to generation. The earliest of all had sailed and buccaneered with Henry Morgan, a great lover and destroyer of life. It was from him that the expression and air of them all had descended. Love and battle had carved his face. Out from behind his bold but easy face peered a prophetic pitifulness, just as behind the loaded brown clouds of drifting storm peers the innocence of blue, and upon it white clouds that are thin and waved like an infant's hair. Upon this model his descendants' faces had been carved, not by love and battle, but by his might alone. Even the tender women flaunted it. It nestled, an eagle, among the old man's snows; it possessed the little child, and he had nothing but the face of the buccaneer, like an eaglet in a cage.

A house is a perdurable garment, giving and taking of life. If it only fit, straightway it begins to chronicle our days. It beholds our sorrows and our joys; its untale-bearing walls know all our thoughts, and if it be such a house as grows after the builders are gone, our thoughts presently owe much to it; we have but to glance at a certain shadow or a curve in the wall-paper pattern to recall them, softened as by an echo, and that corner or that gable starts many a fancy that reaches beyond the stars, many a fancy gay or enriched with regrets. It is aware of birth, marriage and death; and who dares say that there is not kneaded into the stones a record more pleasing than brass? With what meaning the vesperal beam slips through a staircase window in autumn! The moon has an expression proper to us alone, nested among our limes, or heaving an ivory shoulder above the neighbour roofs. As we enter a room in our house we are conscious of a fitness in its configuration that defies mathematics. Rightly used, such a space will inspire a stately ordering of our lives; it is, in another respect, the amplest canvas for the art of life. It becomes so much a part of us that we exclaim:

> This beautiful house is sand and stone:
> What will it be in heaven?

This beautiful house under the Downs was already more than "sand and stone." It was a giant, very gentle but very powerful, and adding to its power the lore of the family it was irresistible. This young mother had all the lore by heart and loved it, yet had fought against it. She had been happy when her child had grown at first unlike her own family and much like her husband's; but no! his hair grew lighter, his nose was as those of her brothers' in bud, and now that he was five he was not a child so much as an incarnation of the family, a sort of graven image to which the old man bowed down, and with all the more fervour because of that weakness in the boy which others thought imbecility. The old man, too, had been not only a man but a family; now that the child was there he waited, garrulously contented, for his release from the post. So contented was he that when the grand-daughter left her child with him, and after delays and excuses and delays disappeared into the blank, indifferent abyss of the multitude far away who knew not the house and the family, he was not only contented but glad at heart, for it was a rebel that was gone.

For several years the white beard and the poor child lived together happily, turning over old memories, old books, old toys, taking the old

walks through the long garden, past, but not into, the beech wood that
a whim of the old man's had closed against even himself, against all
save the birds and the squirrels; over the high downs and back into the
deep vale which had produced that delicate physical beauty and those
gracious lusty ways beyond which it seemed that men and women could
hardly go in earthly life. Very happy were those two, and very placid;
but within a week their tragic peace was perfected. The boy fell out of
one of the apple trees and was killed. The old man could not but stumble
over that small grave into his own, and here is the end, the unnoted, the
common end, and the epitaph written by the auctioneer and the rain.

Much as I love rain, heavy or light, freakish or continuous, I am glad
to be out of it for a little while and to open a book of ballads by a
solitary fire at "The White Horse," and soon to close it after reading
again the lines:

> O then bespake her daughter dear,
>   She was baith jimp and sma':
> "O row me in a pair o' sheets,
>   And tow m owre the wa'!"
>
> They row'd her in a pair o' sheets,
>   And tow'd her owre the wa';
> But on the point o' Gordon's spear
>   She gat a deadly fa'.
>
> O bonnie, bonnie was her mouth,
>   And cherry were her cheeks,
> And clear, clear was her yellow hair,
>   Whereon the red blood dreeps.
>
> Then wi' his spear he turn'd her owre;
>   O gin her face was wan!
> He said, "Ye are the first that e'er
>   I wish'd alive again."
>
> He cam' and lookit again at her;
>   O gin her skin was white!

"I might hae spared that bonnie face
To hae been some man's delight.

"Busk and boun, my merry men a',
For ill dooms I do guess;
I cannot look on that bonnie face
As it lies on the grass."

Wha looks to freits, my master dear,
Its freits will follow them;
Let it ne'er be said that Edom o' Gordon
Was daunted by a dame . . ."

I cannot help wondering whether the great work done in the last century and a half towards the recovery of old ballads in their integrity will have any effect beyond the entertainment of a few scientific men and lovers of what is ancient, now that the first effects upon Wordsworth and his contemporaries have died away. Can it possibly give a vigorous impulse to a new school of poetry that shall treat the life of our time and what in past times has most meaning for us as freshly as those ballads did the life of their time? It is possible; and it is surely impossible that such examples of simple, realistic narrative shall be quite in vain. Certainly the more they are read the more they will be respected, and not only because they often deal with heroic matters heroically, but because their style is commonly so beautiful, their pathos so natural, their observation of life so fresh, so fond of particular detail – its very lists of names being at times real poetry.

Sometimes the style is equal and like to that of the most accomplished poetry, as in the stanza:

The Ynglyshe men let ther boys (bows) be,
And pulde owt brandes that were brighte;
It was a hevy syght to se
Bryght swordes on basnites lyght.

Or in:

God send the land deliverance
Frae every reaving, riding Scot!
We'll sune hae neither cow nor ewe,
We'll sune hae neither staig nor stot.

It is equally good in passages where the poet simply expresses his
hearty delight in something which his own eyes have seen among his
neighbours, as in:

He had horse and harness for them all,
Goodly steeds were all milke-white:
O the golden bands an about their necks,
And their weapons, they were all alike . . .

And, by the way, do not touches like these often reveal the stamp of
individuals upon pieces which are loosely said to have been " composed
by the folk"? They quite do away with the notion that ballads were
composed by a number of people, after the fashion of a story in the
game of "Consequences." In fact, it is one of the pleasures of reading
ballads to watch for those things which show us the heart of one man
who stands out by himself. Such a one was the man who said:

"I dreamt I pu'd the heather green
Wi' my true love on Yarrow."

And who was that unhappy one who served a king for seven years
and only once saw the king's daughter, and that was through a gimlet-
hole? Two were putting on her gown, two putting on her shoes, five
were combing down her hair:

Her neck and breast was like the snow –
Then from the bore I was forced to go.

Was he the man who made it a common thing to speak in ballads of
" combing her yellow hair"?

What a poet, too, was he who put that touch into "Bewick and
Grahame," where the father throws down his glove as a challenge to his
son and the son stoops to pick it up, and says:

"O father, put on your glove again,
The wind hath blown it from your hand."

It is one of the most delicate things, and with it the stanza in the same ballad where the father praises the son for his victory over a friend, but the son, hating the battle which would not have been fought if the fathers had not quarrelled in their wine, says:

"Father, could ye not drink your wine at home
And letten me and my brother be?"

And the mind of a poet is to be seen in the whole of some ballads and in every detail, as for example in the three perfect verses:

O lang, lang may their ladies sit
Wi' their fans into their hand,
Or ere they see Sir Patrick Spens
Come sailing to the land.

O lang, lang may the ladies stand,
Wi' their gold combs in their hair,
Wailing for their ain dear lords,
For they'll see them na mair.

Half-owre, half-owre to Aberdour,
It's fiftie fadom deep,
And there lies guid Sir Patrick Spens,
Wi' the Scots lords at his feet.

This ballad is one peculiar to our island, and no one can seriously deny that some one of its authors was one of the greatest writers of narrative poetry that ever lived.

FIFTEEN

An Outcast

NOT FAR FROM "The White Horse" is a little town upon a stream that waves myriads of reeds and tall purple flowers of hemp agrimony. These are the last shops I am likely to pass in Wiltshire, and it occurs to me that I should like to taste lardy cakes – which I last bought in Wroughton fifteen years ago – before I leave the county. Richard Jefferies' grandfather was "My Lord Lardy Cake" in old Swindon sixty years ago, and his memory is kept alive by those tough, sweet slabs of larded pastry which, in his generous ovens, gathered all the best essences of the other cakes, pies, tarts, and joints which were permitted to be baked with them. In "Amaryllis at the Fair" they are mentioned with some indignity as a ploughboy's delicacy. My lips water for them, and at the first bakery in — I ask for some. The baker tells me he has sold the last one. He is a small, white-haired and white-bearded man with an expression of unctuous repose, assuredly a pillar of his chapel and possibly its treasurer, and though he himself will, by his own telling, have no more lardy cakes until the next morning, he stiffly tries to persuade me that none of his fellow-townsmen bakes them. I disbelieve the man of dough for all his conscious look of sagacity and virtue, and am rewarded for my disbelief by four lardy cakes for threepence-halfpenny not many yards from his accursed threshold. Lardy cakes, I now discover for the first time, have this merit besides their excellent taste and provision of much pleasant but not finical labour for the teeth, that one is enough at a time, and that four will, therefore, take a man quite a long way upon the roads of England.

At the next inn three labourers and the landlord are heated in conversation about some one not present.

"Quite right," says one, a sober carter whose whip leans against the counter, "'tis the third time this week that a tramp has been to his door, and by the looks of them they didn't call for naught."

"One of them didn't, I know," says the landlord. "He came in here once and asked for a job and left without a drink, but after he'd been to Stegbert's Cottage he came straight here and ordered a pint of mild. And I heard as he let a chap and a woman sleep two nights running in that rough patch behind the house. Don't you think the parson ought to hear of that? And what does he do for a living? He looks poor enough himself."

"I don't know. Mr. Jones is a kind-hearted fellow. He stopped my youngest in the street the other day and gave her a penny and measured her hair, and told her she'd have a yard of it some day. They tell me he hasn't a carpet on the floor anywhere, and no parlour, and not even a chest of drawers; and the postman says he hasn't a watch or a clock. What does he do with himself?"

"I reckon he's mad," says the third, chuckling, "and I don't mind if he is. My old dog doesn't need feeding at home since he's been here. He doesn't eat no meat himself neither. The widow Nash was reckoning it up, and she says he spends four shillings a week —"

"And a shilling here regular," interjects the landlord.

"On groceries, including one-and-six for tobacco. He has four loaves, and I know 'Kruger' must have more than half of them."

"And every other week he buys a postal order for two shillings and a penny stamp – "

"Pint of mild, mister," says a tall blear-eyed man who comes in, meekly followed by a small woman, dusty and in rags but neat, to whom he offers the tankard after nearly draining it himself.

"Nice weather," he ventures, smacking his lips.

"Yes," says the landlord discouragingly, and the carter leaves.

"Everybody seems to be gone to the flower show," continues the intruder, "and that's where I'm going" (here he looks at his boots), "but the best way for sore feet is three days in a tap-room in some good sawdust."

The wife sighs.

"The fat woman that weighs twenty-three stone," says her husband to the company, "is a cousin of mine twice removed, and I have done a bit in the show line myself. It's a rum business. Better than working in a brewery stables, though. Me and my mate had to go because we got up so early that we burnt too many candles."

The mention of the fat woman rouses the labourers, and one says:

"They say them fat women eats hardly anything at all."

"Very small eater is Daisy. But you see her food does her good. None of it's wasted."

"That's it. Her food agrees with her."

The wife sighs.

"Now there's my missus here," says the husband. "She was one of these pretty gallus dancing-girls who get their fifteen shillings a week. Her food don't nourish her. Now my brother used to laugh in publics for a pint and he would laugh till they gave him a pint to stop."

"Oh, I can laugh *after* a pint," says the wife, "but then I could just as easy cry, I worries so. There's many a aching heart goes up and down that Great Western Railway in the express trains."

"I never worries, missus," says a labourer with pursy mouth, short pipe, and head straight up behind from his neck.

"Quite right," says the husband. "My old girl here lives on the fat of the land and is always thin. Her food don't nourish her. There's more harm done in the world by a discontented gut than anything else. I think of asking her to try living on her pipe by itself."

"Like Mr. Jones over there," says one of the labourers.

"Mr. Jones? What, my friend Mr. William Jones?" asks the tall man.

"Is he a friend of yours?" asks the landlord, curiosity overpowering his natural caution with a man who is selling spectacles at a shilling a pair.

"He is, and I don't mind letting any one know it. I'm very glad to see him settled down. He's the only one along the road who hasn't gone to the flower show to-day." Here the tall man calls for another tankard, which, as he is doing all the talking, he does not pass to the small neat

woman behind him. Pleased to be civilly used, and warmed by the
liquor, he tells the story of his friend, the little woman helping him out,
and landlord and labourers adding some touches; and Mr. Jones himself
completed the picture during my few days in the village.

The man who fed his neighbour's dog, and sent the beggar satisfied
away, and made presents to the children, and lived on six ounces of
tobacco a week, is a native of Zennor in Cornwall. "Wonderful place
for pedlars is Cornwall. The towns are so few and far between that the
people along the road aren't used to pedlars, and when you do call you
are sure of the best of treatment." He was apprenticed to a shoemaker
in a town in South Devon, and for a time practised his trade there as an
assistant. He was very clever at boxing and wrestling, and a hard fighter,
too, though unwilling to make a quarrel. But he was a queer youth and
took violent likes and dislikes to men, and one day he dropped a boot
and went out into the street and took a young gentleman by the arm
and said to him: "Excuse me, sir, you have passed this shop for five
years nearly every day and I can't stand it any longer." Whereupon he
gave that young gentleman a beating. He was sent to prison; he lost his
employment and went to sea. And at sea or else in foreign countries he
stayed six years. He left the sea only because he broke an arm which
had at length to be amputated above the elbow. He was a changed man
and many thought then that he was mad. When he left the hospital it
was December and bitter weather: he had only five shillings and it was
notorious how he spent it. Every day for a week he bought three loaves
of bread and went out and fed the birds with them. When that week
was over he had to go into the workhouse, and there he stayed until
the spring. It was there that he fell in with the tall man who helped to
tell his tale. They left together and for some time he almost kept the
two by begging, his lack of an arm ensuring his success. But he was not
altogether to his companion's taste, nevertheless. He would stop and
smoke a pipe and admire the view when he was miles from anywhere
and their object was to reach a town and find enough money to pay for
lodgings. He would stand by a hedge, content for an hour to disentangle
the bryony strands that were in danger of straying to the road, and to

restore them to the hazel and thorn where their fellows ramped. He was willing to be foster-father to half the helpless fledglings that he found on the roadside. Sleeping one night in a barn he could not be persuaded to leave until he had decided whether it was better to kill a spider who had a great appetite for flies or to leave it to Fate. Several he rescued from the web and then out of pity for the spider brought it flies already dead; but finding that these were not to its taste he left the difficulty unsolved and went sadly on his way. Almost equal to his pitifulness was his dislike of work and his moral cowardice. Nothing could persuade him to do any work, and such a coward was he that if he failed at the first house where he offered his laces for sale he would not try again in that village or town. Yet he did not scruple to steal – even with a hint of physical violence – if he needed anything which chance presented to him in another man's possession: but he stole only necessaries, having none of the acquisitiveness which is more common to their victims than, in thieves. Few men use leisure as well as he; perhaps no man was ever idle with less harm to his fellows. The rich could have learned many lessons at his feet: they must always be shooting or driving furiously or meddling with politics or stopping footpaths; they cannot be kept out of harm, however rich. How well this man would have employed money: he would have given it away.'

By and by his pity for goaded cattle and his frequent gazings into their brown eyes as they stared at him by a stile still further reduced his necessities – he would touch no meat; so that his companion, finding him no longer of much use in spite of his possession of but one arm, left him and only crossed his path at increasing intervals of time. It was now that Jones remembered with horror a scene which had slumbered in his mind with the fear which it originally roused in youth. He and other boys were in the habit of peeping through a hole in the wall of a slaughter-house and watching the slaughter, the skinning and the cutting up, until their ears became familiar with the groans, the screams, the gurglings, the squelchings in the half-darkness of candle light, the blood and white faces and the knife. But one day there was led into the slaughter-house a white heifer fresh from the May pasture, clean and bright from her

The white heifer

gleaming rosy hoofs to the tips of the horns that swayed as she walked. Her breath made, as it were, a sacred space about her as the light of a human face will do. She stood quiet but uncertain and musingly in the dark, soaked, half-ruinous place, into which light only came in bars through a cob-webbed lattice and fell that day upon her white face, leaving in darkness the tall butcher and the imbecile assistant who held the rope by which the animal's head was drawn down to the right level for a blow. The men were in no hurry and as the heifer was not restive they finished their talk about Home Rule. Then the idiot tried to put her into the right position, but for a time could not get her to see that her head must be drawn tight and somewhat askew against the oaken pillar. He only succeeded by patting her flanks and saying gently as if to a girl: " Come along, Daisy!" She lowed soft and bowed her head; the blow fell; she rolled to the ground and the butcher once more let loose the heavy scent of blood.

The wholesome pretty beast, the familiar "Come along, Daisy!" and the blow and the scent came often into Jones's mind. He ate no meat, but made no attempt to proselytize; he simply retreated deeper and deeper into his childlike love of Nature. The birds and the flowers and the creeping and running things he seemed to regard as little happy, charming, undeveloped human beings, looking down on them with infinite tenderness and a little amusement; with them alone was he quite at home. Nature, as she presented herself to his simple senses, was but a fragrant, many-coloured, exuberant, chiefly joyous community, with which most men were not in harmony. Silent for days and thinking only "green thoughts" under the branches of the wood, he came to demand, unconsciously, that there should be such a harmony. But he loved Nature also because she had no ambiguity, told no lies, uttered no irony. Sitting among flowers by running water he wore an expression of blessed satisfaction with his company which is not often seen at the friendliest table. He drew no philosophy from Nature, no opinions, ideas, proposals for reform, but only the wisdom to live, happily and healthily and simply, himself.

I dare say modernity was in his blood, but no man seemed to belong less to our time. Of history and science he knew nothing, of literature nothing; he had to make out the earth with his own eyes and heart. He had not words for it, but he felt that whatever he touched was God. No myth or religion had any value to him. There were no symbols for him to use. The deities he surmised or smelt or tasted in the air or upon the earth had neither name nor shape. Had he been able to think, he was the man to put our generation on the way to a new mythology. For all I know, he had the vision, the power of the seer, without the power of the prophet. A little more and perhaps he would have invaded Christendom as St. Paul invaded Heathendom. Yet I think he was not wholly the loser by being unable to think. The eye untroubled by thought sees things like a mirror newly burnished; at night, for example, the musing can see nothing before him but a mist, but if he stops thinking quickly the roads, the walls, the trees become visible. So this man saw with a clearness as of Angelico, and in his memory violets and roses, trees and faces were as clear as if within his brain were another sun to light them. He had but to close his eyes to see these things, an innumerable procession of days and their flowers and their birds in the sky or on the bough. And this he had at no cost. He employed only such labour as was needed to make his bread and occasionally clothes and a pipe. Nor did he merely ask alms of Nature and Civilization. He paid back countless charities to flower and bird and child and poorer men, and there was nothing against him of pain or sorrow or death inflicted. And as he was without religion so he was without patriotism. He had no country, knew nothing of men and events. Asked by a person who saw him idle and did not observe his defect, whether he would not like to do something for his country, he replied: "I have no country like you, sir. I own nothing; my people never did, that I know. I admire those that do, for I have been in many a country when I was a sailor, but never a one to beat England, let alone the West Country when it's haymaking time."

He continued to beg with a free conscience, and was always willing to give away all that he had to one in more need. And now chance found him out and gave him ten shillings a week. He rented a cottage in this village, weeded his flower-borders, but let his vegetable-plots turn into poppy-beds. Sometimes he wearied of his monotonous meals; he would then fast for a day or two, giving his food to the birds and mice, until his hearty appetite returned . . .

He did not stay long in the village. He was shy and suspicious of men, and except by the younger children he was not liked. He set out on his travels again, and is still on the road or – unlike most tramps – on the paths and green lanes, the simplest, kindest, and perhaps the wisest of men, indifferent to mobs, to laws, to all of us who are led aside, scattered and confused by hollow goods, one whom the last day of his full life will not find in a whirlpool of affairs, but ready to go – an outcast.

SIXTEEN

The End of Summer

THE ROAD mounts the low Downs again. The boundless stubble is streaked by long bands of purple-brown, the work of seven ploughs to which the teams and their carters, riding or walking, are now slowly descending by different ways over the slopes and jingling in the rain. Above is a Druid moor bounded by beech-clumps, and crossed by old sunken ways and broad grassy tracks. It is a land of moles and sheep. At the end of a shattered line of firs a shepherd leans, bunched under his cape of sacking, to watch his black-faced flock dull-tinkling in the short furze and among the tumuli under the constant white rain. Those old roads, being over hilly and open land, are as they were before the making of modern roads, and little changed from what they were before the Roman. But it is a pity to see some of the old roads that have been left to the sole protection of the little gods. One man is stronger than they, as may be known by any one who has seen the bones, crockery, tin and paper thrown by Shere and Cocking into the old roads near-by as into a dust-bin; or seen the gashes in the young trees planted down Gorst Road, Wandsworth Common; or the saucy "Private" at the entrance to a lane worn by a hundred generations through the sand a little north of Petersfield; or the barbed wire fastened into the living trees alongside the footpath over a neighbouring hill that has lately been sold. What is the value of every one's right to use a footpath if a single anti-social exclusive landowning citizen has the right to make it intolerable except to such as consider it a place only for the soles of the feet? The builder of a house acquires the right to admit the sunlight through his window. Cannot the users of a footpath acquire a right, during the course of half-a-dozen dynasties or less, to the sight of the trees and the sky which that footpath gives them in its own separate way? At least I hope that footpaths will soon cease to be defined as a line – length without breadth

– connecting one point with another. In days when they are used as
much for the sake of the scenes historic or beautiful through which they
pass as of the villages or houses on this hand or that, something more
than the mere right to tread upon a certain ribbon of grass or mud will
have to be preserved if the preservation is to be of much use, and the
right of way must become the right of view and of very ancient lights
as well. By enforcing these rights some of the mountains of the land
might even yet be saved, as Mr. Henry S. Salt wishes to save them (see
his valuable *On Cambrian and Cumbrian Hills*). In the meantime it is to be
hoped that his criticisms will not be ignored by the tourists who leave
the Needle Gully a cascade of luncheon wrappings and the like; for it is
not from a body of men capable of such manners that a really effective
appeal against the sacrifice of "our mountains" to commercial and other
selfishness is like to spring.

And those lone wayside greens, no man's gardens, measuring a few
feet wide but many miles in length – why should they be used either as
receptacles for the dust of motor-cars or as additions to the property
of the landowner who happens to be renewing his fence? They used to
be as beautiful and cool and fresh as rivers, these green sisters of the
white roads – illuminated borders of many a weary tale. But now, lest
there should be no room for the dust, they are turning away from them
the gipsies who used to camp there for a night. The indolent District
Council that is anxious to get rid of its difficulties – for the moment – at
the expense of a neighbouring district – it cares not – will send out its
policeman to drive away the weary horses and sleeping children from
the acre of common land which had hitherto been sacred – to what? –
to an altar, a statue, a fountain, a seat? – No! to a stately notice-board;
half a century ago the common of which this is a useless patch passed
on easy terms to the pheasant lords. The gipsies have to go. Give them a
pitch for the night and you are regarded as an enemy of the community
or perhaps even as a Socialist. The gipsies shall be driven from parish
to parish, and finally settle down as squalid degenerate nomads in a
town where they lose what beauty and courage they had, in adding
to the difficulties of another council. Yet if they were in a cage or a

compound which it cost money to see, hundreds would pay for a stare at their brown faces and bright eyes, their hooped tents, their horses, their carelessness of the crowd, and in a few years an imitation of these things will be applauded in a "pageant" of the town which has destroyed the reality.

The grassy way ends with the moor at a pool beside a road, on one side of it six thatched cottages fenced by sycamore and ash and elm, on the other a grey farm and immense brown barn, within a long wall roofed with mossy thatch; and the swallows fly low and slowly about the trees.

First beeches line the rising and descending road – past a church whose ivied tombstones commemorate men of Cornish name – as far as an inn and a sycamore nobly balanced upon a pedestal of matted roots. Then there are ash trees on either side and ricks of straw wetted to an orange hue, and beyond them the open cornland, and rising out of it an all-day-long procession in the south, the great company of the Downs again, some tipped with wood, some bare; in the north, a broken chain of woods upon low but undulating land seem the vertebra; of a forest of old time stretching from east to west like the Downs. Hither and thither the drunken pewits cry over the furrows, and thousands of rooks and daws wheel over the stubble. As the day grows old it grows sweet and golden and the rain ceases, and the beauty of the Downs in the humid clearness does not long allow the eyes to wander away from them. At first, when the sun breaks through, all silver bright and acclaimed by miles of clouds in his own livery, the Downs below are violet, and have no form except where they carve the sky with their long arches. It is the woods northward that are chiefly glorified by the light and warmth, and the glades penetrating them and the shining stubble and the hedges, and the flying wood-pigeons and the cows of richest brown and milky white; the road also gleams blue and wet. But as the sun descends the light falls on the Downs out of a bright cave in the gloomy forest of sky, and their flanks are olive and their outlines intensely clear. From one summit to another runs a string of trees like cavalry connecting one beech clump with another, so that they seem actually to be moving and adding themselves to the clumps. Above all is the abstract beauty of pure line – coupled with the beauty of the serene and the uninhabited and remote – that holds the eye until at length the hills are humbled and dispread as part of the ceremony of sunset in a tranquil, ensanguined, quietly travelling sky. The blue swallows go slowly along the silent road beside me, and the last rays bless a grooved common grazed upon by cows and surrounded by ranges of low white buildings and a row of lichened grotesque limes, dark of bole, golden-leaved, where children are playing and an anvil rings.

Frost follows after the blue silence and chill of twilight, and the dawn is dimmest violet in a haze that reveals the candied grass, the soaking blue dark elms painted yellow only in one place, the red roofs, all in a world of the unborn, and the waters steaming around invisible crying coots. Gradually round white clouds – so dim that the sky seems but to dream of round white clouds – appear imbedded in the haze; the beams grow hot, and a breeze joins with them in sucking and scattering all the sweet of the first fallen leaves, the weed fires and the late honeysuckle.

Why are there no swifts to race and scream? We fret over these stages of the descending year; we dream on such a day as this that there is no need of farther descent. We would preserve those days of the reaping; we have lost them; but we recall them now when the steam plough has furrowed the sheeny stubble, and long for the day when the gentle north wind can only just stir the clusters of aspen leaves, and the branches are motionless. The nut bushes hang dreamily, heavily, over the white cool roads. The wood-pigeon's is the sole voice in the oak woods of the low hills, except that once or twice a swift screams as he pursues that martial flight of his – as of one who swings a sword as he goes – towards the beeches and hop gardens of the higher hills in the north; it is perhaps the last day for more than eight months that his cry will be heard. A few barley-straws hang from the hazels; some leaves are yellow. Autumn, in fact, seems possible to the mind that is not perfectly content with these calm sweet airs and the sense of the fullness of things.

At a crossing a small island is made amidst this and three other roads, and on the island stands an oast house with two mellow cones and white leaning cowls; and beside it a simple tiled cart-lodge, dimly displaying massive wheels, curving bulwarks of wagons and straight shafts behind its doorless pillars of rough-hewn wood. Making one group with these, though separated from them by one road, is an old red farm-house, of barely distinguishable timber and brick, with white-edged dormers and lower windows and doors, entrenched behind hollyhocks of deepest red and the burning disks of everlasting sunflowers. Behind the gates stand four haystacks brightly thatched, and one that is dark and old and carved into huge stairs.

Notice the gate into the rickyard. It is of the usual five oak bars; and across these is a diagonal bar from the lowest end nearest the hinge to the upper end of the opposite side, and from top to bottom a perpendicular cross-bar divides the gate. The top bar marks it as no common gate made at a factory with a hundred others of the same kind, though there are scores of them in Kent. It thickens gradually towards the hinge end of the gate, and then much more decidedly so that it resembles a gun-barrel and stock; and just where the stock begins it is carved with something like a trigger-guard; the whole being well proportioned, graceful but strong. In all the best gates of Kent, Sussex and Surrey and the South Country there is an approach to this form, usually without the trigger-guard, but sometimes having instead a much more elaborate variation of it which takes away from the dignity and simplicity of the gate. At the road's edge crooked quince trees lean over a green pond and green but nearly yellow straight reeds; and four cart-horses, three sorrels and a grey, are grouped under one stately walnut.

These things mingle their power with that of the silence and the wooded distance under the blue and rosy west. The slow dying of a train's roar beats upon the shores of the silence and the distance, and is swallowed up in them like foam in sand, and adds one more trophy to the glory of the twilight.

Night passes, and the white dawn is poured out over the dew from the fold in low clouds of infinitely modulated grey. Autumn is clearly hiding somewhere in the long warm alleys under the green and gold of the hops. The very colours of the oast houses seem to wait for certain harmonies with oaks in the meadows and beeches in the steep woods. The songs, too, are those of the drowsy yellow-hammer, of the robin moodily brooding in orchards yellow spotted and streaked, of the unseen wandering willow-wren singing sweetly but in a broken voice of a matter now forgotten, of the melancholy twit of the single bullfinch as he flies. The sudden lyric of the wren can stir no corresponding energy in the land which is bowed, still, comfortable, like a deep-uddered cow fastened to the milking-stall and munching grains. Soon will the milk and honey flow. The reaping-machine whirrs; the wheelwrights have mended the wagons' wheels and patched their sides; they stand outside their lodges.

There is a quarter of a sloping wheat-field reaped; the shocks stand out above the silvery stubble in the evening like rocks out of a moonlight sea. The unreaped corn is like a tawny coast; and all is calm, with the quiet of evening heavens fallen over the earth. This beauty of the ripe Demeter standing in the August land is incomparable. It reminds one of the poet who said that he had seen a maid who looked like a fountain on a green lawn when the south wind blows in June; and one whose smile was as memorable as the new moon in the first still mild evening of the year, when it is seen for a moment only over the dark hills; and one whose walking was more kindling to the blood than good ale by a winter fire on an endless evening among friends; but that now he has met another, and when he is with her or thinks of her he becomes as one that is blind and deaf to all other things.

But a few days and the bryony leaves are palest yellow in the hedge. Rooks are innumerable about the land, but their cawing, like all other sounds, like all the early bronze and rose and gold of the leaves, is muffled by the mist which endures right through the afternoon; and all day falls the gentle rain. In the hillside hop-garden two long lines of women and children, red and white and black, are destroying the golden green of the hops, and they are like two caterpillars destroying a leaf. Pleasant it is now to see the white smoke from the oast house pouring solidly like curving plumes into the still rain, and to smell the smell, bitter and never to be too much sniffed and enjoyed, that travels wide over the fields.

For the hop-drier has lit his two fires of Welsh coal and brimstone and charcoal under the two cones of the oast house, and has spread his couch of straw on the floor where he can sleep his many little sleeps in the busy day and night. The oast house consists of the pair of cones, white-vaned and tiled, upon their two circular chambers in which the fires are lit. Attached to these on one side is a brick building of two large rooms, one upon the ground, where the hop-drier sleeps and tends his fires, lighted only by doors at either side and divided by the wooden pillars which support the floor of the upper room. This, the oast chamber, reached by a ladder, is a beautiful room, its oak boards polished by careful use and now stained faintly by the green-gold of hops, its roof raftered and high and dim. Light falls upon it on one side from two low windows, on the opposite side from a door through which the hops arrive from the garden. The wagon waits below the door, full of the loose, stained hop-sacks which the carter and his boy lift up to the drier. From the floor two short ladders lead to the doors in the cones where the hops are suspended on canvas floors above the kilns. The inside of the cone is full of coiling fumes which have killed the young swallows in the nests under the cowl – the parents return again and again, but dare no longer alight on their old perches on the vanes. When dried, the hops are poured out on the floor of the vast chamber in a lisping scaly pile, and the drier is continually sweeping back those which are scattered. Through a hole in the floor he forces them down into a sack reaching to the floor of the room below. He is hard at work making these sacks or "pokes," which, when full and their necks stitched up, are as hard as wood. Before the drying is over the full sacks will take up half the room. The children tired of picking come to admire and to visit all the corners of the room; of the granary alongside and its old sheepbells, its traps, a crossbow and the like; of the farmyard and barns, sacred except at this time. For a few minutes the sun is visible as a shapeless crimson thing above the mist and behind the elms. It is twilight; the wheels and hoofs of the last wagon approach and arrive and die away. And so day after day the fires glow with ruby and sapphire and emerald; the cone wears its plume of smoke; and everything is yellow-green – the very scent of the drying hops can hardly be otherwise described, in its mixture of sharpness and mellowness. Then, when the last sack is pressed, benches are placed round the chamber and a table at one end. The master, who is giving up the farm, leans on the table and pays each picker and pole-puller and measurer, with a special word for each and a jest for the women. Ale and gin and cakes are brought in, and the farmer leaves the women and one or two older men to eat and drink. The women in their shabby black skirts and whitish blouses shuffle through a dance or two, all modern and some American. One old man tipsily tottering recalls the olden time with a step-dance down the room; some laugh at him, others turn up their now roseate noses. Next year the hops are to be grubbed up; the old man to be turned out of his cottage – for he has paid no rent these seven years; but now it is cakes and ale, and the farmer has hiccupped a lying promise that his successor will go on growing hops.

HAMPSHIRE

To-day is fair day. The scene is a green, slightly undulating common, grassy and rushy at its lower end where a large pond wets the margin of the high road, and at the upper end sprinkled with the dwarf and the common gorse out of which rise many tumuli, green or furzy mounds of earth, often surmounted by a few funereal pines. The common is small; it is bounded on every side by roads, and on one by a row of new mean houses; there is a golf-house among the tumuli; in one place a large square has been ploughed and fenced by a private owner. But the slope of the sandy soil is pleasant; in one place it is broken into a low cliff overhanging the water, and this with the presence of the gorse give it a touch of the wildness by which it may still deserve its name of "heath." Most powerful of all in their effects upon the place are the tumuli. They are low and smooth; one or two scarcely heave the turf; some have been removed; and there is no legend attached to them. Yet their presence gives an indescribable charm and state, and melancholy too, and makes these few acres an expanse unequalled by any other of the same size. Not too far off to be said to belong to the heath, from which they are separated by three miles of cultivated land and lesser beechen hill, are the Downs; among them one that bears a thin white road winding up at the edge of a dark wood. In the moist October air the Downs are very grave and gentle and near, and are not lost to sight until far beyond the turreted promontory of Chanctonbury.

Early in the morning the beggars begin to arrive, the lame and the blind, with or without a musical instrument. King of them all certainly is he with no legs at all and seeming not to need them, so active is he on a four-wheeled plank which suspends him only a foot above the ground. Many a strong man earns less money. The children envy him as he moves along, a wheeled animal, weather-beaten, white-haired, white-bearded, with neat black hat and white slop, a living toy, but with a deep voice, a concertina and a tin full of pence and halfpence.

These unashamed curiosities line the chief approaches down which every one is going to the fair except a few shabby fellows who offer blue sheets full of music-hall ballads to the multitude and, with a whisper, indecent songs to the select. Another not less energetic, but stout and condescending, yellow-bearded, in a high hard felt hat, gives away tracts. The sound of a hymn from one organ mingles with the sound of "Put me among the girls" from another and the rattle of the legless man's offertory tin.

The main part of the fair consists of a double row, a grove, of tents and booths, roundabouts, caravans, traps and tethered ponies. A crowd of dark-clad women goes up and down between the rows; there is a sound of machine-made music, of firing at targets, of shouts and neighs and brays and the hoot of engines. Here at the entrance to the grove is a group of yellow vans; some children playing among the shafts and wheels and musing horses; and a gipsy woman on a stool, her head on one side, combing her black hair and talking to the children, while a puppy catches at the end of her tresses when they come swishing down. Beyond are coconut-shies, short-sighted cyclists performing, Aunt Sallies, rows of goldfish bowls into which a light ball has to be pitched to earn a prize, stalls full of toys, cheap jewellery and sweets like bedded-out plants, and stout women pattering alongside – bold women, with sleek black or yellow hair and the bearing and countenance of women who have to make their way in the world. Behind these, women are finishing their toilet and their children's among the vans, preparing meals over red crackling fires, and the horses rest their noses on the stalls and watch the crowd; the long yellow dogs are curled up among the wheels or nosing in the crowd.

There are men selling purses containing a sovereign for sixpence, loud, fat cosmopolitans on a cockney basis with a ceaseless flow of cajolery intermingled with sly indecency; the country policeman in the background puzzling over his duty in the matter, but in the end paralyzed by the showmen's gift of words. One man has before him a counter on which he asks you to cover a red-painted disk with five smaller disks of zinc, charging twopence for the attempt and promising a watch to the great man who succeeds. After a batch of failures, he himself, with a good-natured but bored face, shows how easily it is done, and raising his eyes in despair craves for more courage from the audience. The crowd looks on, hesitating, until he singles out the most bashful countryman at the back of the throng, saying: "I like your face. You are a good sort. You have a cheerful face; it's the rich have the sad faces. So I'll treat you to a go." The hero steps forward and succeeds, but as it was a free trial he receives no watch; trying again for twopence he fails. Another tries: "By Jove! that was a near one." A woman tries, and just as she is finishing, "You're a cute one, missus," he ejaculates, and she fails. Another tries, and the showman has a watch ready to hand over, and only at the last moment says excitedly (restoring the watch quietly to its place): "I thought you'd got it that time . . . Come along! It's the best game in the world." Once more he repeats the trick himself without looking, and then exclaims as he sweeps the disks together: "It's a silly game, I call it!" He is like the preachers who show the stupid world how virtue is won: he has a large audience, a large paunch, and many go away disappointed. The crowd stares, and has the one deep satisfaction of believing that the woman who travels with him is not his wife.

At the upper end of the grove is the gaudy green and gold and scarlet-painted and embossed entrance to the bioscope, raised a few feet above the crowd. On the platform before the door stand two painted men and a girl. The girl has a large nose, loose mouth and a ready, but uneasy, discontented smile as if she knows that her paint is an imperfect refuge from the gaze of the crowd; as if she knows that her eyes are badly darkened, and her white stockings soiled, and her legs too thin under her short skirt, and her yellow hair too stiff. She lounges wearily with a glib clown who wears a bristly fringe of sandy hair round his face, which tickles her and causes roars of laughter when he aims at a kiss. The other performer is a contortionist, a small slender man in dirty, ill-fitting scarlet jacket with many small brass buttons, dirty brown trousers criss-crossed by yellow stripes; his hands in his pockets; his snub nose deep pink, and his lean face made yet leaner and more dismal by a thin streak of red paint on either cheek. His melancholy seems natural, yet adds to his vulgarity because he forsakes it so quickly when he smirks and turns away if the girl exposes her legs too much. For she turns a somersault with the clown at intervals; or doubles herself back to touch the ground first with her yellow hair and at last with her head; or is lifted up by the clown and, supported on the palm of one of his hands, hangs dangling in a limp bow, her face yet gaunter and sadder upside down with senseless eyes and helpless legs. The crowd watch – looking sideways at one another to get their cue – some with unconscious smiles entranced, but most of them grimly controlling the emotions roused by the girl or the contortionist or the clown and the thought of their unstable life. A few squirt water languidly or toss confetti. Others look from time to time to see whether any one in the county dare, in broad daylight, enter the booth for "gentlemen only," at the door of which stands a shabby gaudy woman of forty-five grinning contemptuously.

Up and down moves the crowd – stiffly dressed children carrying gay toys or bowls of goldfish or coconuts – gipsy children with scarves, blue or green or red – lean, tanned, rough-necked labourers caged in the best clothes, except one, a labourer of well past middle age, a tall straight man with a proud grizzled head, good black hat of soft felt low in the crown, white scarf, white jacket, dark-brown corduroys above gleaming black boots.

On the open heath behind the stalls they are selling horses by auction. Enormous cart-horses plunge out of the groups of men and animals and carry a little man suspended from their necks; stout men in grey gaiters and black hats hobble after. Or more decorously the animals are trotted up and down between rows of men away from the auctioneer and back again, their price in guineas mingling with the statement that they are real workers, while a small boy hustles them with whip and shout from behind, and a big stiff man leads them and, to turn them at the end of the run, shoves his broad back into their withers. The Irish dealers traffic apart and try to sell without auction. Their horses and ponies, braided with primrose and scarlet, stand in a quiet row. Suddenly a boy leads out one on a halter, a hard, plump, small-headed beast bucking madly, and makes it circle rapidly about him, stopping it abruptly and starting it again, with a stiff pink flag which he flaps in its face or pokes into its ribs; if the beast refuses he raises a high loud "whoo-hoop" and curses or growls like an animal. For perhaps five minutes this goes on, the boy never abating his oaths and growls and whoops and flirtings of the pink flag. The horse is led back; a muttering calm follows; another horse is led out. Here and there are groups of cart-mares with huge pedestalled feet and their colts, or of men bending forward over long ash sticks and talking in low tones. Horses race or walk or are backed into the crowd. Droves of bullocks are driven through the furze. Rows of bulls, sweating but silent and quiet, bow their heads and wait as on a frieze. Again the pink flags are flourished, and the dealer catches a horsy stranger by the arm and whispers and shows him the mare's teeth. This dealer is a big Irishman with flattened face and snaky nose, his voice deep and laughing. He smiles continually, but when he sees a possible buyer he puts on an artful expression so transparent that his merry face shines clearly underneath and remains the same in triumph or rebuke – is the same at the end of the day when he leads off his horses, and stopping at a wayside inn drinks on the kerb, but first gives the one nearest him a gulp from the tankard.

All night – for a week – it rains, and at last there is a still morning of mist.

A fire of weeds and hedge-clippings in a little flat field is smouldering. The ashes are crimson, and the bluish-white smoke flows in a divine cloudy garment round the boy who rakes over the ashes. The heat is great, and the boy, straight and well made, wearing close gaiters of leather that reach above the knees, is languid at his task, and often leans upon his rake to watch the smoke coiling away from him like a monster reluctantly fettered, and sometimes bursting into an anger of sprinkled sparks. He adds some wet hay, and the smoke pours out of it like milky fleeces when the shearer reveals the inmost wool with his shears. Above and beyond him the pale blue sky is dimly white-clouded over beech woods, whose many greens and yellows and yellow-greens are softly touched by the early light which cannot penetrate to the blue caverns of shade underneath. Athwart the woods rises a fount of cottage-smoke from among mellow and dim roofs. Under the smoke and partly scarfed at times by a drift from it is the yellow of sunflower and dahlia, the white of anemone, the tenderest green and palest purple of a thick cluster of autumn crocuses that have broken out of the dark earth and stand surprised, amidst their own weak light as of the underworld from which they have come. Robins sing among the fallen apples, and the cooing of wood-pigeons is attuned to the soft light and the colours of the bowers. The yellow apples gleam. It is the gleam of melting frost. Under all the dulcet warmth of the face of things lurks the bitter spirit of the cold. Stand still for more than a few moments and the cold creeps with a warning, and then a menace into the breast. That is the bitterness that makes this morning of all others in the year so mournful in its beauty. The colour and the grace invite to still contemplation and long draughts of dream; the frost compels to motion. The scent is that of wood-smoke, of fruit and of some fallen leaves. This is the beginning of the pageant of autumn, of that gradual pompous dying which has no parallel in human life, yet draws us to it with sure bonds. It is a dying of the flesh, and we see it pass through a kind of beauty which we can only call spiritual, of so high and inaccessible a strangeness is it. The sight of such perfection as is many times achieved before the end awakens the never more than lightly sleeping human desire of permanence. Now, now is the hour;

let things be thus; thus for ever; there is nothing further to be thought
of; let these remain. And yet we have a premonition that remain they
must not for more than a little while. The motion of the autumn is a
fall, a surrender, requiring no effort, and therefore the mind cannot long
be blind to the cycle of things as in the spring it can when the effort
and delight of ascension veils the goal and the decline beyond. A few
frosts now, a storm of wind and rain, a few brooding mists, and the
woods that lately hung dark and massive and strong upon the steep hills
are transfigured and have become cloudily light and full of change and
ghostly fair; the crowing of a cock in the still misty morning echoes up
in the many-coloured trees like a challenge to the spirits of them to come
out and be seen, but in vain. For months the woods have been homely
and kind, companions and backgrounds to our actions and thoughts,
the wide walls of a mansion utterly our own. We could have gone on
living with them for ever. We had given up the ardours, the extreme
ecstasy of our first bridal affection, but we had not forgotten them. We
could not become indifferent to the Spanish chestnut trees that grow at
the top of the steep rocky banks on either side of the road and mingle
their foliage overhead. Of all trees well-grown chestnuts are among the
most pleasant to look up at. For the foliage is not dense and it is for the
most part close to the large boughs, so that the light comes easily down
through all the horizontal leaves, and the shape of each separate one is
not lost in the multitude, while at the same time the bold twists of the
branches are undraped or easily seen through such translucent green.
The trunks are crooked, and the handsome deep furrowing of the bark
is often spirally cut. The limbs are few and wide apart so as to frame
huge delicately lighted and shadowed chambers of silence or of birds'
song. The leaves turn all together to a leathern hue, and when they
fall stiffen and display their shape on the ground and long refuse to be
merged in the dismal trodden hosts. But when the first one floats past
the eye and is blown like a canoe over the pond we recover once more
our knowledge and fear of Time. All those ladders of goose-grass that
scaled the hedges of spring are dead grey; they are still in their places,
but they clamber no longer. The chief flower is the yellow bloom set

in the dark ivy round the trunks of the ash trees; and where it climbs over the holly and makes a solid sunny wall, and in the hedges, a whole people of wasps and wasp-like flies are always at the bloom with crystal wings, except when a passing shadow disperses them for a moment with one buzz. But these cannot long detain the eye from the crumbling woods in the haze or under the large white clouds – from the amber and orange bracken about our knees and the blue recesses among the distant golden beeches when the sky is blue but beginning to be laden with loose rain-clouds, from the line of leaf-tipped poplars that bend against the twilight sky; and there is no scent of flowers to hide that of dead leaves and rotting fruit. We must watch it until the end, and gain slowly the philosophy or the memory of the forgetfulness that fits us for accepting winter's boon. Pauses there are, of course, or what seem pauses in the declining of this pomp; afternoons when the rooks waver and caw over their beechen town and the pigeons coo content; dawns when the white mist is packed like snow over the vale and the high woods take the level beams and a hundred globes of dew glitter on every thread of the spiders' hammocks or loose perpendicular nets among the thorns, and through the mist rings the anvil a mile away with a music as merry as that of the daws that soar and dive between the beeches and the spun white cloud; mornings full of the sweetness of mushrooms and blackberries from the short turf among the blue scabious bloom and the gorgeous brier; empurpled evenings before frost when the robin sings passionate and shrill and from the garden earth float the smells of a hundred roots with messages of the dark world; and hours full of the thrush's soft November music. The end should come in heavy and lasting rain. At all times I love rain, the early momentous thunderdrops, the perpendicular cataract shining, or at night the little showers, the spongy mists, the tempestuous mountain rain. I like to see it possessing the whole earth at evening, smothering civilization, taking away from me myself everything except the power to walk under the dark trees and to enjoy as humbly as the hissing grass, while some twinkling house-light or song sung by a lonely man gives a foil to the immense dark force. I like to see the rain making the streets, the railway station, a pure desert, whether bright with lamps or not. It foams off the roofs and trees and bubbles into the water-butts. It gives the grey rivers a demonic majesty. It scours the roads, sets the flints moving, and exposes the glossy chalk in the tracks through the woods. It does work that will last as long as the earth. It is about eternal business. In its noise and myriad aspect I feel the mortal beauty of immortal things. And then after many days the rain ceases at midnight with the wind, and in the silence of dawn and frost the last rose of the world is dropping her petals down to the glistering whiteness, and there they rest blood-red on the winter's desolate coast.

LITTLE TOLLER BOOKS republishes classics of
nature writing and rural life.
Please contact us to join our mailing list or for
more information on current and forthcoming titles.

Current Titles

THE SOUTH COUNTRY   *Edward Thomas*
RING OF BRIGHT WATER   *Gavin Maxwell*
MEN AND THE FIELDS   *Adrian Bell*
THE UNOFFICIAL COUNTRYSIDE   *Richard Mabey*
SALAR THE SALMON   *Henry Williamson*
FOUR HEDGES   *Clare Leighton*

LITTLE TOLLER BOOKS
Stanbridge Wimborne Minster Dorset BH21 4JD

Telephone: 01258 840549
ltb@dovecotepress.com
www.dovecotepress.com